THE
EARLY ENGLISH BAPTISTS

BENJAMIN EVANS
1803-1871

THE

EARLY ENGLISH BAPTISTS.

VOL. I.

BY

B. EVANS, D.D.

LONDON:

J. HEATON & SON, 21, WARWICK LANE,
PATERNOSTER ROW.

—

1862.

 **he Baptist Standard Bearer, Inc.**
NUMBER ONE IRON OAKS DRIVE • PARIS, ARKANSAS 72855

Thou hast given a *standard* to them that fear thee;
that it may be displayed because of the truth.
-- *Psalm 60:4*

Reprinted by

THE BAPTIST STANDARD BEARER, INC.
No. 1 Iron Oaks Drive
Paris, Arkansas 72855
(501) 963-3831

THE WALDENSIAN EMBLEM
lux lucet in tenebris
"The Light Shineth in the Darkness"

ISBN #1-57978-897-1

TO MY

MINISTERIAL BRETHREN,

MEN OF SIMILAR DEVOTEDNESS AND OF KINDRED SPIRIT,

AND OF EQUAL

ATTACHMENT TO THE GREAT PRINCIPLES OF RELIGIOUS LIBERTY,
WITH THOSE WHOSE HISTORY IS HERE RECORDED,

THESE MEMORIALS

OF THE

"Early English Baptists"

ARE AFFECTIONATELY INSCRIBED BY THEIR FRIEND AND
FELLOW LABOURER,

B. EVANS.

Sicut lilium inter spinas sic amica mea inter filias

On The Cover: We use the symbol of the "lily among the thorns" from Song of Solomon 2:2 to represent the Baptist History Series. The Latin, *Sicut lilium inter spinas sic amica mea inter filias*, translates, "As the lily among thorns, so is my love among the daughters."

PREFACE.

I DO not offer this volume as a history of the English Baptists. It aims at no such dignity. The time has not yet come for the production of such a work. Other materials have yet to be collected, and vast and varied stores of information have yet to be explored. From the national archives, the Bishops' courts, the writings of their opponents, and the productions of their own pens, much new and very valuable information will be gleaned. Hitherto, very little has been done in this department. Previous writers in our history, either from ignorance or other causes, have made no research. Ivimey is only the bare copyist of Crosby, and adds scarcely a grain of information to the stock the latter had accumulated. Facilities for investigation have now increased. The labours of the Record Commission are laying open to the public the rich stores of important historical materials which have lain unheeded for generations. It is matter of deep regret to the writer, that his distance from London, and pastoral and public duties, have rendered it all but impossible for him to avail himself of these to any great extent. The present work is simply, therefore, offered as a small contribution to the elucidation of the history of the Baptists.

A brief sketch of the labours of my predecessors may not be out of place here, and will not be uninteresting to many of my readers.

The first attempt at a history of the denomination was made by Thomas Crosby. He was a deacon of the church in Goat Street, over which the excellent Benjamin Stinton presided, and kept a school in Southwark. His work is in four volumes, and is now somewhat scarce. Materials for a similar work had been collected by his pastor. These he placed in the hands of the celebrated historian of the Puritans. The unfair use, scarcely, indeed, the use at all, of the information by Mr. Neal, induced the author to write and issue his work. There is much valuable information of men and events, of one of the darkest and most humiliating periods of our national history, contained in this work. Crosby was probably conversant with some of the sufferers. His intimacy with the leading ministers in the metropolis was close. Keach and others had ministered to the church with which he was officially connected. From men, competent to speak, he has told us much which, otherwise, would have been lost. To the future historian this writer's work will always be of value.

Next in this field of denominational literature appeared Mr. A. Taylor. His work is in two volumes, and was issued more than half a century ago. It is avowedly a History of the English General Baptists. It contains a mass of important information in reference to this increasing section of the body, especially of the New Connexion, formed principally by the late Dan Taylor. Many of Mr. Taylor's conclusions will be found more than vindicated, by the documents which will appear in this and the subsequent volume.

The History of the English Baptists, by the Rev. J. Ivimey, in four volumes, appeared in 1811—1830. The author was a laborious and useful minister, and for many years the successful pastor of the church in Eagle Street, London. The early part of his work supplies us with only a few fragments of additional information, beyond what the pages of Crosby had already given. It is far more copious in after periods, detailing public events in which Baptists took part with other bodies, and supplying us with sketches of biography and of the history of individual churches, which can be found nowhere else. The work is remarkably heavy, whilst its extent places it beyond the reach of the vast mass of the community. Its materials will be of great value to some future historian of the later periods of Baptist history.

In 1847, appeared a condensed History of the General Baptists of the New Connexion, by J. H. Wood, with a recommendatory preface by the late Rev. J. G. Pike. As its title indicates, the volume is devoted to one section of the body. There is a large mass of information, especially on the operations of the New Connexion since the close of Taylor's work. Mr. Wood designed his volume for popular use; and though it will not occupy the same position as its predecessor, yet it will be a good substitute, in the absence of this, to many readers.

Of the admirable sketches of Mr. Underhill, in the various volumes of the Hansard Knollys Society's publications, it would be worse than idle to speak. In reading them, one only regrets that he has not laid his brethren under larger obligations. Beyond these we have no independent works. Rippon's Registers, the Magazines, Histories of Associations, Circular

Letters, &c., supply epitomes, &c. Other writers have not done us justice. The complaint has been uttered again and again. Crosby complained of Neal; Ivimey is equally loud against Messrs. Bogue and Bennett. Wales utters the same complaints still.*

This practice cannot be too strongly censured. Truth should be more precious than party. By Christian men, at least, her supremacy should be acknowledged. If they mangle or distort her fair form, to whom can she look for protection? Only as she is honoured, will principle triumph; only as her sweet voice regulates our conduct, and her instruction moulds our character, will society be purified in its lowest depths, and the empire of light and love be extended. The age is one of loud and large professions of liberality; but it would be a more satisfactory sign of its genuineness, to see Christian men, on the points which divide them, contending for truth, and not for victory. Under the influence of such a spirit, discussion would be a blessing, and controversy would strengthen, rather than impair, the outworks of Christianity. Earnestly does the writer pray for the growth of this spirit; because, as its influence is felt, the spiritual life of Christ's true church will be vigorous and aggressive on the masses of depravity around it.

The period of our history which this volume covers is one of a transition state. Principles were working which have exerted a mighty influence on the Church

---

* "The Rev. Thomas Rees, of Beaufort, in his work, *The History of Nonconformity in Wales*, is guilty of doing the Welsh Baptists a flagrant injustice. His conduct is unfair, unjust, and unworthy of any historian, if that historian does not wish the English reader to believe that the Nonconformists of Wales are the *Independents*."—*The Welsh Baptists*, by the Rev. T. Price.

and on the State. The different standpoints from which writers have viewed it, and the great actors in the struggle, have influenced the estimate which they have formed of the results. Impartiality is difficult. Writers near to the events are frequently most wanting in this. Their sympathies with certain principles, their prejudices, and their ignorance, have often led to the omission of certain things, to the discolouring of others, and to conclusions which subsequent investigations have shown to be unfounded. No class of men have, probably, suffered more from this than those to whom this volume refers. I do not claim entire exemption from this imperfection. I have tried in every case to be impartial; but, perhaps, in some instances I may have failed. Still, I trust that, notwithstanding my attachment to the principles of these persecuted ones, and my intense admiration of their moral heroism, in no instance have I acted unfairly towards their bitter and malignant foes.

My aim in this work, has been to present to the minds of my readers as graphic a sketch of the illustrious founders of our body as possible. Their rise,—their principles and ecclesiastical polity,—their public and social life,—their sufferings,—and, finally, their triumphs,—will form prominent features in the picture. Only in part is this accomplished in the present volume.

In preparing it, I have had constantly in view the interests of a large and important class of the denomination. Thousands of young men and maidens are growing up around us. Many are anxious for information and mental culture. Their means are limited. Large historical works they cannot purchase, nor have they time to read them if they could. To familiarize their minds with the moral heroism of our fathers,—to indoctrinate them with those deathless principles which they were the first to promulgate, and to which the true Church of Christ is now doing homage,—is a work of incalculable importance. Never was it more so. The conflicts of to-day clothe it with the deepest interest. Men of like principles and of kindred spirit are most fitted for the struggle. Their weapons are the keenest, and from their vantage ground can success only be secured. Only as the spirituality of Christ's Church is exhibited, and a living union with the Saviour urged, as essential to its members, will truth triumph. Finer models of the true, the noble, the holy, and morally great, cannot be set before them. They were men of whom the world was not worthy. Should any one, therefore, find fault with the details which I have supplied on collateral matters, I point to this class, and urge its wants as my chief apology.

The reader will see that I have used in the text, and equally so by a reference to the notes, a class of writers whose views on ecclesiastical polity are widely different from our own. No one more highly values the labours of my friends, Dr. Price and Mr. Underhill, and others who had preceded them, than I. I have read them again and again with profit; and, no doubt, for many a thought I am indebted to their lucid pages. But, after all, I preferred my own independent inquiry: the reading of a class of writers who had no sympathy with the Anabaptists, and from their pages to draw ample materials for the present work. I could present a long list of authors read, many of whom have repaid the toil with only a small grain of material. I will only add, that whilst this course has involved more labour, I have no regret now it is done.

Upon some points I have ventured to differ from my predecessors, though sanctioned by Danvars, and a numerous class who have repeated from him, or from one another. I have not done so hastily. When I have calmly examined their opinions, and found evidence against them, I have not hesitated for a moment in entering my dissent. Some may blame me for this as weakening our defences. I am content to bear it. Only that which is true is really of any worth. The value of our principles is not dependent upon the practices of the Early British Christian— Wickliff, or any other of the illustrious saints, who shed the light of Christ's truth, and the beauty of a holy life, on the ages of the past. To a higher source we can go. Whatever will not bear the severest scrutiny, let it be rejected. History should deal only with fact, not with theory. With evidence, not with mere conjecture. Any other course will only be a source of weakness, and not of strength. Upon these convictions I have acted. It has been the rule to which I have sought to conform. About its results I am not careful. Consequences which necessarily follow great principles we should always welcome. The cherished opinions of some, and men for whose judgment I have great respect, may be disturbed by the facts and conclusions which I have recorded. All I ask is, that they will candidly examine, before they reject, the conclusions to which I have been led.

It was originally intended to complete this work in one volume. The plan of it was constructed in harmony with this design. But I soon found this impossible. The new and valuable documents placed at my command, some of which are given in the present volume, and others reserved for the next, which throw much light on churches and proceedings in connexion with our body, in the early periods of the reign of the first Charles, demanded an alteration. In addition to a valuable series of letters, giving much new and very valuable information on one of the obscurest, and yet interesting, periods of our history, the proceedings of our brethren in Holland, the Confession of Faith published by the remainder of John Smith's company, and known only to us by the fragments given by Robinson in his reply to it, are given in the present volume. There is also an elaborate work by the same author, on the subject of Baptism, in reply to Clifton, still in MS. It is lengthy for publication in connexion with this undertaking; but the former are too precious to be withheld. The Publishers mnst be exonerated from all blame. They have done all they could to prevent it. The responsibility is mine. I unhesitatingly avow it. If after the volumes are published, my judgment in this matter is impeached, I will bow to the decision with as much dignity as I can.

To my friend Professor Muller, of Amsterdam, I am very, very deeply indebted. His profound scholarship and Christian courtesy excite my warmest admiration and command my esteem. The valuable documents, preserved under his care in the archives of the church at Amsterdam, by his ready kindness, were placed at my disposal; whilst with the deepest interest and untiring patience he has examined other records for me, and thus thrown a flood of light on many obscure points on the state of our brethren in Holland. Some of these documents, both in the text and appendix, were in Latin, others in Dutch; and when I failed to find a Dutch scholar in this country able to translate the language of the sixteenth century, Dr. Müller kindly undertook and accomplished the task for me. His English I have not altered. If censure is uttered, I must calmly bear it. This simple statement will show the extent of my obligations; but no words can express the warmth of my gratitude.

I have only to add my deep regret, that with all my anxiety to present this volume as correct as possible, I find, when too late for alteration, several errors have crept into the text. The work, though laborious, has been a labour of love; and it would be to the writer a source of unmingled thankfulness if, whilst his name is associated with these memorials of the great and the good, he could emulate their faith and rival their devotedness.

B. EVANS.

SCARBOROUGH,
August 5th, 1862.

CONTENTS.

	PAGE
PREFACE	vii
INTRODUCTION:	
Early Baptists	1
Were the British Churches Baptist?	2
Austin's questions	5
Baptist sufferers in Henry the Second's time	10
Wickliffe—sentiments on Baptism	12
The Lollards	14
Anabaptist—its misapplication	16

CHAPTER I.

THE TUDOR DYNASTY.

State of the nation	18
Discovery of Printing	18
Commerce	19
The Papacy	19
The spirit of Civil Liberty	21
Accession of Henry the Seventh	21
His policy—favourable to the Church	23
Persecution—the Lollards	23

CHAPTER II.

HENRY THE EIGHTH.

State of Europe on Henry's Accession	25
His character and magnificence	25
Causes which led to the Reformation	27
Low state of religion	27

xviii   CONTENTS.

	PAGE
Moral condition of the people	31
Glimpse of the popular superstitions	32
Wolsey—his influence with Henry	33
Aspires to the Popedom	37
Conflicting interests of parties in the State	37
Baptists, persecution of, by Wareham	41
Henry head of the Church	42
James Bainham suffers	43
Anne Boleyn elevated to the throne	45
Dutch Baptists—their sufferings	46
Elevation of Cranmer to the Primacy	48
Baptism—its varied Ceremonies	48
The Pilgrimage of Grace	50
Commissions to hunt for Anabaptists	51
Elector of Hesse urges Henry to persecute them	52
Proclamations against them	53
Excluded from a general pardon	54
Death of Cromwell	55
Condition of the Anglican Church	56

CHAPTER III.

EDWARD THE SIXTH.

The joy of the nation at Edward's birth	57
His Accession to the throne	58
Parties in the State and the Church	59
Urgent need of Reform	60
Moral state of the People	61
Cranmer's efforts	63
The Prayer-Book on Baptism	64
Mode of Baptism	65
Significancy of Baptism	67
Influence of Continental Reformers in England	67
Extent of the Reformation	68
Baptists persecuted	69
Commission to Cranmer to seek them	69
Calvin excites persecution against them	70
Ridley's Enquiries	71
Joan of Kent	72

CONTENTS.   xix

	PAGE
Putts suffers at Colchester	75
Baptists in Kent	76
———— and Essex	77
Hart and the Free-Willers	79
Family of Love	79
George Van Pare	80
Giles Van Bellan	81
Death of Edward	82

CHAPTER IV.
MARY.

Accession of Mary	82
State of Parties	84
———— of the Church	84
Mary's early Character	86
Influence of the Papacy	88
Gardiner	88
The Spanish Ambassador	90
Cardinal Pole in England	91
Reconciliation to Rome	92
The form of ditto	93
Articles issued to the Bishops	94
General Apostacy	95
Martyrs	97
Enquiries about Dissidents	98
Baptist Martyrs	99
Robert Cooke	102
Smith and others	103
Discussion in Prison	108
Philpot on Baptism	109
Baptists in East Anglia	109
Charge against them	111
Bonner's complaints	114
Growing hatred to Rome	114
Death of Gardiner	115
Misery of the Queen	116
Her death	119
Death of Pole	119

CHAPTER V.

ELIZABETH.

	PAGE
Hostility to Elizabeth	121
Her danger from Papal influence	121
True estimate of her reign	122
State of the Church	123
———— society	124
———— the Universities	125
The Reformation more political than religious	127
Elizabeth's difficulties	131
Her policy	132
Debate between Romanists and Protestants	133
Defects of Elizabeth's Reform	135
Act of Uniformity	138
Controversy about vestments	138
Influence of the Separatists from the Church	141
Destitution of ministers	142
Moral state of the people	143
Rise of the Presbyterians	144
———— Romanists	146
Wide diffusion of Baptist principles	147
The cause	149
Anabaptists ordered to leave the country	149
The minister of the Dutch Church	150
Dutch Baptists suffer	151
Their examinations	152
Their complaints	153
Apostacy of some	155
Fox's sympathy with them	156
Their confession	157
The order for their execution	158
Somers's account	159
Perverted account by historians	165
Spread of Anabaptists	166
Hatred of Elizabeth to the Puritans	166
Strengthened by the Episcopate	167
Spread of Puritanism	168
Personal character of Elizabeth	169
State of religion	171
Closing scenes	172
The Family of Love (note)	174

CHAPTER VI.

THE STUART DYNASTY.—JAMES THE FIRST.

	PAGE
The Stuart Princes	176
Influence at work	176
Accession of the King	181
All parties hopeful	182
James's principles	184
Appeal of the Puritans	186
Hampton Court discussion	187
James patronises the Episcopates	191
Cause of this	191
Bancroft raised to the Primacy	192
The Puritans—their position	193
Separatists in Holland	196
John Smith, Helwys, &c.	197
Smith's self-baptism, &c.	198
History of it	200
Action of the Dutch Baptists	203
Subsequent history of the English Baptists in Holland	212
Helwys in England	217
D'Ewes's testimony to the spread of our principles	220
Leonard Busher—Plea for Religious Liberty	221
Pilgrim Fathers	223
Edward Wightman—his opinions	232
Consigned to the secular power—martyrdom	233
Close of James's reign	234
Personal and social character	235
Immoral state of his court	236
His death and funeral	237

APPENDICES.

A.

Rites and Ceremonies observed about Baptism . . 239

B.

The sentence against Joan of Kent, with the certificate made upon it 242

CONTENTS.

C.

	PAGE
Examination of Giles Vanbeller	243

D.

Names of the English who confess their errors, &c. . .	244

E.

A short Confession of Faith, by John Smith and his friends .	245

F.

Confession of Faith, by John Smith	253
——————————— Richard Overton . . .	254

G.

Confession by the remainder of John Smith's company . .	257

H.

Letter of Henry Hart, &c.	272

EARLY ENGLISH BAPTISTS.

THE

EARLY ENGLISH BAPTISTS.

INTRODUCTION.

"THE true origin of that sect which acquires the denomination of Anabaptists by their administering anew the rite of baptism to those who come over to their communion, . . . is hid in the remote depths of antiquity, and is, of consequence, extremely difficult to be ascertained."* No one conversant with the records of the past can doubt this. The whole facts of history place the truth beyond dispute. "I have seen enough to convince me that the present English dissenters, contending for the sufficiency of Scripture, and for primitive Christian liberty to judge of its meaning, may be traced back in authentic manuscripts to the Nonconformists, to the Puritans, to the Lollards, to the Vallenses, to the Albigenses, and, I suspect, through the Paulicians and others, to the apostles."† Dissidents from the popular church in the early ages, compelled to leave it from the growing corruption of its doctrines and morals, were found everywhere. Men of apostolic life and doctrine contended for the simplicity of the church and the liberty of Christ's flock, in the midst of great danger. What the pen failed to do, the sword of the magistrate effected. The

---

* Mosheim, vol. iv., cent. xvi., chap. iii., p. 439.
† Robinson's Claude, vol. ii., p. 53.

Novatians, the Donatists, and others that followed them, are examples. They contended for the independence of the church; they exalted the divine Word as the only standard of faith; they maintained the essential purity of the church, and the necessity of a holy life springing from a renewed heart.* Extinguished by the sword, not of the Spirit, —their churches broken and scattered,—after years of patient suffering from the dominant sect, the seed which they had scattered sprang up in other lands. Truth never dies. Its vitality is imperishable. In the wild wastes and fastnesses of Europe and Africa it grew. A succession of able and intrepid men taught the same great principles, in opposition to a corrupt and affluent *State* church, which distinguish modern English Nonconformists; and many of them taught those peculiar views of Christian ordinances which are special to us as Baptists. Beyond all doubt such views were inculcated by the Paulicians, the primitive Waldenses, and their brethren. Over Europe they were scattered, and their converts were very numerous,† long before the Reformation shed its light on the darkness of Europe. But our design is to trace the history, not of Foreign, but of Early English Baptists.

Were the ancient British Christians Baptists? This question meets us on the threshold, and asks our attention for a time. Writers on both sides the Atlantic, claim for Wales the honour of retaining primitive ordinances and church polity beyond any other nation of Europe. Removed

---

* That these early separatists taught doctrines now held by the English Baptists, might be made to appear by their own works and the statements of their adversaries. Long. Hist. Donatists. Lardner's Works, vol. iii. Jones's Ch. Hist. Robinson's Hist. of Baptism.

† The reader will find much information on the former in Lardner, Jones, Robinson's Ecclesiastical Researches, and Mosheim. Dr. Allix says, "They, with the Manichees, were Anabaptists, or rejectors of infant baptism, and were, consequently, often reproached with that term."—Rem. Ch. Pied., p. 138. Orchard's Hist. F. Baptists, &c.

INTRODUCTION.

from the influence of Rome, the authority of the ambitious and worldly-minded Pontiffs who ruled in that city was not acknowledged in Wales till about A.D. 600, and the growing corruptions of the Western church had not penetrated the fastnesses of that country. Some of our American brethren speak of the churches there as corresponding, up to the time of Austin's invasion, with our present polity. National Christianity was unknown, and everywhere the churches were based on Congregational principles, and union with them was the result of individual conviction, and was professed and secured by the immersion of the body in water. In other words, in a true and important sense they were Baptist churches. We cannot speak with the same confidence. The fact is not so clear to us as to some, and we feel that there are elements of doubt about it, the solution of which we should be glad to find. It is not as to the mode of baptism. That is unquestioned. No man would risk his claim to accurate acquaintance even with English history, by denying that the ancient mode of baptism was immersion. Wales knew nothing else. Christendom knew nothing else. Trine immersion was,* probably, all but universal. It is questionable if any other modes were recognized, except in the case of the sick. Austin and his companions, beyond all doubt, practised immersion.† The question for settlement is not respecting mode, but simply this: *Had the practice of infant baptism at this time made its way into Wales, or was it unknown amongst these primitive disciples till the Roman missionary forced it on them by the sword of his murderous Saxons?* We shall place the evidence in as clear a light as we can before our readers. It is only

---

* From the writings of many Fathers, Bingham places this beyond all controversy. E. Ant., vol. iv., pp. 355—358, 360—362. "If a Bishop or a Presbyter use not three immersions in the mystery of baptism, but only one immersion unto the death of Christ, let him be deposed."—Apostolic Canons, 50; *Ibid*, viii., p. 65.

† Bede, by Giles, pp. 112, 113, 115, 171, 277.

as an historical fact that we deal with it. Beyond this it is really of no moment.*

The Saxon invasion of Britain was followed by cruelty and oppression. Religion suffered. Churches were demolished, and ministers slain. The worshippers of Wodin had no sympathy with the forms of faith which prevailed in the island. To the fastnesses and morasses of Wales many retired. Austin was sent by Gregory to convert the Saxons. Success crowned his efforts. Thousands, in various parts of the country, nominally raised Christ to the place of their idols. They called themselves Christians; but their knowledge of the great truths of the religion of Jesus was very limited, and the influence of those truths on their life and character was as feeble. Elevated to the episcopacy, the ambition of Austin took a wider flight, and he sought to bring the Cambro-Britons under his episcopal control, and to extort from them the acknowledgment of the spiritual supremacy of Rome. A meeting was convened, at which many British ministers attended. The discussion was long, and they did not comply with the exhortations or rebukes of the proud monk, but preferred their own traditions before all the churches in the world.† At another meeting, Austin presented his demands in the following form, consenting to allow their independence in other matters, if they would yield obedience in these : "To keep Easter at the due time; to

---

* That difference existed in the Irish church from the Saxon baptism admits of no doubt. *Vide* Todd's Irish Church, pp. 97, 99. In letters from some Irish bishops to Lanfranc, they ask the primate—If it was necessary to the salvation of infants that they should receive the eucharist as well as be baptized? So late as A.D. 1172, a Synod at Cashel directed "that *infants* be catechised before the door of the church, and baptized in the holy font in the baptismal churches." *Ibid*, pp. 100, 125. "The Britons were contrary to the whole world, and enemies to the Roman custom." Usher's Religion of the Anct. Irish, pp. 33, 34, 108, 109. Hostility to Rome, p. 110. Thierry supplies us with abundant evidence to the same effect. Norman Conquest, vol. i., pp. 64—69, 82; vol. iii., p. 4.

† Bede, by Giles, p. 82.

administer baptism, by which we are again born to God,* according to the custom of the Holy Roman Apostolic Church; and jointly with us to preach the Word of God to the English nation. We will readily tolerate all the other things you do, though contrary to our custom."† This sainted monster threatened them with war, and finally induced the Northumbrians to invade their lands with fire and sword. Thousands then fell victims to priestly pride and the love of Romish dominion.

Now, it is on the form of the second of these propositions that the whole dispute turns. As it stands before us, we should have no difficulty in the matter; but we are stopped by the fact, that the next writer who gives a report modifies the statement of Bede. Fabian, in his Chronicle, states the proposition as follows: "*That ye give Christendom to children.*" Bede, the father of English ecclesiastical history, died in 735. Fabian, the merchant and chronicler of his day, died in the year 1512. Now which of these is the true report ? We shall lay before our readers the best evidence we can collect, and allow them to form their own judgment. Of Fabian's Chronicle five editions have been published, viz., 1516, 1533, 1542, 1549, and the last in 1811, under the superintendence of Sir H. Ellis. In this edition the words agree with Bede, "*as to the manner of the Church of Rome;*" but Sir Henry tells us that this phrase is wanting in the editions of 1542 and 1549. It is right to add, that the edition of 1549, which omits the clause, was professedly compared with the first.‡

---

* The words of Bede are: "Ut ministerium baptisandi, quo Deo renascimur, juxta morem sanctæ Romanæ Apostolicæ Ecclesiæ, compleatis."

† Bede, p. 82.

‡ "Because the last print of Fabian's Chronicle was in many places altered from the first copies, I have caused it to be compared with the first print of all, and set it further in all points according to the author's meaning."—*The Printer to the Reader.* Holinshed and Stowe in their Chronicle report the same as Bede. Grafton refers his reader to Fabian. Harding, earlier still, thus notices it :—

But assuming the correctness of Bede, what did Austin mean? Only one of two things: either that they were to baptize their children because Rome did, or that they should baptize them in the same way. The latter is affirmed by Baxter, Wall, Murdock, and others: it is not the mode which Austin means, but the ceremonies which at that time had gathered around it. Let Baxter speak: "*And who knows not that the Church of Rome, and all its communions, then called the Universal church, used in baptism the white garment, milk and honey, as an apostolical tradition?*" Only this interpretation can be put upon it, say they. It admits o fno other. In opposition to this, D'Anvers, Davye, and Ivimey, in England, and several Cambro-Americans, maintain that it refers exclusively to the baptism of children. It would occupy too much space, and be too large a demand on the patience of our readers, to enter fully into the grounds of their widely-different opinions. We shall rather suggest some facts which are patent to both parties. It is manifest, then, that Austin himself was not fully satisfied about the baptism of infants. About that of children he might; but his correspondence with Gregory makes it manifest that the former idea had not lost the feature of novelty. Look at these questions: "May a woman with child be baptized? or how long after she is confined may she come into the church? Also, after how many days the infant born may be baptized, lest he be prevented by death?"* It must not be forgotten, either, that up to this time the baptism of children, though

---

"To converte and to teache the Saxons all,
  The English also, in Christian faith and treive,
  And baptize them; through Brytaine over all
  The pasche to keep, as Rome did then full dewe."

There is no allusion to this in the "Brut, or Chronicles of the Kings of England," an early work, translated from the Welsh by the Rev. P. Roberts. London, 1811. *Vide* p. 178. Appendix vi., p. 317.

* Bede, p. 52. Widely different on this subject are the opinions of the Fathers. Greg. Naz. thinks that healthy children should wait for three years.—Bingham, vol. iv., p. 218-9. Hagenbach's Hist. Doctrines, vol. i., p. 363.

in many parts prevalent, was purely voluntary. No canon had been passed by any Council of importance on this subject. At a meeting—what ecclesiastical writers would call a Council, very likely—of seven Spanish bishops, A.D. 517, the subject was discussed. Robinson says, "*That they agreed (not commanded) to baptize catechumens only at Easter and Pentecost, except in case of sickness. Also in case of infants, if they were ill, and would not suck their mothers' milk, if they were offered to them, to baptize them, even though it were the day they were born.*"* Later still, it is obvious, from a law of Charlemagne, that the baptism of infants was not regarded in the same light as by Romanists in subsequent times. He enacted, A.D. 789, a law *by which his Saxon subjects were obliged, on pain of death, to be baptized; and of heavy fines, to baptize their children within the year of their birth.*

Independently of these facts, which must not be overlooked in this inquiry, there are other considerations of some weight, but at which we can only hint at present. For example: Infant baptism, at this period, was by no means universal. It had not yet everywhere superseded that of believers. In the fifth century, Mabillon says, "Children were baptized at six years of age." Catechumens still were found nearly in all countries where Christianity was recognised; whilst by most, we might probably be justified in affirming that by all, of the dissidents from Rome, the baptism of infants was rejected. The supposition, therefore, that the British churches retained the primitive practice,

---

* Before this time, baptism was regarded as essential to salvation. Pages could be filled by showing the exaggerated importance which the singular old gentlemen called the Fathers attached to this simple rite. One example shall suffice: "The pertinacious wickedness of the devil hath power up to the saving water, but that in baptism he loses all the poison of his wickedness. When, however, they come to the saving water, and to the sanctification of baptism, we ought to know and be confident that the devil is then overcome," &c.—Cyprian's Letters, p. 69. *Vide* Coun. at Carthage. Cyprian's Letters, Lib. of Fathers, p. 233.

involves no violation of existing facts or probabilities. May we not also regard this supposition as strengthened by the fact, that up to this time they had not recognised the usurpation of the Roman Pontiff?* Bede more than warrants the conclusion, that on many points they differed widely from the church at Rome; and states positively, that when Austin asked them to relinquish their mode of keeping Easter, and adopt that of the West (the badge, let it be remembered, of union with Rome), they absolutely refused. No one can read the accounts of this Father of Ecclesiastical history, and we have none else, without feeling that the pretensions and claims of this haughty monk were regarded by the sturdy Cambrians as an invasion of their independence. In fragments of poems, written soon after, the hostility to Rome is unmistakable. Old Thomas Fuller gives us this:—

> "Wo be to the priest unborn,
> That will not cleanly weed his corn,
> And preach his flock among.
> Wo be to that shepherd, I say,
> That will not watch his flock away,
> As to his office doth belong.
>
> "Wo be to him that doth not keep
> From Romish wolves his sheep,
> With staff and weapon strong."

From Sharon Turner we select another:—

> "I will not receive the Sacrament
> From the detestable monks,
> With their gowns upon their haunches;
> May the Sacrament be administered to me
> by God himself."

The causes which contributed to shut out the influence of Rome from Wales till the time of Austin, are too obvious to be mentioned. The church was not yet lifeless. Forms had not yet destroyed the realities of spiritual life. In-

---

* Thierry's Norman Conquest, vol. iii., p. 4, 5.

dividual freedom was not yet crushed by the iron rod of spiritual despotism. Its vitality was wounded, but not annihilated. Uniformity of worship, in rites and ceremonies, in doctrine and discipline, did not exist universally. Variety in all these prevailed, and was held to be compatible with the unity of the Spirit. The correspondence of Gregory with the missionary priest is valuable on this account, and places the matter very distinctly before us. "It *pleases* me that if you have found anything, either in the Roman or the Gallican or any other church, which may be more acceptable to Almighty God, you carefully make choice of the same." "Choose, therefore, from any church, those things that are pious, religious, and upright." The argument from uniformity against the Baptist view, utterly fails.*

We offer these considerations, not in the spirit of partizanship, but with calmness and impartiality. The question cannot be decided with positivity. No evidence we think exists to warrant it. The utmost we can do is to reach the probable. From this point we have looked at it, and ventured to submit reasons which, to us, demolish much if not the whole of the ground, on which Baxter, Wills, Wall, and others, have based their case. Our own judgment, in the main, is concurrent with that of our early writers, although we have arrived at it by a process somewhat

---

* "As late as A.D. 747 it was enjoined that the priests should take care to discharge the duty of apostolic commission in baptising according to lawful right; and in the II. Canon of Clovashoo, the priests are directed to study to perform this sacerdotal ministry in one and the same mode of baptising." Wilkins Consil, vol. i., p. 96. Denne on Fonts, p. 116. By a canon of Edgar, A.D. 960, every priest was instructed to perform baptism as soon as it was required of him; and he was to give it in charge to his parish, that the baptism of an infant was not to be delayed beyond thirty-seven days. But by a law of Northumberland, A.D. 950, the child was to be baptised within nine days.—Wilkins Consil, vol. i., p. 218. *Apud* Denne on Fonts, pp. 116–7.

Hostility to Rome equally marked the Irish church. Examples of this will be found in Usher, and especially in Todd's Ancient Irish Church, pp. 84, 103-4, 131.

different to theirs. We think the preponderance of probabilities decidedly in favour of the opinion that the British church at this time did not practise infant baptism.*

The Anglo-Saxon church presents but very little on which the mind of an intelligent Christian can rest with satisfaction. The corruptions of Rome here found a rich soil, and they flourished with increased vigour. Its darkness was that of midnight, relieved only here and there by the feeble glimmer of some small star. Controversies about forms—multiplied ceremonies clothed with some undefined supernatural power—conflicts between the secular and spiritual powers—and the rapid decay of all spiritual life, prove the sad and prominent characteristics of this era.† No trace of the Baptist element appears till some generations after, under the government of the Norman dynasty. During the reign of the Second Henry we have a glimpse of it. Historians of a certain stamp tell us that this was the first appearance of heresy in this kingdom. Not of hostility to Papal oppression, but to the doctrine of the Holy See. The seamless coat of the unity of the church till now had been untouched. The horrid crime which called forth the holy indignation of the church was perpetrated by Baptists. The facts of the case, as we gather them from the pages of their enemies, are these. From their language they were from Holland. These "publican" heretics were about thirty of both sexes. They pretended to visit this country on business. They were rustic in their manners, and were headed by one

---

* The reader will find this matter fully discussed in the following works: D'Anvers's Treatise on Baptism. Reply to Wills, Baxter, &c. Benedict's History of Baptists; New York, 1848.

† The reader who would form an accurate opinion of the true spiritual character of the Anglo-Saxon church, must do more than familiarize himself with the pages of Lingard and Soame. Both were written for a special purpose, and leave untouched the ignorance, the superstition, and immorality, which everywhere prevailed. Let him master the old chronicles of the period, and his views will approximate nearer to the reality.

Gerhard, a man of some learning. The watchmen of the church soon detected their secret foes. Before a synod at Oxford the transgressors were called. Their leader replied to the questions of their judges, on behalf of the rest. He avowed their attachment to Christ, and that the doctrine of the apostles was their sole rule of faith. On the Trinity and incarnation they were sound, but they *rejected baptism*, the eucharist, and other dogmas of Rome. Entreaty and menace alike failed. To their opinions they adhered, and in reply to the threat of punishment as heretics, calmly replied: "*Blessed are they that suffer in persecution for righteousness' sake, for theirs is the kingdom of heaven.*" Compassion for their souls, and anxiety for the commonwealth which might be diseased by the contagion of their wicked example, induced the bishops to transfer them to the secular magistrate as confirmed heretics. Upon this the king ordered them to be branded on the forehead and publicly whipped out of the town; strictly forbidding all persons either to entertain them or give them any manner of relief. They suffered the execution of this sentence very cheerfully, their ringleader marching at the head of them, and singing, "*Blessed are ye when men shall hate you.*" In short, the rigour of the sentence and the season were such (it being winter), that these poor wretches sunk under their punishment and were all despatched.*

Doubtless these martyrs were Paulicians.† Under this name they appear as dissidents from the Greek church about the middle of the seventh century. Amidst persecutions, war, and sufferings, they spread over Europe. Doctrines, as usual, the most revolting, were attributed to them by their enemies. Rome, at an early period, excelled in this. She

---

* Collier's Ecclesiastical History, vol. i., pp. 347-8.

† "They called themselves the true Catholic church, opposed to the corrupt and ruling establishment." They were also styled Publicans, but this was more particularly in the southern provinces of France.—Neander's Life of Brainard, p. 338.

laid no restraint on her fancy. She renounced her allegiance to truth when dealing with her adversaries. Cleared from the calumnies of these men, their doctrines were far more evangelical than those of the corrupt church, and their lives far more holy than those of the recognized priesthood. No doubt the unbroken testimony of history justifies the statement of Dr. Allix :—" They were Anabaptists, or rejectors of infant baptism, and were consequently often reproached with that name."*

Was Wickliffe a Baptist? Many of our writers have claimed the illustrious reformer as one of a long list of witnesses who through many ages have borne their testimony against the baptism of infants, and have stated that, through the ministry of his poor priests, these opinions were widely diffused through this land.† We may be permitted to quote from an article of our own, our matured opinion on this question : "It is beyond all doubt that his opponents charged him with denying it. Walden, one of his most violent and unscrupulous opponents, again and again urges it; and subsequent writers, historians and others, repeat the statements of the monk, without, it is to be feared, examining the writings of the reformer. It is beyond all controversy that he rejected many of the superstitious notions which the Romish church had gathered around the sacrament. Not only is it probable that he relinquished many of the absurdities which distinguished the outward ceremony, but rejected it altogether as productive of those saving effects which Rome attached to its valid administration. Of this there can be little doubt, as one of the charges against him, in the Council of 1396, was, that he affirmed in his writings that the

---

* Rem. Ch. Piedmont, p. 138. Gibbon has devoted a chapter to this sect; on the whole, fair and candid. The reader may consult also Robinson's Ecc. Researches, Jones's Ecc. Hist., Orchard's F. Baptists, Dr. Lardner's work, vol. iii. 8vo. Ed. To these he may add Mosheim and Milner, on the sect.

† *Vide* D'Anvers, Ivimey, and others.

children of the righteous might be saved without baptism. As held by the church, baptism was a saving ordinance. The damnation of all infants who died without it was certain.* Now the modification of these views would be ground sufficient on which his adversary would base his charges. Truth was not his aim. Any misrepresentation which would damage his adversary would be allowed. No men are less to be trusted than the monkish historians, when they speak of the character and doctrine of dissidents from Rome.

"No doubt the sentiments of the reformer on some dogmas were Baptist, and I think it is more than probable that many of his followers were consistent, and rejected the baptism of infants; but I know at present no document which warrants this conclusion in relation to Wickliffe himself. His Triologues, those on which his enemies rested their charges, certainly, as given by his latest biographer, supply no proof. The following may be taken as embodying his views on this ordinance at the time of their publication:—'*On account of the words of the last chapter in Matthew, our church introduces believers who answer for the infant which has not yet arrived at years of discretion,*' &c.† '*Nor is it of moment whether the baptized be immersed once, or thrice, or whether the water be poured on the head; but the ceremony must be performed according to the usage of the place, and is as legitimate one way as another; for it is certain, that bodily baptism or washing is of little avail, unless there goes with it the washing of the mind by the Holy Spirit from original or actual sin. For herein is a fundamental article of belief, that wherever a man is duly baptized, baptism destroys whatever sin was found in the man.*'‡ Of children dying unbaptized, he says,—'*I think it probable*

---

* A writer in the Dublin Quarterly Review affirms the absolute damnation of all infants dying unbaptized.

† Triologue x., p. 156 (Wickliffe Society). ‡ *Ibid*, pp. 156–7.

that Christ might, without any such washing, spiritually baptize, and by consequence save, infants.'* 'When an infidel baptizes a child, not supposing that baptism to be of any avail for his salvation, such a baptism we are not to regard as serviceable to the baptized. Yet we believe that where any old woman or despised person duly baptizes with water, God completes the baptism of the Spirit along with the words of the sacrament.'"

At the same time it is only right to add, that it is certain the Lollards, who had long preceded Wickliffe, and had diffused their opinions far and wide throughout this country, repudiated infant baptism. Walter Lollard had visited this country early in the fourteenth century; a man of enlightened views, of inflexible courage, and impassioned eloquence; and he had widely extended the circle of his influence.† The followers of both soon united. The name of the latter marked the sectarians. In a few years after the death of Wickliffe, more than half the nation were imbued with the principles of the *"Bible Men."*‡ East Anglia, Middlesex, Kent, Hereford, and the Midland Counties, were the chief places of their abode. The relations of England to Rome, the state of the Papacy throughout Europe, had been favourable to their peace and prosperity. But the tide soon turned. The repression of Episcopal anger only made it more fearful.

Arundel and Chicheley, successively Archbishops of Canterbury, distinguished themselves in this service of blood. In their hands, the laws enacted against the Lollards were

---

* Triologue xi., pp. 159-60 (Wickliffe Society).   † Mosheim.

‡ "Some of his followers," Knyghton testifies, "in a very short time became eloquent preachers, and very powerful disputants." The monkish chronicles attribute this to the devil. "The heretics and Lollards of Wickliffe's opinions were suffered to preach abroad so boldly, to gather conventicles unto them, to keep schools in men's houses, to write books, compile treatises, and write ballads, to teach privately in angles and corners, as in woods, pastures, meadows, groves, and caves of the ground, &c." Bales' Works (Parker Society).

INTRODUCTION. 15

by no means a dead letter. Multitudes were forced to recant or to expiate their crime at the stake.* Arundel employed twelve magistrates to search for information against them, and got an Act passed forbidding the reading of the Scriptures.† The first who fell a prey to the malice of this prelate, and the first martyr in England, was Sautrey, supposed by some to have had Baptist views, but, we think, without clear proof of the fact.‡ The illustrious Cobham, who sealed his testimony with his blood, may again come under our notice. The king thought heresy very dangerous, and under the advice of his Episcopal councillors, he burnt more of the followers of Wickliffe than any, since the first of the Lancastrian kings. Yet the doctrine of this archheretic struck deeper root in the minds of the people.§ Amongst them the prevalence of Baptist principles admits of no doubt.

"I have now before me," says Robinson, "a MS. register of Grey, Bishop of Ely, which proves that in the year 1457, there was a congregation of this sort (Baptist) in this village, Chesterton, where I live, who privately assembled for divine worship and had preachers of their own, who taught them the very doctrine which we now preach. Six of them were accused of heresy before the tyrants of the district, and condemned to abjure heresy, and do penance half naked, with a faggot at their backs, and a taper in their hands, in the public market-place of Ely and Cambridge, and in the churchyard of Great Swaffham."—Claude's Essay, vol. ii., p. 54. Dr. Richard's Welsh Nonconformist Memorials, p. 436.

---

* "Their necks were tied fast to a post with towels, and their hands holden, that they might not stir; and so the hot iron was put to their cheeks. It is not certain whether branded with L for Lollard, or H for heretic, or whether it was only a formless print of iron."—Fuller's Ch. Hist., p. 164.

Bishop Longland, of Lincoln, enjoined, in 1521, that none of these persecuted Christians "should hide their marks upon their cheek, neither with hat, cap, hood, kerchief, napkin, or otherwise, nor shall suffer their beards to grow past fourteen days."—Foxe, p. 765. *Apud* Soame's Refor., vol. i., p. 159.

† Parliamentary History, vol. i., pp. 323–4.

‡ Crosby and others. § Forster's Essays, 1. Plantagenet et Tudor, 2.

Walsingham, referring to the examination of some of these men, says, "That they would by no means bring an infant to the church to be baptized by the parish priest, because, in their opinion, the Holy Trinity would be profaned by the sinfulness of such a ministry, and the dead be in a worse condition by being put into the priest's hands."*

The Lollards' tower, with its rings and chains of iron, stands still, as the monument of the bitter hostility of their mitred tyrants, and the fidelity to their tenets of these noble and holy men.

Before entering on the history, the reader may be detained by a sentence or two on another topic. Historians of a certain class, and partisan writers, have been fond of designating us as "Anabaptists," and gathering around us all those elements of social disorder and fearful profligacy which the scenes of Munster, and the mad vagaries of Stork and his brethren, ever suggest.† Hard have they laboured to identify us with these men. We are not careful to answer them in this matter. The men that shrunk not from the severe privations of the jail, and the more terrible punishment of the stake, were not affected much by a name. It answered the purpose of their adversaries for a time; but they were blind to the logical consequences of their own position. They forgot, in the fulness of their malice, the retribution to which they were exposing themselves. To trace the sad events which resulted from the efforts to secure social freedom, to the doctrines that the individual

---

* Walsingham, *apud* Collier, vol. i., p. 619. Other evidence may be seen in Crosby, vol. i., pp. 19–24.

† Robertson, ch. v., book v. On the other side, consult Robinson's Ecc. Res., ch. xiv., p. 535. It is no part of our plan to enter on this subject, or it would not be difficult to prove how prejudice on the one hand, and ignorance on the other, have warped the judgment of most of our popular historians. Mr. Underhill intimated, some years ago, his intention to give to the world his researches on this subject. As yet that promise is unredeemed. Its fulfilment would rectify many of our popular writers on these events.

consciousness of God's claim on man's affections, and that the Christian profession is only made by an immersion of the individual in water, "in the name of the Father, of the Son, and of the Holy Ghost," is only to lay open their own system to the most crushing retort. It were just as easy to demonstrate that the world has been the vast theatre on which Pædobaptists have perpetrated crimes at which humanity shudders, and over which piety and virtue must weep, as that the Anabaptists, as a body, were found steeped in crime, and revelling in lust.* The term, always one of reproach, is now scarcely ever used, except by a few remaining types of the condensed bigotry and ignorance of the past. The error in which it originated, and the injustice on which it was based, are passing away. In no sense was it ever applicable to our Fathers. No individuals would more strongly condemn Anabaptism than the persons to whom the charge was applied. They never advocated the repetition of baptism. Such a practice they would have repudiated. The sprinkling of infants they never recognised as Christian baptism. It not only violated their vital principles in relation to the individual, but not less their views of the scripturalness of the mode. With equal justice might the charge of Anabaptism be applied to Cyprian and his African brethren, to Dionysius and his brethren in Egypt, to Novatian at Carthage, and Novatus at Rome, and the churches they founded; whilst Donatus and his followers, Arius and his followers, all rejected the baptism of those who have since been designated Catholics, and regarded their churches as habitations of impurity, and invariably baptized all who came from them,— not as a repetition of baptism, but from the conviction that their previous baptism wanted some essential element. The morality of some of these dissidents was more rigid than that of the favoured sects, yet they invariably inculcated

---

* Henry the Eighth "charges the commotions and revolts in Germany upon Luther's doctrines, and that he had been the occasion of a great deal of rapine and disorder in the world."—Collier, vol. ii., p. 21.

"one Lord, one faith, one baptism."* The task would be easy of accomplishment to show, that, on the principles involved in the application of this term, nearly all the purity and truth in the world, for generations, was found in the community of Anabaptists. Dr. Wall, with a candour which distinguishes him from many of his brethren, felt the impropriety of this appellation, and used the term Anti-pædobaptists.†

Upon the narrative itself we now enter. Our starting-point will be the Tudor dynasty; and, passing on to the most eventful periods of British history, we shall close with the final expulsion of the Stuarts from the throne of these realms.

CHAPTER I.

THE TUDOR DYNASTY.

THE era which marked the accession to the throne of England of the descendant of the Welshman, was one pregnant with the most important consequences. Causes were operating which, in their ultimate issues, not only affected the social, the religious, and the commercial life of England, but more or less the condition of the civilized world. On some of these causes, we shall be pardoned if, for a moment, we detain the reader's attention.

The discovery of the art of printing placed within the hands of the people a power, the influence of which is even yet augmenting. It gave a mighty impulse to the awakened mind of Europe, which led to the study of those great masterpieces of thought, which had lain entombed

---

* Cyprian's Letter. Robinson's Hist. of Baptism, ch. xxxiv.
† History of Infant Baptism.

amidst the dust and neglect of the cloister for ages. Refined taste, mental culture, marked improvement in artistic effort and scientific inquiry, were the result. Dante, Petrarch, Boccaccio, had thrown the splendour of their genius over Italy, and its radiance had illumined other lands. In every way humanity was benefited by the discovery of printing. Dogmatism, especially, was smitten in its high places, and free inquiry was everywhere encouraged.

The spirit of commerce had opened new regions to the rivalry and enterprise of Europe,—regions clothed with all the attractions with which the most romantic ardour could invest them. Columbus had centred in himself the hopes of thousands.* The envied of multitudes, the daring spirits of the age sought to emulate him. Everywhere the influence of his movement was felt. From every seaboard adventurers started in the search of unknown lands and exhaustless wealth. The effect of this on mind, liberty, and social life, need not be indicated.

A series of events had contributed, for generations, to invest the Papacy with spiritual supremacy. The iron sceptre of Christ's vicar had broken in pieces every opposing power. Secure under his triple crown, emancipated from all fear of rebellion against his vicariate, the insolence of the successor of the Galilean fisherman was unbounded, and "*the servant of the servants of God*" exclaimed, "*Thou shalt trample on the lion and the adder*," as he placed his foot on the neck of kings.† But in the day of his mightiest prowess there were signs of weakness. The conflicts of the civil and spiritual powers had been frequent. The soil of England had witnessed many a struggle. The blood of martyred millions was crying for vengeance; and reason and truth were shocked at the cruelties which were inflicted on men,

---

* On the subject of the visit of this great man to England, the reader may consult Sharon Turner's Henry VIII., and Washington Irving's Life of Columbus. † Ranke's History of the Popes.

far more honest and holy than the very best of their persecutors. Virtue could find no resting-place within the palace of the Vatican.*

> "Long had the Pope proclaimed himself to the world
>   Half man, half God;
> Now, by God's blessing, we are enabled to see him
>   Half man, half Satan."

Alexander had left a memory far more execrable than that of Nero or Caligula. The enormous wickedness of his son, Cæsar Borgia, stamps his pontificate with unmixed infamy.† His successor was Julian the Second. This Vicar of the Prince of Peace was the most warlike Pontiff who had worn the tiara. The booming of cannon, the ring of the war cry, and the groans of the dying, appear to have been more melodious in his ears than the all but ravishing music of the Lateran. Turbulent, plotting, ambitious of power and dominion, Europe was ever agitated by his malignant genius.‡ Immorality, moreover, afflicted the whole body. From the conclave down to the humblest monastery, vice flourished. Arrogance, wealth, the love of power, everywhere seen, had operated on the public mind, and extorted from Europe a long and loud cry " for a reformation in the head and members." For generations, hostility to Rome had been growing. The noble, the moral, the enlightened, had denounced her.§ Only by the Inquisition and the stake, by massacre and carnage, had she repelled their attacks. The efforts of Luther were only the utterance of the past; the

---

* *Vide* Epis. of Petrarch. He calls Rome "a school of error, a temple of heresy; once Rome, now Babylon, the fallen and wicked, the hell of the living."

† Villiers on the Influence of the Reformation, &c.

‡ Ranke's History of the Popes, chap. ii.

§ The reader will find abundant proof of this in Rosetti's interesting volumes on the Anti-papal Spirit which preceded the Reformation, vol. i., chap. i., ii., &c. Spottiswood gives a melancholy account of the church of Scotland, lib. ii., pp. 59-60.

weapons with which he smote, with such terrific power, the very centre of Catholic unity, were forged by the martyred host which had fallen in the conflict.

The spirit of civil liberty was shedding her light over a wider circle, and putting forth higher claims, and calmly but firmly asking for broader privileges. Feudalism was losing its hold on the nations, and the peoples of Europe were rapidly improving their political condition. Society was struggling, like some great giant bound in fetters, to emancipate itself from those restraints which civil and spiritual despotism unitedly had imposed upon it. In no country was this struggle, probably, more marked than in England, and no people were more disposed to realise to the full extent the influence resulting from it. The recollection of these things is essential to the correct understanding of the great and rapid changes which marked the close of the fifteenth, and the greater portion of the sixteenth, century. The events which transpired during these periods, which shed such glory on the world, and opened to humanity at large long-hidden sources of happiness, were only the harvest of those seeds which the persecuted had sown,—the liberty and the purity which they had died to secure to us.

Amidst the groans of the wounded, and the struggles of the dying, the diadem was placed on the head of the first of the Tudors; and on the field of Bosworth, Henry was hailed by the mailed warriors as monarch of England.* From early youth his life had been tried, and his character formed, by a discipline by no means uncommon in those days to the class to which he belonged. Upon the whole, his mind had been well cultivated; and one of his eulogists tells us that he was master of several languages. The circumstances of his early life would more than warrant this opinion. Uniting in himself, by marriage, the rival claims of York and Lancaster, he finally succeeded in consolidating a policy, from which

---

* Lord Bacon's Henry VII., p. 1. London, 1622.

sprang results which ultimately changed the condition of the whole island.* Up to this period two classes appear to have held the throne in subjection, and ever and anon to have retarded the prosperity of the nation by their struggles for supremacy in the State. The great feudal barons, and the church, were the chief sources of power. Royalty was often a mere puppet in their hands; whilst the wealth and numerous retainers of both were a source of frequent, if not perpetual, oppression to the commonwealth.† Henry wisely sought to curb the power of both.‡ In all the plots which disturbed his reign some of them were engaged. Around the pretenders to his throne, churchmen threw their influence. The ecclesiastical body was very corrupt. The inferior clergy were almost lawless, till, by an enactment in A.D. 1497, he authorized the bishops to punish them "by such imprisonment as they should think expedient."§ Intelligent piety was unknown, except in the few dissidents scattered here

---

* "His direct male line ceased in Queen Elizabeth, but the descendants of his daughter Margaret succeeded in the Stuarts. The superior Brunswick line, which has given a stability to our civil and religious liberties, &c., is also, through her, a branch of Henry's descendants."—Sharon Turner's Middle Ages, vol. iv., p. 165.

† Turner's Middle Ages, vol. iv., p. 149. Grafton, Leland, and others, supply ample materials illustrative of these statements. The income of these nobles would range from £6,000 to £7,000 per annum. Wheat was worth from 1s. 6d. to 2s. the quarter. Lambs were worth 1s., fat sheep, 3s. 4d., and fat oxen would only realize £1 3s. 8d. These figures, multiplied by twelve, will give the reader their value in our present money.—Froude's History, vol. i., chap. i.

‡ Grafton says, "He used this rigour only, as he said himself, to bring low and abate the high stomachs of the wild people nourished and brought up in seditious factions and civil rebellion," &c.

§ "So much reverence was attributed to the holy orders, that although a priest had committed high treason against his sovereign lord, and to all other offenders in murder, rape, or theft, yet the life was given, and the punishment of death relaxed." During this reign, a petition was presented by the gentlemen and farmers of Carnarvonshire, accusing the clergy of systematic seduction of their wives and daughters. Grafton, p. 931. The privilege of sanctuary was greatly reformed by Henry.

and there, who worshipped the Saviour in the solitude of the woods, or by stealth in some obscure place, for fear of the spies of the mitred lords. That profligacy of the worst kind flourished in the monasteries, and was indulged by the priests, admits of no doubt. It would be difficult for language to exaggerate the enormity of their crimes. The evidence of this is overwhelming.

The wise and cautious policy of Henry grappled with these evils. Under the control of law both these powerful elements were brought; and by the marriage of his children he laid the foundation, though unwittingly, first of the Reformation, and then of the accession of the Stuarts to the throne of these realms. Royalty from his reign became a reality, and not a form.

Partly, perhaps, to gratify the clergy, whose influence he had weakened, and whose immoralities he tried to check, he allowed their hostility to the godly to display itself. Of the sentiments held by many of their victims we have no distinct record. With the opinions of Lollardism they were tainted, there is no doubt. How far they rejected the baptism of infants, so common at this time, the evidence is not so certain. It is not improbable that some of them may have been foreign Baptists, who fled from their continental enemies. The first victim was a poor old woman, who was, A.D. 1494, burnt at the stake. Two years later, the church was gratified by the spectacle of many Lollards bearing faggots at St. Paul's Cross, whilst they listened to the edifying exhortations of some fiery zealot.* In A.D. 1498, public curiosity was gratified by the exhibition of twelve of this

---

* "The Lollards, after abjuration, were forced to wear the fashion of a faggot, wrought in thread or painted, on their left sleeves, all the days of their lives: it being death to put on their cloaks without that cognizance. And, indeed, to poor people it was true,—put it off, and be burned; keep it on, and be starved: seeing none generally would set them on work that carried that badge about them."—Fuller's Church History, book v., p. 165.

class; and a few years later, the prior of a monastery, and five others, were doomed to the same humiliating penance. These cruelties were enacted in the metropolis; and though we have but little information, no doubt provincial zeal would burn with as bright and steady a flame at Norwich, Lincoln, and York, as it did at Fulham and Lambeth.

We are now approaching a period when history throws a clearer and steadier light on the subject of our inquiries; and, guided by her records, we may trace, with unmistakable distinctness, the action and principles of our forefathers.

CHAPTER II.

HENRY THE EIGHTH.

No monarch had ever ascended the throne of England with such promise as Henry. Young, cultivated, and endowed with many of those social and mental qualities which inspire the most sanguine with brighter hopes, and give confidence to the most cautious and prudent, his advent to the throne was hailed with rapture. The heart of the nation thrilled with ecstacy. He was, to some extent, the embodiment of the spirit of the age. Chivalrous, fond of gorgeous splendours, indulging in all the martial and manly exercises which distinguished his era, yet free, and throwing around him a gladsome influence, all concurred in laying at the feet of the young and ambitious monarch the most glowing tribute of their admiration.* Educated for the church,

---

* Details will be found in Fabian, pp. 529—535. Turner's Henry VIII., ch. i. "This most serene king is not only very expert in arms and of great valour and most excellent in personal endowments, but is likewise so gifted and adorned with mental accomplishments of every sort, that we believe him to have few equals in the world. He speaks English,

and conversant with theological doctrines, the episcopate counted on his favours, whilst the politician and the warrior anticipated the fullest opportunity for displaying their peculiar prowess. Everything around him was favourable to the development of the peculiarities of his nature, and the gratification of his desires. The heir of both Roses, no competitor for the throne was feared, and he had only to consolidate his empire, and augment the nation's glory. The state of Europe too was singularly felicitous. It is an interesting fact, that on the thrones of the three great monarchies young men were seated,—Charles of Germany, Spain, and the New World; Francis of France; and our Henry. These men had much in common. They were all endowed with great mental qualities, well trained and disciplined according to the spirit of the age, and glowed with intense desire for distinction in all those things which monarchs so dearly love. They enjoyed, too, the full affections of the church. Their courtiers and nobles sympathised with their masters and emulated their display; their people, delighting in shows and martial grandeur, thought, in common with their chiefs, that the greatness and glory of a nation were the savage war spirit by which it was animated, and the physical prowess of its people. To this the history of the past scarcely furnishes a parallel.*

The accumulations of his father supplied Henry with an ample treasure from which he could gratify his love of display, and he opened his reign with a magnificent coronation. His marriage of his deceased brother's wife, Catherine of Spain, after a solemn repudiation of the lawfulness of

---

French, Latin; understands Italian well; plays almost on every instrument; sings, and composes fairly: is prudent and sage, and free from every vice." So wrote the Venetian Ambassador.

* Froude presents us with a truthful and graphic picture of the social condition of the various classes in England at this time, vol. i., ch. i. Turner's Henry VIII., vol. i. Latimer gives us many interesting glimpses of social life. *Vide* Sermons (Parker Society).

the contract, was ultimately the cause of events which have gathered around him the most conflicting opinions. The pages of the ultra-Protestant history are full of light and brilliancy; he is the central figure, around which are gathered the great and the good of that age: whilst the Romanist clothes him with all those attributes which are repulsive to our moral sense, and makes him pass before us as a fiend incarnate. Both extremes need modifying. No doubt circumstances influenced his conduct and prompted his actions. Truth must trace up the cause of his conduct in the divorce exclusively to Romish influence. The doubt, and protest against the marriage, were almost forced by the Legate of England. A French bishop awakened the doubt by asking about the legitimacy of Mary, and Wolsey himself had instituted inquiries before Henry had troubled his own conscience.* We have no cause, in reality there is none, to attribute to him the selfish and brutalised nature to which one class would trace all the actions of his life; nor, on the other, can we admit the encomiums of his eulogists without considerable allowance. The Tudor dynasty was essentially iron-willed, and fond of power. In Henry, both these features were exemplified. A modern writer, whose recent researches and broad sympathies with liberty have illumined many a dark page of our history, speaks of the family "as strong-willed, but able to put a restraint on their passions. Their tyranny fully indulged

---

* The reader will find this placed in a clear light by Turner, and later still by Froude, vol. i., ch. ii. "Of this trouble I only may thank you, my Lord Cardinal of York," said Catherine; "for because I have wondered at your high pride and vain glory, and abhor your voluptuous life, and little regard your presumptuous power and tyranny, therefore of malice you have kindled this fire, and set this matter abroad, and in especial for the great malice you bare to my nephew, the Emperor." Hall, p. 755. Bishop Godwyn's Annals of Henry VIII., p. 101. Tyndale says he did this through his tool, the Bishop of Lincoln, confessor to the King. In another place he says, that the Emperor affirms that Wolsey did this, because he would not aid him in his efforts for the triple crown. Tyndale's Works, vol. i., pp. 463, 465-6.

in the court, but watched and conciliated the people. Henry the Eighth spurned, renounced, and utterly cast off the Pope's authority, without too suddenly revolting the people's usages and habits: to arrive at blessed results by ways that a better man might have held to be accursed; to persecute with an equal hand the Romanist and Lutheran; to send the Protestant to the stake for resisting Popery, and the Roman Catholic to the scaffold for not admitting him to be Pope." *

To unfold the causes which produced the Reformation,— causes which had been working before either Henry or Catherine was born,— to mark the influence which that great event exerted on this nation and Europe at large, is not the object of this volume.† Yet a glance at the condition of the church cannot be withheld, without manifold injustice to the subject, as well as to the reader.

It is saying but little, that at this era evangelical religion was low. Effects never exist apart from causes; and as the ministry was a mass of ignorance and superstition, no one has a right to expect grapes from thorns, or figs from thistles. The people never rise in moral excellence and social virtues higher than their teachers. The religious state of a community can never be accurately gathered from the page of history. To other sources we must repair; and from writers equally honest, but of a widely different class, we must gather the materials absolutely necessary for such a work. We shall be forgiven if we select from other pens a few facts and illustrations. The people relied "on the merit of their own works toward their justification, such as pilgrimages to images, kneeling, kissing, and cursing of them, as well as many other hypocritical works in their store of religion; there being marts or markets of merits, full of holy relics, images, shrines, and works

---

* Forster's Essays: Plantagenet et Tudor, p. 222.
† *Vide* Villiers's Influence of the Reformation.

of supererogation, ready to be sold; and all things they had were called holy: holy cowls, holy girdles, holy pardons, holy beads, holy shoes, holy rules." * "They were greatly seduced by certain famous and notorious images, as by our Lady of Walsingham, our Lady of Ipswich, St. Thomas of Canterbury,† St. Anne of Buxton, the Rood of Grace. . . . To these they made vows and pilgrimages, thinking that God would hear their prayers in that place rather than in another place. They kissed their feet devoutly, and to these they offered candles, and images of wax, rings, beads, gold, and silver abundantly. And because they that taught them had thereby great commodity, ‡ they maintained the same with feigned miracles and erroneous doctrines, teaching the people that God would hear their prayers made before these images rather than in another place." § "Sometimes," says Cranmer, "the people would run from their seats to the altar, and from altar to altar, and from sacring (as they call it) to sacring, peeping, toating, ǁ and gazing at that thing which the priest held up in his hand." ¶ Sometimes the shout was heard to the priest, "Hold up, hold up!" and one would say to the other, "*This day I have seen my Maker; and I cannot be quiet, except I see my Maker once a day.*" ** Rough, racy, good old Father Latimer, gives us many glimpses of the dark and gloomy superstition enthroned everywhere in the kingdom. †† The moral and

---

* Homily of Good Works. *Apud* Todd's Cranmer, vol. ii., pp. 14, 15.

† Todd's Illustrations of the Lives of Chaucer and Gower supply us with some curious information about the worship of this saint. The reader may also consult Hume, vol. vi., p. 181., ed. 1796.

‡ Gains.   § Cranmer's Catechism, Todd's Cranmer, vol ii., p. 50. "We will have the Sacrament hung over the high altar, and there to be worshipped as it was wont to be; and they which will not thereto consent, we will have them die like heretics against the holy Catholic faith." —Petition of the Devonshire Rebels, art. iv.

ǁ Gazing about.   ¶ The elevation of the host.
** Todd, vol. ii., p. 319.   †† *Vide* his Sermons (Parker Society).

intellectual condition of the clergy can scarcely be described. Their power over the masses was complete. The destiny of the people for both worlds was in their hands. With their influence they encircled them from the cradle to the grave. Claiming to be the vicegerents or the representatives of the Holy One, their lives were a perpetual exposition of the hypocrisy which marked them. Decency was thrown aside, and morality unknown. Brothels were kept in London for the especial use of the priesthood. The confessional was abused, and profligacy was all but universal. The punishment for their flagitious crimes was trifling. Five paternosters, a few aves or credos, with the present of a waxlight to some altar, would cleanse the sinner from his pollution.* Tyndale's description of this class is abundantly sustained by other writers of that age: "The priests of the country be unlearned, as God knoweth. There are a full ignorant sort, which have seen no more Latin than that they read in their portesses † and missals, which yet many of them can scarcely read, except it be *Albertus de Secretis Mulierum*, in which yet, though they be never so lowly learned, they pore day and night, and make notes therein, and all to teach midwives, as they say; and Linwode, a book of constitutions, to gather together mortmains, offerings, customs, and other pillage, which they call not theirs but God's part, and the duty of holy church, to discharge their consciences withal." ‡

---

* *Vide* Froude's History, vol. i., pp. 178-9. "Moreover, besides daily corrupting other men's wives, and open whoredom, unto what abominations, too filthy to be spoken of, hath their voluntary chastity led them!" Tyndale, vol i., pp. 38-39. Also, Simon Fish, in 1531, said to the government: "Tie the holy idle thieves to the cart, to be whipped, naked, till they fall to labour, that they by their importunate begging take not away the alms that the good charitable people would give unto us sore, impotent, miserable people, your bed men."—Fox, vol. iv., p. 664. Froude, vol. i., p. 47. † The Breviary.

‡ Works of Tyndale and Frith, by the Rev. T. Russell, M.A., vol. i., p. 3. "In the rural districts the clergy were universally ignorant, idle, slothful, superstitious, proud, and vicious; preaching very seldom, and

Referring to the same class, Latimer says: "Ever since the prelates were made lords and nobles, their plough standeth, there is no work done. They hawke, they hunt, they card, they dice, they pastime in their prelacies with gallant gentlemen, with their dancing minions, and with their fresh companions, so that ploughing is set aside; and by the lording and loitering, preaching and ploughing is clean gone." *
"They are so troubled with lordly living, they be so placed in palaces, couched in courts, ruffling in their rents, dancing in their dominions, burdened with embassages, pampering of their paunches, like a monk that maketh a jubilee: munching in their mangers, and moiling in their gay manors and mansions, and so troubled with loitering in their lordships, that they cannot attend. They are otherwise occupied: some in the king's matter, some are ambassadors, some of the privy council, some to furnish the courts, some are lords of parliament, and some are presidents and controllers of the mint." † "I hear that some of these men wear velvet shoes and velvet slippers; such fellows are more fit to dance the morris-dance than to be admitted to preach." ‡ Like clouds of locusts, the friars penetrated every nook and corner of the land, obtruding their dirty bodies and their shameless faces into every family. To these cormorants nothing came amiss. Their bag was open for a bushel of wheat, or malt, or rye: a piece of cheese, a side of bacon, or a good cut of beef. Old Chaucer has painted these locusts of his age with great accuracy. The Wife of Bath is the reporter:—

> "For now the grete charites and prayers
> Of limituous, and other holy freres:
> That serchen every land and every streme,
> As thicklie as motes in the sonne beame;

teaching the people fables and legends, rather than the true and wholesome word of God."—Burnet's History of the Reformation, vol. i., p. 21.

* *Vide* Sermons (Religious Tract Society), p. 40.
† *Ibid* (Parker Society), p. 67. ‡ *Ibid* (Parker Society), p. 289.

> Blessing halles, chambers, kichenes, and boures,
> Citees and burghs, castles highe, and towers,
> Thropes * and bernes, shepenes and diavies.
> This maketh that ther ben no faeries :
> For ther as wont to walken was an elf,
> Ther walketh now the limiton himself,
> In undumeles and in mor neninges,
> And saith his matins and his holy thinges,
> As he goeth in his limitations." †

To form accurate conceptions of the moral state of the people is all but impossible. By no effort can we throw the mind back so as fully to realize the past. It is less difficult with the secular than with the moral. The reasons are so obvious that we need not detail them. The data on which we can rest our conclusions are necessarily limited. Ignorance, superstition, and immorality, however, are features which stand out with prominency. The implicit obedience which the people rendered to their spiritual guides necessarily produced these results. Doubts, the freedom of inquiry, are requisite to spiritual life and moral power. Limit the range, raise up barriers beyond which no thought shall go, and you retard the progress of truth, and imperil the highest interests of society. At no time were these evils more rife. The spiritual power was supreme, and hostility to it was death. ‡ Above all law the priesthood placed themselves. As fathers had a right to control and punish their children, so these spiritual fathers could deal with the laity. Emperor and monarch must bow to their will. §

Occasionally we get a glimpse of the popular religion of

---

* Villages. † Wife of Bath, v. 6447–59.

‡ "The very prelates are now so sore changed, that if they smell that one of their flock do but once long or desire for the true knowledge of Christ, they will slay him, burning him with fire most cruelly."—Tyndale, vol. i., p. 229.

"There is not the poorest desolate widow, but with his fair flattery he will so deceive her, that he will be sure either of money or meal."—Frith's Mirror, Works of Tyndale and Frith, vol. iii., p. 275.

§ Burnet, vol. i., pp. 12—17.

this era, like the following, though we can scarcely credit the representation, so perfectly destitute is it of anything which is consistent with the immaculate purity and dignity of the Great Supreme, and of the most obvious necessities of man's moral nature. Tyndale thus describes many of the ceremonies in which religion consisted, and for which more or less money was paid:—

"Christenings, churchings, banns, weddings; offerings at weddings, offerings at buryings, offerings to images, offerings of wax and lights, which come to their damage; besides the superstitious waste of wax in tapers throughout the land. These brotherhoods and pardoners,[1] what get they by confession? Yea! and many enjoin penances, to give a certain (sum) for to have so many masses said, and desire to provide a chaplain themselves. Soul masses, dirges,[2] month minds,[3] peace minds, all souls' days, and trentals.[4] The mother church and high altar must have something in every testament. Offerings at priests' first masses. No man is professed, of whatsoever religion it be, but he must bring something. The hallowing, or, rather, conforming of churches, chapels, altars, superaltars, chalice, vestments, and bells. Then book, bell, candlestick, organ, chalice, vestments, copes, altar-clothes, surplices, towels, basins, ewers, sheep, censors, and all manner of ornaments, must be found them freely, they will not give a mite thereunto. Last of all, what swarms of begging friars there are! The parson shareth, the vicar shareth, the parish priest pulleth, the friar scrapeth, and the pardoner pareth; we lack but a butcher to pull off the skin." *

"The people are thoroughly brought in belief," says the same writer, "that the deed in itself, without any further respect, saveth them: if they be so long at church; or say so many paternosters; or read so much in a tongue which they understand not; or go so much on a pilgrimage; and take so much pain; or fast such a superstitious fast; or observe such a superstitious observance, neither profitable to himself nor to his neighbours, but done by a good

---

(1) A seller of pardons. (2) A hymn in the Romish service, beginning "*Dirige gressos meos.*" (3) Days when the soul was had in special remembrance. (4) A service of thirty masses.

* Works, vol. i., p. 270. The language of religion was unknown to the people. "They pray in Latin, they christen in Latin, they bless in Latin, they grant absolutions in Latin; only curse they in the English tongue." *Ibid*, vol. i., p. 305.

intent, say they, to please God withal. Yea, to kiss the pax they think it a meritorious deed, when before their neighbours." *

Religion with the mass of the people, then, was a mere form. Multiplied ceremonies had scarcely left a trace of the Divine original. Taught to regard the priesthood as the representatives of Christ, and crushed with the most fearful power, their obedience was implicit, though the tyranny exercised over them was without a parallel in the world's history. To submit to penances, to wear hair-shirts, to go barefoot and with head uncovered, to repeat vows the meaning of which they knew not, to fast on bread and water—some once, some twice a week, some all the week; some for one, two, or even ten years; and to lie in filth; to go on pilgrimage and visit the memorials of saints, and expend their resources on the church: this was their faith. Or, if these sacrifices were too great, others could be purchased to do all the work for them which religion demanded. The moral state of the people under such teaching was almost beyond conception. Ignorance, vice, and immorality of the worst kind, reigned all but universally.†

"The soul of religion, however, had died out of it for many generations before the Reformation. Faith had sunk into superstition; duty had died into routine." ‡

Wolsey, for years the leading counsellor of the king, and the most influential man in the nation, was a genuine type of the dignified clergy of his day. Low in his origin, he rose to an eminence which cast into the shade all his rivals. We state the former fact, respecting his origin, not from any sympathy with those who look on it as a blot. Birth and wealth are accidents men cannot control. There is no virtue in being born to a coronet, or to the possession of vast estates. To conquer circumstances, and to make the elements of adversity minister to your elevation, is true greatness.

---

* Tyndale, vol. i., p. 312.   † *Vide* Tyndale, vol. ii., p. 413; also p. 415.
‡ Froude, vol. ii., p. 408.

They only are true men, who leave the impress of their own genius or moral power on the ranks of society below which they were born. Other features marked Wolsey, than his being a butcher's son. His first parishioners gazed at their pastor as he sat in the stocks for drunkenness. Property belonging to the Bishop of Lincoln he appropriated to his own use; whilst the powerlessness of his vow of celibacy was manifest in living proofs to multitudes.* Brought into contact with the youthful monarch by mere accident, by his servile arts and his more loose morality he ministered to his master's gratification, and daily rose in the estimation of the pleasure-loving king.† His progress was rapid. To the highest pinnacle in Church and State his ambition carried him. Swayed only by one ever-present and all-absorbing motive, he hesitated at no means, and was deterred by no moral principle, in the gratification of his insatiate love of power.‡ Archbishop, chancellor, and cardi-

---

* "Wolsey had a son and daughter, by the daughter of a man of the name of Lark. The daughter was a nun at Shaftesbury—what became of the son is uncertain."—Galt's Life, p. 181. *Vide* Articles of Impeachment. *Vide* Campbell's Lives of the Chancellors, vol. i., pp. 439—445, 449. Respecting his magnificence, *vide* pp. 455—457, 459. Burnet says that "later on in life he had an infamous disease," vol. i., p. 8.

† "Every age," said he, "of man had its seasons and delights agreeable. They did not do well that would force the king to act an old man before his time—youth being utterly averse from wrinkled society. . . . . Until the time came, he should enjoy the present, and not by hearkening to others' needless persuasions, any way interrupt the course of that felicity which the largeness of his dominions could easily afford him to."—Godwyn's Annals of Henry VIII., p. 29. In this tone did this teacher of morality discipline his patron, even offering to free him from the cares of the council table, by reporting to him the chief points of discussion.—*Ibid*, p. 29.

‡ The ambition of this unprincipled priest was boundless. Nothing could impede his gratification. Upon all law he would trample, over all ranks he would pass. By his insatiable thirst for power, he shed some of the noblest blood in the realm. Charles said, when referring to the death of the Duke of Buckingham, that "*the butcher's dog had killed the fairest hart in England*," &c.—Godwyn's Annals of Henry VIII., p. 47. His appearance is thus described by a cotemporary poet :—

nal, all but royalty centred in him.* Mingling with emperors and monarchs, his state was little inferior to theirs; and the enormous wealth which he drew from his multiplied offices and ecclesiastical dignities, not only enabled him to gratify this love of display, but to subordinate almost every element of civil and religious power to his own sordid interest. Bishop Godwyn remarks, that except the Bishops of Rome, all Europe never saw a more potent prelate. It is doubtful if the bishop's language admits even of this qualification. His splendour was quite imperial. "His retinue consisted of near about a thousand persons, among which was one earl, commonly nine barons, many knights and gentlemen, and officers belonging to his house above four hundred—besides their servants, which far exceeded the former number. His chapel was served by a dean, a sub-dean, a chanter, thirty-five singers (sixteen of whom were clergy). In addition to these were sixteen chaplains of the most

---

"A great carl he is, and fat;
Wearing on his head a red hat,
Procured with angels' subsidy;

"And, as they say, in time of rain
Four of his gentlemen are fain
To hold o'er it a canopy.

"Besides this, to tell them more news,
He hath a pair of costly shoes,
Which seldom touch the ground:

"They are so goady and curious,
All of gold and stones precious,
Costing many a thousand pound.

"And who did for these shoes pay?
Truly, many a rich abbay,
To be eased of his visitations."
—Galt's Life of Wolsey, p. 168.

* He was Archbishop of York, Bishop of Winchester and of Bath, and Abbot of St. Alban's. The income from such pluralities was enormous. That of the Archbishopric of Canterbury alone was estimated at £6,000 per annum. Multiply this by twelve, and the reader will then have its value according to our present standard.—Froude, vol. i., pp. 35, 88.

learned in the kingdom, with two cross-bearers and as many pillar-bearers," &c.* Only the diadem and the triple crown were above him.† To the latter he aspired more than once, and he thought the dazzling bauble was just within his reach. He bribed largely, through his agents, in order to neutralize hostility to his claim.‡ The moral state of the conclave and court of Rome was very low. "I should say, myself (and I have said it often before), that your majesty may have the whole college at your devotion, for ever, if you will spend 20,000 ducats amongst the leading cardinals, in pensions and benefices. Give one of them a thousand, and these 2,000 or 3,000, and you will find the money well laid out to your advantage." § In the twelfth century the same corruption prevailed. "Our lord the Pope, indeed, is a holy and righteous man, and his abbot, as I am told by many, does his best to imitate him; but their necessities are so great, and the dishonesty and cupidity of the Romans are so standing, that the Pope, sometimes under his prerogative, and by dispensation, obtains what may benefit the state, but cannot benefit religion." ‖ "I will not apply to those Roman robbers, for they do nothing but plunder the needy without compunction." ¶

We have seen that revenge for his disappointment at the

---

* Godwyn's Annals, p. 113.

† "For pride, covetousness, and ambition, he excelled all others, as you shall hear after." . . . "When he was once a perfect cardinal, he looked then above all estates, so that all men almost hated him and disdained him." . . . "In other presence he would lye and say untruth, and was double both in speech and meaning : he would promise much and perform little. He was vicious of his body, and gave the clergy evil example. The authority of this cardinal set the clergy in such a pride that they disdained all men," &c., &c.—Hall, pp. 567, 583, 774. London, 1809.

‡ Galt, p. 379; Burnet, vol. i., p. 19.

§ Letter from the Spanish Ambassador at Rome to Charles V., August 5th, 1529.—The Pilgrim. *Apud* Append., p. 84.

‖ John of Salisbury.

¶ Giles's Life of Becket, vol. ii., pp. 18, 157, 171, 201.

loss of the Papacy prompted Wolsey to suggest thoughts to Henry which led to the overthrow of the Papal authority in this country, and which, in the end, exhibited him crushed by the power which he had created, forsaken of the king whom he had served, and hated by all the other grades of society below him.* With the spirit of Wolsey the inferior grades of the clergy were animated. Around him they moved, as the centre of their hopes and fears; whilst the worldliness and insensibility to high moral principle which ever marked him, found its reflex in the vices and immoralities which rioted in monastic establishments and in the homes of the priesthood. "*The whole head was sick, and the whole heart faint.*"

One of the necessary results which sprang from this religious movement—a movement which had long been foreshadowed, which would have transpired in spite of Henry, which the cardinal saw, and, striving to arrest its progress, was crushed beneath its power†—was the conflicting prin-

---

* Tyndale says that "when his hat was brought to Westminster, it was set on a cupboard, and taken about, so that the greatest duke in the land must make courtesy thereto; yea, and to his empty seat."—The Practice of Prelates, vol. i., p. 484. Cavendish says that "he was the haughtiest man that lived."—Life, vol. ii., p. 126.

† Froude, vol. i., chap. 2. We gather the progress of this conflict from the letters of the French Ambassador, from which we give an extract or two :—

"The bishops have had a grand struggle. Part desired to retain the mass complete, part to make a new service. The majority were with the conservatives, who have carried the day. The king, as the leader of this party, said all which ought to have been said. He maintained that the holy sacrament ought to be believed and adored, and to be honoured with the ceremonies observed in the church from immemorial time. Evil speaking, therefore, against the sacraments is prohibited under pain of death; and priests are forbidden to marry." (Maillac to Francis I. 1539.) —Froude's Pilgrim, p. 128.

In another letter, Maillac says that "the king's declaration about the sacrament has given wide pleasure and satisfaction. The people in general are inclined to the old religion, and only a few bishops support the new opinions. These bishops are in a bad humour," &c. (Maillac to the Constable. June, 1539.)—*Ibid*, p. 128.

ciples and parties it brought into opposition. It opened the prison-house of mind, and gave liberty to thought. Rome had its partizans—numerous, active, stern; men blind to every defect in the sensuous and superstitious forms of the old faith; men who, from passion, self-interest, or sincerity, believed all the claims which the Vatican put forth to spiritual supremacy as the representative of Christ on earth, and who thought all means lawful to sustain its pretensions, and life a trifling sacrifice to lay on its altar. Above all human law, and responsible only to God, they clung to the old system, and battled long for its integrity.*

In antagonism to these was another party, less numerous, perhaps, but living and acting under the protection of the

---

"The Lords about the Council, and the greater part of the people, are with him" [the king]. (Chastelleon to the Bishop of Paris.)—*Ibid*, p. 69, note B.

"Things are now at a pass when either Cromwell's party or the Bishop of Winchester's party must fall; and although both are in high favour and authority with the king their master, fortune will most probably turn in favour of Cromwell. The Dean of the Chapel, the Bishop of Winchester's best friend, is struck down; the Archbishop of Canterbury, his greatest adversary, has been deputed to preach in the bishop's place at St. Paul's, and has begun to argue against his doctrines in the same pulpit where the bishop preached in Lent. . . . Another doctor, named Latimer, who last year surrendered his see rather than subscribe to the Six Articles, is recalled, and will shortly be replaced on the bench. . . . The state of religion continues most unfortunate. The bishops are divided, and hate one another. The people know not what to believe; for those who are inclined to the reformed views are called heretics—those who adhere to the old faith are charged with papistry." (Maillac to the Constable. June 17, 1540.)—*Ibid*, p. 143.

"The Bishop of Chichester and the Dean of the Chapel Royal have been arrested on a charge of high treason, &c. The rest of the bishops are in terror. They are afraid that they also may be made out guilty; and their fate will be certain. The religious strife has become so bitter, that each party will destroy their antagonists if they can. There will be prisoners enough between them by and by." (Maillac to Francis I. June 1st, 1540.)—*Ibid*, p. 143.

* "For who can doubt," said Becket, "that Christ's priests are the fathers and masters of kings, and princes, and all the faithful?"—Giles's Life of Becket, vol. i., p. 336.

royal authority. Their views of Christian doctrine had been considerably modified—their hostility to the Papal power was unmixed. Aiming to reform the church, they abolished many forms of superstition which for ages had gathered round the great verities of the Gospel, and had impaired, if not quite destroyed, their vital energies. Their minds were largely imbued with the spirit and teaching of Moses. Everything was viewed by them through a Jewish medium. Things that differed they confounded, and the beauty and simplicity of the Gospel were lost amidst the splendour of the sanctuary. Participating in this, in common with the first class, their pretensions to priestly power were not lower, and they enforced them with a power and earnestness which evinced that their claim to alliance with the Aaronic order was not a form, but a terrible reality.

"There was a third party in the country—the only one which, in a true high sense, was of importance at all, and for the sake of which, little as it appeared, the whole work was to be done:—composed at that time merely of poor men,—poor cobblers, weavers, carpenters, trade apprentices, and humble artizans,—men of low birth and low estate, who might have been seen at night stealing along the lanes and alleys of London, carrying with them some precious load of books, which it was death to possess, and giving their lives gladly, if it must be so, for brief tenure of so dear a treasure." *

In this latter class, regarded by both the other parties with deadly hatred, as disturbers of public order; as men who ventured to think for themselves on the most vital matters, and to express their opinions as they had opportunity; men, the triumph of whose convictions would involve in utter ruin the religious theories of the old and the new form of ecclesiastical order; men who, drawing their inspirations from the fountain of Eternal Truth, held the sacred volume as

---

* Froude, vol. i., p. 152.

dear as life;—amongst these we shall have to trace the footsteps of our fathers.

It is difficult for us to realize their condition, or the moral courage which was requisite to sustain them. From the Chancellor down to the merest parish constable, an oath had been taken to hunt them to the death. Wolsey* and his colleagues had a keen scent for heresy, and pursued it with a vigour which success only augmented. Spies met the dissident at all points. In the solitude of the woods, in the obscurity of some dark narrow alley in the city, or in the quiet of the home circle, these wretches obtruded themselves. Like wild beasts, the people were hunted from one covert to another. Day and night the fear of detection was upon them. Escape at one time only increased the conviction of their danger.

Their end was ever before them. Amidst the joys and endearments of their homes, they knew that the informer might step in at any moment, and that then the prison, the rack, or the stake would await them.† They were men; men of tender sympathies and lofty principles; men of noble daring and holy aspirations for their country and the world; God's heroes, whose life was a daily martyrdom. Many of them we can only trace by the edicts of the council or the convocation of the clergy, as we gaze with rapture on their manly and Christian steadfastness in the presence of the haughty prelate, or their heroic fortitude at the martyr's stake. Beyond this we have no record. The pen of history has preserved none. Their names are embalmed amongst those who have willingly sacrificed their life for the world's freedom. There is their sole record.

---

* Justice to the Cardinal demands from us the acknowledgment, that More, Longland, and others of the episcopal bench, had a greater thirst for Protestant blood than Wolsey.

† In the country any unknown face was challenged and examined; if the account given was insufficient, he was brought before the justice.—Froude, vol. i., p. 36.

Proceedings in the Court of Wareham, at Knoll, A.D. 1511, give a glimpse of some who taught "*that the sacrament of baptism and confirmation is not necessary nor profitable for man's soul.*" * Crosby regards these as Baptists. We think the evidence is not complete. There were ten altogether—six men and four women. They were residents at Tenderden. Their faith embraced some ten articles, differing from that of the mitred prelate. They are points of dissidence in which all Baptists would agree, and such as we know were held by them in other times. In the histories of the Reformation fuller details are given;† it is enough for us to say that the prelate succeeded in terrifying them and others to a renunciation of their supposed errors, and bound them by an oath, not only to this, but degraded them to the betrayal of their brethren. Some were condemned to carry faggots and leave them at the church door; others, to go barefoot, with a lighted taper in their hands; others, to lay an offering on the high altar when mass was said.‡ In this way the ministers of truth sought to repress error. Their efforts were powerless.

In 1528 a similar process was carried on against seven individuals, who had probably fled from the demon of persecution in the Netherlands. The usual course was adopted. Imprisonments, and blandishments, and threats, overcame the constancy of five. They recanted, and bore the faggot in the usual way. Woman's nature triumphed. Stowe tells us that one woman and a man sealed their testimony with their blood, and, in the presence of a multitude, were burnt in Smithfield.§

In 1530, Wareham, anxious for the spiritual well-being

---

* Collier, vol. ii., p. 2.   † *Vide* Burnet, Collier, Crosby, &c.

‡ Collier, vol. ii., p. 2. Burnet adds,—"And to wear the badge of a faggot in flames on their clothes during their lives, or till they were dispensed with for it," vol. i., p. 27.

§ Chron., p. 576. D'Anvers, p. 306. Strange that he should mention these as coming in with Anne of Cleves!

of the nation, issued an elaborate address, in which he says: "Many books in the English tongue, containing many detestable errors and damnable opinions, are printed in countries beyond the seas, to be brought into divers towns and sundry of this his realm in England, and sown abroad in the same, to the great decay of our faith and the perilous corruption of the people, unless speedy remedy were briefly provided," &c. Then the works and doctrines are specified. From "The Sun of Scripture"* we quote the following on baptism:— "The water in the font has no more virtue in it than the water of the river: the baptism lies not in hallowed water, or in any other outward thing, but in the faith only. The water of baptism is nothing but a sign, that we must be under the standard of the cross." Collier supplies much more.

Invested with the full powers of supreme head of the church, his claims to spiritual supremacy recognized by the legislature and by the clergy, Henry manifested his anxiety for the souls of his people by warning them of errors, and by denunciations of those who propagated them. "*Forasmuch*," says one of his proclamations, "*as divers and sundray strangers, of the sects and false opinions of the Anabaptists and Sacramentarians,† being lately come into this realme, where they lurke secretely in divers corners and places, minding craftely and subtilly to provoke and stir the king's loving subjects to their errors and opinions,*" &c. Full of holy indignation, he denounces "their wicked and abominable errors," and enjoins their departure from the country within eight days.

The martyr spirit never quails before such agency. Its voice falls powerless on the ears of such men. In the "corners and lurking-places," in the alleys and lanes of the city, they

---

* Collier, vol. ii., pp. 49, ‧50. We think it more than probable that at least this work was of Baptist paternity.

† The followers of Zwingle.

remained. Stronger denunciations were hurled against them. The public were warned of many strangers, baptized in infancy, but who, despising the holy sacraments, had been rebaptized, and were spreading their damnable heresies throughout the land, to the fearful injury of holy church, and the great annoyance of its spiritual chief. Exile or death were the terms. Twelve days were granted to the moral lepers to seek refuge in other lands. If dragged from their hiding-places after that, death would be the consequence.*

An Englishman now claims our sympathy. James Bainham, a barrister of the Middle Temple, and styled by Crosby a knight, appears on the stage. His matrimonial connexion had excited the suspicions of the sleepless guardians of the faith. His wife was the widow of Simon Fish, the author of "The Beggar's Petition."† That he was connected with the Christian brethren appears probable; and Fox assures us that he repudiated the baptism of infants.‡ To be suspected, however, was enough. He was called before the ecclesiastical tribunal. Dissent from the leading doctrines of the church was the crime of which he was guilty. Refusing

---

* Wilkins, vol. iii., p. 779. Tracts on Liberty of Conscience, vol. i., p. 88 (Introduction).

† The following is an extract from it:—"This is the great scab, why they will not let the New Testament go abroad in your mother tongue, lest men should spy that their cloaked hypocrisy do translate thus fast your kingdom into their hands: that they are cruel, unclean, unmerciful, and hypocrites: that they seek not the honour of Christ, but their own." —The Beggar's Petition against Papacy, presented to Henry VIII., 1538; Harlean Miscellany, vol. ii., p. 539.

‡ "Likewise, touching the sacrament of baptism, his words were these: 'That as many as repent and do on them Christ, shall be saved; that is, as many as dye concerning sin shall live by faith with Christ. Therefore, it is not we that live after that, but Christ in us. And so, whether we live or dye, we are Christ's by adoption; and not by the water only, but by water and faith, that is, by keeping the promise made. For ye are kept by grace and faith, saith St. Paul, and that not of yourselves, for it is the gift of God.'"—Fox, vol. ii., p. 246.

to recant, he was, with his wife, committed to prison. Sir Thomas More, who had succeeded Wolsey in the Chancery, was more learned and had more culture than the great high priest, but he had more cruelty. By his orders, the prisoner was stretched on the rack, and tortured with severity. On the 17th of February he was carried before the Lord Bishop of London. Suffering from his torture, his spirit failed him, and he abjured his errors. Fearful as the rack may be, it is feeble compared with the pangs of conscious guilt. His misery was unutterable. The following Sunday, the congregation which had assembled in the church of St. Augustine, was startled during the service. A man rose in their midst, pale from recent suffering, holding in his hand a copy of the New Testament, and with tears flowing down his cheeks, confessed his crime in denying God in a moment of weakness. "If," said he, "I should not return to the truth, this Word of God would damn me body and soul, at the day of judgment." He urged the people to fidelity, declaring that he would not feel such a hell again for all the world's good.

The die was now cast. On endless ruin he was now bent. Spiritually dead, it was the loftiest exercise of mercy on the part of the spirituality to save him. What mattered a moment's torture of the body, even the roasting of it at the stake, if the soul could be saved from everlasting burning? This doctrine soothed the conscience, whilst it inflamed the zeal, of the spiritual man. We now find Bainham manacled and in the stocks, in the coal-cellar at Fulham, the residence of his lordship of London. The chill winds of March, and the damp and gloom of his prison, only augmented his zeal. The bishop failing, the chancellor would try his hand. Before him many a criminal had quailed. Will Bainham tremble? Of the power of More's persuasive eloquence we have no record. Of other arguments the martyrologists give us some report. In his house at Chelsea the confessor was kept, and for two nights was fastened to a post and whipped. The lash drew blood, but it produced no conviction. A week at Fulham was again tried; then the Tower for a fortnight, where the gaoler attempted, but ineffectually, to flog the heresy from him. A month later sentence was pronounced. The charity of the church was exhausted; and, at the close of the month of April, Smithfield witnessed the blazing faggots which consumed the hero, and the crowd listened to his last words. Thus died one of the noble army of martyrs.*

The elevation of Queen Anne to the throne was an event of some importance. The men of the new learning held it to be pregnant with everything which could contribute to the success of the Reformation: on the other hand, the Romanists denounced it everywhere, and the clergy sought by their inflammatory appeals to excite the people against it.† The power of the pulpit then was no insignificant thing. The character of this princess is still an unsolved problem in our annals. The pages of Saunders, and his copyists since, whilst they invest her with the most bewitching influence over the monarch, portray her as the embodiment of moral and physical repulsiveness; on the other hand, her advocates see no fault in her.‡ Be this as it may, one thing admits of no dispute : her influence over Henry was powerful. The beauty of her person, the liveliness of her wit, and her quenchless hatred to the Pope, enabled her to check the spirit of persecution. During the tide of her prosperity, the war of words went on, but the spirit of cruelty was held in check. But though she shielded others, the weight of royal and episcopal wrath still fell heavily on our forefathers. England had been an asylum for the persecuted brethren in the Low

---

* Fox, vol. iv., pp. 702—705. A shorter account is given by Burnet, vol. i. : Froude, vol. ii., pp. 85—87. Crosby has six lines, vol. i., p. 31.

† Burnet, vol. i., p. 127.

‡ *Vide* an elaborate examination of her character, in Froude, vol. ii., chap. 11. In justice to her memory, it should be read with other accounts (Burnet, vol. i., p. 188).

Countries. Again and again reference is made to these Dutch Anabaptists. During this period, twenty of these quiet and industrious men were secured. They were brought before the bishops' council. The accusation was, their denying of Christ's humanity, &c. This was a common charge. The views held by the Netherland Baptists on this matter are before the reader. Ten of these heroic men held fast to their profession; and the remainder, seduced by the promises, or terrified by the threats, of the bishops, submitted to the usual degradation of those who recanted.*

The old chronicler, Stowe, gives us the following details, A.D. 1535 :—

"The 25th day of May, were—in St. Paul's church, London—examined, nineteen men and six women, born in Holland, whose opinions were—first, that in Christ is not two natures, God and man; secondly, that Christ took neither flesh nor blood of the Virgin Mary; thirdly, that children born of infidels may be saved; fourthly, that baptism of children is of none effect; fifthly, that the sacrament of Christ's body is but bread only; sixthly, that he who after baptism sinneth wittingly, sinneth deadly, and cannot be saved. Fourteen of them were condemned; a man and woman were burnt in Smithfield; the other twelve of them were sent to other towns, there to be burnt."

It is more than probable that old Father Latimer refers to some of them, in one of his sermons. He not only records the facts, but the noble spirit of the men :—

"I should have told you here of a certain sect of heretics, that

---

* Wall's History of Infant Baptism, p. 423; Crosby, vol. i., p. 31. The attitude of the emperor and the Pope abroad, and the influence of the clergy at home, alarmed the people. It is thus described :—"The common people, foreseeing these inconveniences, are so violent against the queen, that they say a thousand shameful things of her, and of all who have supported her in her intrigues. On them is cast the odium of all the calamities anticipated from the war." (D'Intevelle to M. de Turbes, October, 1534.)—The Pilgrim, note B., p. 101.—The same writer insinuates that the king's "regard for the queen is less than it was, and diminishes every day. He has a new fancy, as you are aware."—*Ibid.*

spake against their order and doctrine; they will have no magistrates nor judges on the earth.* Here I have to tell you what I heard of late, by the relations of a credible person and a worshipful man, of a town in this realm of England that hath about 500 of heretics of this erroneous opinion in it" [Anabaptists are mentioned in the margin].† "The Anabaptists that were burnt here, in divers towns of England (as I have heard of credible men, I saw them not myself), met their death even intrepid, as you will say; without any fear in the world. Well, let them go. There was, in the old times, another kind of poisoned heretics, that were called Donatists; and those heretics went to their execution as they should have gone to some jolly recreation or banquet." ‡

We cannot deny ourselves the gratification of adding to this a sentence or two from a writer whose pages we never read but with advantage :—

"The details are gone—their names are gone. Poor Hollanders they were, and that is all. Scarcely the fact seemed worth the mention, so shortly is it told in a passing paragraph. For them no Europe was agitated, no courts were ordered into mourning, no Papal hearts trembled with indignation. At their death the world looked on complacent, indifferent, or exulting. Yet here, too, out of twenty-five poor men and women were found fourteen who by no terror of stake or torture could be tempted to say they believed what they did not believe. History for them has no word of praise; yet they, too, were not giving their blood in vain. Their lives might have been as useless as the lives of most of us. In their deaths they assisted to pay the purchase-money for England's freedom." §

The progress of dissent from the old faith, and the spread of baptistical opinions, are indicated unmistakably at this time. ǁ Cranmer, on the death of Wareham, had been raised to the primacy. Much more moderate than his predecessor, but more anxious for a thorough reformation

---

* Latimer more than once brings this charge against them; one which has no foundation in fact.

† Sermons, p. 151 (Parker Society, vol. v).   ‡ *Ibid*, p. 60.

§ Froude, vol. ii., p. 365.

ǁ John Frith, one of the choice spirits of the age, found time, amidst the solitude of his wretched confinement, to write against them.

in the church than Wareham or Henry, the spirit of the churchman was strong in him. Under his presidency the Convocation met in 1536. It was an important gathering. The struggle was long and fierce. Canterbury and York headed different factions, and around their standards bishops, doctors, and mitred abbots, gathered as interest or principle prompted. Passing over various matters unconnected with our subject, and which may be found in the ordinary histories indicated below,* we select the utterances of these holy men on the subject of baptism, and its bearing on our brethren :—

"That the sacrament of baptism was instituted and ordained in the New Testament by our Lord and Saviour Christ, as a thing necessary for the attaining of everlasting life, according to that saying of Christ, *Nisi quis renatus fuerit ex aquâ et Spiritu Sancto, non potest intrare in regnum cœlorum.*

"*Item:* That it is offered unto all men, as well infants as such as have the use of reason, that by baptism they shall have the remission of sins, and the grace and favour of God; according to that saying of St. John, *Qui crediderit et baptizatus fuerit, salvus est.*

"*Item:* That the promise of grace and everlasting life, which promise is adjoined unto the sacrament of baptism, pertaineth not only unto such as have the use of reason, but also to such, to infants, innocents, and children, and that they ought, therefore, and must needs be baptized; and that by the sacrament of baptism they do also obtain remission of their sins, the grace and favour of God, and be made thereby the very sons and children of God; inasmuch as infants and children, dying in their infancy, shall undoubtedly be saved thereby, or else not.

"*Item:* That infants must needs be christened, because they be born in original sin; which sin must needs be remitted, which cannot be done but by the sacrament of baptism, whereby they receive the Holy Ghost, which exerciseth his grace and efficacy in them, and cleanseth and purgeth them from sin, by his most secret virtue and operations.

"*Item:* That children or men, once baptized, cannot (nor ought) ever be baptized again.

---

* Fuller, Collier, Burnet, &c. Not less than sixty errors are mentioned by the latter, as submitted to the Convocation by some heresy hunter.

"*Item:* That they ought to repute and take all the Anabaptists' and the Pelagian opinions, contrary to these premises, and every other man's opinions, agreeable to the said Anabaptist or the Pelagian opinions in their behalf, for detestable heresies, and utterly to be condemned.

"*Item:* That men or children having the use of reason, willing and desirous to be baptized, shall, by virtue of that holy sacrament, obtain the grace of the remission of all their sins, if they shall come thereunto perfectly and truly repentant and contrite of all their sins before committed, and also perfectly and constantly confessing and believing all the articles of our faith, according as it was mentioned in the articles before; or else not. And finally, to all, they shall also have firm credence and trust in the promise of God, adjoined to the said sacrament: that is to say, that in and by this sacrament which they shall receive, God the Father giveth unto them, for His Son Jesus Christ's sake, remission of all their sins, and the grace of the Holy Ghost, whereby they be newly regenerated, and made the very children of God, according to the saying of Christ, and His apostle St. Peter, *Penitentiam agite, et baptizatur unusquisque vestrum, in nomine Jesu Christi in remissionem peccatorum, et accipietis donum Spiritus Sancti;* and, according to the saying of St. Paul, *ad Titum,* 3, *Non ex operibus justitiæ quæ fecimus nos, sed secundum suam misericordiam, salvos nos fecit, per lavacrum regenerationis et renovationis Spiritus Sancti, quem effudit in nos opulentè per Jesum Christum Servatorem nostrum, ut justificati illius gratia hæredes efficiemur, juxta spem vitæ æternæ.*"*

These dogmas of baptismal regeneration, subversive alike of Christ's teaching and of intelligent piety, would be regarded as detestable heresies, and utterly condemned, by all holding the views of the Anabaptists.

Henry had stood unmoved before the most hostile of his foes. Pope and Cæsar, as they uttered their threats of invasion, only caused a deeper frown to gather around his massive brow. In vain did his Holiness hurl the greater excommunication, and, rising in all his strength, seek to smite by one blow the detested heretic to the ground; it only called into stronger play all the elements of his Tudor nature, and widened the gulf which lay between them. Difficulties

---

* The whole of the articles are given by Burnet, vol. i. (Addenda), p. 283; Collier, vol. i., p. 123.

never made Henry quail. He was firm when others hesitated; bold when others trembled; and never shrunk from an encounter with any foe.* Hitherto the Reformation had made gradual progress. Steadily it had marched onwards, securing a deeper hold on the minds of the community. Untouched by the thunders of the Vatican and the wiles of her adherents, it was gathering around it the intelligence of the nation, and exerting an influence over a circle which was widening daily. It awaited one fiery trial more. The hour was now come. Lincoln and the northern counties soon poured forth their bands. Now came "*the Pilgrimage of Grace.*" The clerical element pervaded it.† Abbots, monks, and village priests, raised the war cry. The destruction of heresy, the overthrow of the detested Cromwell, and the restoration of the monastery and the shrine, were the avowed ends of this holy war. The struggle was fearful. The barons and churchmen of the north headed the hostile forces; the commanders of the royal troops were doubtful; and in many parts of the country thousands were waiting for the issue of the first fight. The king and his minister were equal to the crisis. They rolled back the tide of rebellion, and secured an all but bloodless victory. Into details we cannot enter. To do so would overstep the boundaries of our design. Against the reformed doctrines, and those of the Anabaptists in particular, the "Pilgrims of Grace" breathed the fiercest hatred. Their first proposition, in the list of grievances they presented to Henry, was this :—

"Touching our faith, we have the heresies of Luther, Wickliffe,

---

* The following, from More, is rather a significant view of the irritable temper of the monarch :—"Howbeit, son Roper, I may tell them I have no cause to be proud thereof; for if my head would win him (Henry) a castle in France, it should not fail to go."—Butler's Memoirs of English Catholics, vol. i., p. 62.

† There were ten thousand priests in the Rebellion, in 1536, "who never ceased to stir them on to their work, and to tell them what great things they would achieve." (Letter to the Queen Regent at Brussels.) —Collier, p. 113.

Huss, Melancthon, Œcolampadius, Bucer's Confessio Germanica, Apologia Melancthonis, the works of Tyndale, of Barnes, of Marskal, Raskal, St. Germain, and such other heresies of Anabaptists, clearly within this realm, to be annihilated and destroyed." *

The year 1538 opens a new chapter. Henry's compliance with the request of the northern rebels was exact in relation to the Anabaptists. He was powerless in reference to the other parts. A commission of inquiry was issued. Cranmer, Stokesley, Sampson, and others, were empowered to hunt out these men. Their authority was plenary. To the fire all the books of the accused were to be consigned: the penitent were to be restored to the embraces of their affectionate mother; but the obstinate, the men of faith and hightoned principle, must be transferred to the secular power, as the executioner of the church's will.† Bishops might declare men worthy of death, but their tender natures forbade their executing their own decrees. Diligently the secular power executed the task given to it. Two Dutch Anabaptists—a man and a woman—in the course of a month, paid the penalty of their faith. Beyond this bare fact we know nothing. To them truth was precious, and life was willingly sacrificed as the highest homage they could offer to it. ‡ Nor was this all. The spirit of persecution was everywhere rampant. None of the early reformers were free from its influence. The cry for vengeance on the Anabaptists rose not only from the rebels, but the Elector of Hesse about this time threw the weight of his influence into the already deep and rapid current. To Henry he addressed the most exciting appeals. His malignity is

---

* Froude, vol. iii., pp. 156–7. The whole of this remarkable document is given from the MS. in the Rolls' House.

† Fuller, vol. ii., p. 152; Burnet, vol. iii., p. 159. *Vide* Tracts on Liberty of Conscience, vol. i., pp. 87—90 (Introduction).

‡ Todd's Cranmer, vol. i., pp. 256–7. On the former page we have a specimen of the ignorant and frantic abuse so frequently lavished on our brethren.

obvious; the dangers which surrounded these confessors for Christ are not less so. We can only quote a sentence here and there from the iniquitous production of the Elector:— "There are no rulers in Germany, whether they be Papists or professors of the doctrines of the Gospel, that do suffer these men if they do come into their hands. All men punish them quickly. We use a just moderation, which God requireth of all good rulers." Then he tells Henry how some are corrected by these means, and are led home again. But, "If any do stubbornly defend the ungodly and wicked errors of that sect, yielding nothing to such as can and do teach them truly, these are kept a good space in prison, and sometimes sore punished there; yet in such sort are they handled, that death is long deferred, for hope of amendment: and as long as any hope is, favour is showed to life. If there be no hope left, then the obstinate are put to death." Urging the king to make a difference between the Lutherans, who "mislike the abuses of the Bishop of Rome's baggage, and those that be Anabaptists," he says:—"In many parts of Germany, where the Gospel is not preached, cruelty is exercised upon both sorts without discretion. The magistrates which obey the Bishop of Rome (whereas severity is to be used against the Anabaptists), they slay good men utterly alien from their opinions. But your Majesty will put a difference great enough between these two sorts, and secure Christ's glory on the one side, and save innocent blood on the other." * The tender mercies of the wicked are always cruel. The appeal was not in vain. Immediately proclamations were issued, denouncing the dangerous tenets of the Anabaptists, condemning their books, and threatening very heavy punishment on those who circulated them. Many of their tracts were printed abroad, and very widely circulated in this country. Ever ready to co-operate, the Commons passed an act of grace

---

* Froude, vol. iii., p. 337, 338.

about the same time, covering almost every delinquency, but from which the Anabaptists were excluded.

Racy old Fuller tells us, that on the marriage of Henry with Anne of Cleves "Dutchmen flockt faster than formerly unto this England. Many of them had active souls, so that whilst their hands were busied about their manufactories, their heads were also beating about points of divinity. Hereof they had many rude notions, too ignorant to manage them themselves, and too proud to crave the direction of others. Their minds had a *by-stream* of activity more than what sufficed to *drive* on their vocation, and *this waste of their souls* they employed in needless speculations, and soon after began to broach their strange opinions, being branded with the general name of Anabaptists. These Anabaptists for the main are but *Donatists new dipt.*" *

Early in 1539 Henry tried to lessen the prevailing errors. In spite of his efforts, and the rigour of the civil and spiritual powers, dissenters from his theological dogmas increased. In February, he tells us, in a proclamation issued by him, that "of late certain Anabaptists and Sacramentarians, coming out of outward parts unto this realm, have, by divers and many perverse and crafty means, seduced many simple persons of the king's subjects, which, as his highness trusteth, now be sorry for their offences, and minding fully to return again to the Catholic church." "Like a loving parent" he weeps over them, deplores their wanderings, promises the most ample forgiveness on their repentance; but if any fall, or continue in their "detestable and damnable opinions," then the full vengeance of the law will fall on them. †

---

* Fuller's Church History, b. v., p. 229. *Vide* Stowe's Chron., p. 576. "Their morality was rigid, their exterior simple; they disdained riches, or affected to do so; and their austere demeanour impressed the multitude with reverence, at the same time that their doctrine seduced them." —J. G. Hess's Life of Zuingle, p. 221.

† Wilkins Corr., vol. iii., p. 843. Tracts on Liberty of Conscience, vol. i., p. 91.

Again the lion growled, and the detested heretics were exposed to his fury. A general pardon was proclaimed on the 5th of July, 1540, but these exceptions marked it:— "These heresies and erroneous opinions hereafter ensuing: that infants ought not to be baptized, and if they be baptized, they ought to be re-baptized when they come to lawful age; that it is not lawful for a Christian man to bear office or rule in the commonwealth; that no man's laws ought to be obeyed; that it is not lawful for a Christian man to take an oath before any judge; that Christ took no bodily substance of our blessed lady; that sinners after baptism cannot be restored by repentance," &c.* Some of these monstrous errors are loved as precious truths by thousands in our day. They leave us in no doubt as to the character of the individuals who held them in the time of Henry. Their opinions on magistracy, oaths, the humanity of the Saviour, are the common property of the early Baptists. The former have given rise to the notion that they were hostile to all governments, as such; that if their opinions prevailed, anarchy and confusion would be universal.† The conclusion was monstrous. It is not difficult to conceive that men whose minds were imbued with intelligent notions of the purity, the spirituality, and the lofty tendency of Christianity, and who contrasted these

---

* 32nd Henry VIII., c. 49 (Froude, vol. iii., p. 501). The French ambassador, in April of this year, thus writes:—"The see of Rome and the institutions of the monks were the sole points on which differences were left remaining; and as to the monks, there is not one in all England who is not now dressed as a secular priest. But in matters of doctrine, the orders then taken have been ill observed. The statute has been infringed by the Anabaptists and the Germanizers. . . . Ten or twelve London citizens and fifteen or twenty foreigners have been arrested. The latter are chiefly Flemish Anabaptists." (Maillac to Francis I.; April 10, 1540.)—The Pilgrim, pp. 139, 140.

† I am surprised that so acute an observer, and generally so fair and liberal an investigator, as Mr. Froude, should fall into the vulgar error, and charge these innocent people, against whom a single act of treason was never brought, with such aims.—See his third volume, p. 389 (Note).

with the wretched character of the governments of Europe, should arrive at the conclusion that no good man could fill office in the commonwealth. Beyond this we know of no evidence to criminate them.

Age and growing infirmities by no means calmed the temper of Henry. Cromwell, one of the greatest men of his age, was removed. His death was everywhere hailed by the enemies of England with joy. "The news is more than grateful to me," said Francis I. "It is such as I give most hearty thanks for to Almighty God, who has been my brother's perpetual friend."* Cromwell's noble aim was the freedom of his country, and the destruction of her spiritual bondage. Under the shadow of his all but limitless authority, many dissidents found mercy. † His removal threw back the Reformation for a time, and Anglo-Catholic influence became paramount. Opposition to his spiritual, was as distasteful to Henry as treason against his temporal authority. Unconquerable in his aversion to all sectaries, yet many acts during his eventful reign had contributed to their increase and augmented their power : ‡—the liberation

---

* Francis I. to Maillac; 1540.—The Pilgrim, by Froude, p. 146.

† "Cromwell has lent himself to the Lutherans, and has abused his authority to show favour to the teachers of false opinions, and to oppress and hinder their opponents. . . . . He said he hoped to put down altogether the old preachers, and to have none but the new." (Maillac to Francis I. ; June 10th, 1540.)—The Pilgrim, p. 144.

"Lord Cromwell's party appeared the strongest : a few days since he was able to arrest the Bishop of Chichester and the Dean of the Chapel. But the party have now fallen in the fall of the Lord Cromwell himself; there remains of them only the Archbishop of Canterbury, whose mouth for the future will be closed, and the Lord Admiral, who has long learnt to trim his sails to the wind. Against them are the Duke of Norfolk and all the rest." (Maillac to the Constable; June 10th, 1540.)—*Ibid*, p. 145.

‡ Sir Thomas More anticipated some of these results :—"And yet, son Roper, I pray that some of us, high as we seem to sit on the mountain, treading heretics under feet like ants, live not to see the day that we would gladly be at league and composition with them, to let them have their churches quietly to themselves, so that they would be contented to let us have ours quietly to ourselves."—Butler's Memorials of English Catholics, vol. i., p. 62.

of the Divine Word from the bondage in which for centuries it had been held;* the destruction of the monasteries, those sinks of corruption;† the influence permitted to Cromwell, Cranmer, and their colleagues, in removing from the churches a variety of objects which only gendered superstition, and gave to the crafty and unprincipled spirituality a power which was destructive to all morality; and the wider circulation of the simple but sublime verities of Christ's holy Gospel,—all, in various ways, contributed to this result. The influence of Queen Catherine Parr, and the threatening attitude of the Papal power, had in one way worked well, by preparing the public mind for a calmer examination of the higher truths, as well as for a simpler form of worship. The Anglican church, at the death of Henry, was but little reformed. "The Six Articles" embodied nearly all the essential elements of the old faith. The Papal supremacy, and some of the evils incident to it, were thrown off; but the core of the evil was left untouched.‡

---

* *Vide* Anderson's Annals of the English Bible,—a work which is an honour to our body.

† For the opinion of Cardinal Pole on the moral state of these houses of ill fame, *vide* Madden's Life of La Savanarola. We give an extract:— "*Another abuse to be corrected is in the religious orders, many of which have become so defiled* that their example has become a scandal to the laity, and noxious to the latter. We think all conventual orders should be abolished; not however to inflict injury on any, but to prohibit the reception of any novices, so that, without injury to the existing orders, they shall be suppressed, and good and religious men may be substituted for them. Now, we think it would be best if all youths who are not professed should be sent away from these monasteries." [The Cardinals Pole and Caraffa signed this report.]

‡ "He has been forced to arrest many changes which were in progress before his last parliament. To satisfy this country, and to silence the Christian powers, he has restored all the old opinions and constitutions, save the authority of the See of Rome and the orders of the monks and nuns; while two bishops, who were the chief promoters of the new opinions, have been deprived of their sees, and if they will save their lives, they must make the best of the time of grace which is allowed

Other generations, and other conflicts, must come and go, before "soul liberty," even as a theory, shall be recognised; and others, longer still, before it shall be realized as a fact.

CHAPTER III.

EDWARD THE SIXTH.

THE birth of Edward was hailed by the nation with raptures. Many a perplexing question was now settled. The evils of a disputed succession were at least suspended, if not quite annihilated. Latimer, in his own way, embodied the gladsome feelings of thousands:—"There is no less rejoicing for the birth of our prince, whom we have hungered for so long, than there was, I trow, *inter vicinos*, at the birth of John the Baptist. God give us grace to yield due thanks to our Lord God, the God of England! For verily he hath showed himself the God of England, or rather an English God, if we will consider and ponder his proceedings with us. He hath overcome our illness with his exceeding goodness, so that we are now more compelled to serve him and promote his word, if the devil of all devils be not in us. We have now the staff of various sects, and the stay of vain expectations. Let us all pray for his preservation."

A nation's hopes, for a nation's welfare in every sense, hung on the life of this infant. Extreme caution watched over him. None were allowed to approach his cradle but his authorized attendants. His food was tasted, and his clothes washed only by trusty servants. Night and morning

---

them, and relinquish their errors." (Mavillac to Francis I. ; July 13th, 1539.)—The Pilgrim, p. 130. (Note F.)

high officers of state watched whilst the royal babe was washed and dressed; and all the avenues of approach to him were guarded with sleepless solicitude.* There was a needs-be for all this. Not only did Henry intensely desire a son to perpetuate his race; but powerful parties in the state had the greatest interest in his death. The sickly child gathered around him the hopes and the fears of the men who had smitten the spiritual head of Christendom with a force from which it has never recovered, and disturbed the faith and social state of the whole of Europe.

The accession of Edward to the vacant throne was in January, 1567. His youth,† his amiability, his cultivated taste,‡ and apparent devotion, inspired the heart of the nation with the most powerful emotions. Hope predominated; and a bright vista of peace and prosperity opened to the eyes of the people. To trace the political intrigues of this short reign,—the rising of the commonalty, partly, if not entirely, from the crushing oppression and grasping selfishness of the higher classes §—the wars in which the nation was involved—and the fall of the Protector—would conduct us over a field far too wide to be compatible with the limits of this work. To other topics our attention must be confined.

The conflict of principles, which had somewhat subsided during the closing period of Henry's life, was now recommenced with new vigour. Both parties put forth strenuous efforts. Cranmer, high in official rank, was recognized as

---

* Froude, vol. iv.   † He was only ten years of age.

‡ His knowledge of French, Latin, and Greek, appears to have been considerable. Strype's Life of Cheke, one of his tutors, supplies much information. Burnet has published, in his second volume, some of the literary remains of the young king, and also his journal.

§ Latimer, Gilpin, and Lever supply us with overwhelming evidence. Strype's Memorials, and his Life of Cranmer, may be consulted. Turner and Froude have crowded their pages with the most painful proofs. The religious element is unfolded in the pages of the latter more than in those of the former.

the leader of the progressionists; whilst Gardiner, the Bishop of Winchester, wielded the conservative power. In many respects the two men were unlike. In all the prominent attributes of their character, the contrast was great. With mental powers inferior to none of his contemporaries, the bishop had been trained to all the arts of diplomacy from his youth, and in all the cunning of the profession he had made rapid progress. The archbishop was no courtier. His early life had been spent in comparative scholastic seclusion, and he had little fitness for the stormy period on which his lot was cast. Honesty, the love of the truth, and anxiety for the nation's welfare, ever marked him.* The skill of both parties was admirable. With sleepless vigilance they watched every movement, and with consummate art tried to foil each other. Upon many points their agreement was perfect. Gardiner, Bonner, and Tunstall repudiated with as much distinctness the supremacy of the Pope, as Cranmer, Ridley, and Latimer. The former pleaded not for a return to Rome, only that things should remain as Henry had left them;† whilst the others pleaded for a more extensive and thorough reform. One party was satisfied with the mere semblance of spiritual life—the forms and ceremonies which still remained were dear to them; the other was anxious to make the church, as far as they knew, a living power, and to remove from it everything which would weaken its influence or narrow the

---

* Strype's Memorials of Cranmer.

† Gardiner, Tonstal, Bonner, and other bishops, took an oath "never to consent that the Bishop of Rome should exercise or have any manner of authority, or jurisdiction, or power within this realm, or any other of the king's dominions; but that he would resist the same, at all times, to the utmost of his power; but that, from henceforth, he would accept and repute the king's majesty to be the only supreme head of the Church of England; and that to the utmost of his power he would observe all acts and statutes, made and to be made, for the extirpation of the Bishop of Rome and his authority, and for the corroboration of the king's supremacy, against all persons whatsoever."—The Oath of Bonner.

circle of its operations. The old and the new life of England were brought thus into collision.

Henry had composed the council of nearly equal numbers of each party; though, dreading the restless, the intriguing spirit of Gardiner, and well knowing his bitter hostility to Cranmer, he had left him no share in the government. Still, the sympathies and the convictions of the youthful monarch were yielded up to Cranmer. Somerset also threw the whole weight of his authority around him and his friends. Only for a short time could the issue be doubtful. The transfer first of Gardiner, then Bonner, and finally Tunstall and others, from their episcopal palaces to the gloom and seclusion of the Tower, and the elevation of Ridley and other friends of the archbishop to the vacant thrones, show at once the magnitude of their power and the extent of their triumph.

The spirit of reform was needed. Only here and there a branch had been cut off the great upas-tree. Corruption and vice were everywhere prevalent. Into all circles they had penetrated.* Moral principle was feeble in the extreme. Gain, not the Gospel, was the spirit which influenced some. The want of preachers was severely felt. Calvin, in a letter to Cranmer, says "that a parcel of slowbellies were nourished from the revenue of the church, to sing vespers in an unknown tongue." "The great ones, in the minority of the king, took their opportunity to fly on the spoils of the church and charitable donations, little regarding anything else than to enrich themselves. Very vicious and dissolute they were in their lives, as the soberer sorts in those days complained."† The great chiefs appropriated the ecclesiastical revenues to their own use.‡ Many of the

---

* *Vide* Froude, vol. v., chap. 26; Latimer's Sermons; Turner, vol. iii. (Modern History, chap. 8).

† Memorials of Cranmer, vol. ii., p. 161.

‡ "It may seem strange," says Burnet, "that the Earl of Hertford had six good prebends offered him, two of them being afterwards converted into a deanery and treasurership. But it was ordinary at that

worst features of the old superstitions remained, and the mass of the people were shrouded in darkness, and watched with a sullen countenance the removal of many of those objects which had been enthroned in their affections from their earliest youth.* If the reader could, by an easy fiction of the imagination, throw back his mind to the time of this monarch, he would probably see, in many a church, "the minister kiss the Lord's table; wash his fingers at any time in the communion; wiping his eyes with the pater or sudery, or crossing his head with the paters; shifting of the book from one place to another; laying down and licking the chalice of the communion; holding up his fingers, hands, or thumbs, joined towards his temple; breathing upon the bread or chalice; shewing the sacrament openly before distribution of the communion; ringing or sacrying bells; or setting any light upon the Lord's board at any time." †

---

time. The Lord Cromwell had been Dean of Wells; and many other secular men had these ecclesiastical benefices without cure conferred on them."—History of the Reformation, vol. ii., p. 8 (edit. 1683). *Vide* Strype's Cranmer; Turner, vol. ii., p. 234; Soame's Reformation, vol. iv.

* Edward himself gives an affecting view of the moral and social condition of the people:—"The country people generally loved all those shrines, processions, and assemblies, as things of diversion; and judged it a dull business only to come to church for divine worship and the hearing of sermons; therefore, they were much delighted with the gaiety and cheerfulness of these rites."—Burnet's History of the Reformation, vol. ii., p. 59.

† Articles put forth by the King (Burnet's Reformation, vol. ii., Appendix, p. 165; Instructions to Bishop Ridley, p. 205). In various forms many of these errors were exposed. Poems, moralities, ballads, were all employed by the men of progress. The following is a sample:—

"Holy pardons, holy beads,
Holy saints, holy images,
With holy, holy blood.
Holy stocks, holy stones,
Holy chests, holy bones,
Yea, and holy, holy wood.

"Holy days, holy fastings,
Holy twitchings, holy tastings,
Holy visions and sights;
Holy wax, holy lead,
Holy water, holy bread,
To drive away sprites."

—Hawkin's Origin of the English Drama. *Apud* Todd's Cranmer, vol. i., p. 330.

Ignorant of religion, insensible to the spiritual wants of the people, grasping only at the wealth of the church, the patrons, the council, and even "*the gospelers*," entered into cures, or had three or four served by half-famished ignorant monks,—men, from their lives and vicious habits, totally unfit for the ministry. Some placed their stewards in the pulpit, others induced their huntsmen and gamekeepers to doff their forest green and adorn themselves with clerical attire.* The influence of all this was disastrous in the extreme. Society was agitated. The nation, from one cause or another, was heaving with deep feeling, and gave unmistakable indications of anger. Lever has embodied these in one of his indignant outbursts of holy passion:—"You maintain your chaplain to take pluralities, and your other servants take more offices than they can discharge. Fie, fie; for shame! Ye imagine there is a parish priest's curate which does the parson's duty. Yea, forsooth, he ministereth God's sacraments, he sayeth the service, he readeth the homilies. The rude lobs of the country, too simple to paint a lie, speak truly as they find it, and say, 'He ministereth the sacraments, he slubbereth the service, he cannot read the homilies.'" †

Hooper, in a letter to his friend Bullinger, thus describes the religious condition of the nation:—"As far as true religion is concerned, *idolatry* is nowhere in greater vigour. Our king has destroyed the Pope, but not Popery; he has

---

* Bucer to Bishop Hooper, in Strype's Cranmer. Collier has given the substance of this, vol. ii., p. 294. Froude, vol. v.

† Strype's Memorials, vol. iii. Bacon gives a darker picture. *Vide* Works (Parker Society), p. 415. An extract is given in Strype's Cranmer, vol. i., p. 421. "Edward, in 1547, issued articles and injunctions to certain divines, for a visitation of the various dioceses. In these it is ordered 'that all dignified clergy should preach personally twice a year,' and 'that all bishops should preach four times a year in their dioceses, unless they had a reasonable excuse for the omission.'"—Burnet's History of the Reformation, vol. ii., pp. 28, 29. In Ireland it was still worse. St. Leger informed the Council, in 1549, that "there had been but one sermon made in the country for three years, and that by the Bishop of Meath."—Froude, vol. i., p. 419 (Note).

expelled all the monks and nuns, and pulled down their monasteries; he has caused all their possessions to be tramped into his exchequer; and yet they are bound, frail female sex, by the king's command, to perpetual chastity. England has at this time 10,000 nuns, not one of whom is allowed to marry. The impious mass, the most shameful celibacy of the clergy, the invocation of saints, auricular confession, superstitious abstinence from meats, and purgatory, *were never held by the people in greater esteem than at the present moment.*" *

We will only add another sentence or two on this matter, chiefly because they will enable the reader to understand the facility with which, in the next reign, the "old faith" resumed its empire over the nations. The writer is Cecil, now appearing on the political theatre:—"The majority of our people will be with our adversaries; and it is reasonable to think that, although so long as all is quiet the crown can maintain tranquillity, should war break out, they will listen rather to what they consider the voice of God calling on them to restore Popery, than to the voice of the king calling on them to obey. The great body of the peers, some of the council, all of the bishops except three or four, almost all the judges and lawyers, almost all the justices of the peace, the priests and vicars, will be on the same side; and the commons are in such a state of irritation, that they will rise at a word." †

Steadily did the archbishop and his colleagues seek to lessen the number and magnitude of these evils. To secure the spread of sound doctrines, and partly on account of the ignorance of the priesthood, a number of homilies were prepared, to be read to the people. Visitors were appointed

---

* Letters of the Bishops (Parker Society), vol. i., p. 36.

† Froude, vol. v., p. 304. Dr. Lingard says that eleven-twelfths of the people were in favour of the old faith. He bases his estimates on a statement of Paget's to the Protector (vol. vii., p. 81).

to inspect the churches in every parish, to remove any objects of superstition, and diminish the senseless ceremonies. Light will be thrown on the state of the church by the following practices which were to be abolished:—" Casting holy water on the beds, on images, and other dead things; or bearing about holy bread, or St. John's Gospel; or keeping of private holy days—as bakers, brewers, smiths, shoemakers, and others do; or ringing of holy bells, or blessing with the holy candle, to the intent to be discharged of the burden of sin, or to drive away devils, or put away dreams or fantasies." * Later on, the new English Prayer Book, sanctioned by the senate, was issued; and articles of faith—after many trials of strength in the convocation and both houses—were given to the nation, with the hope that uniformity of faith and practice would be secured. † It was vain. Nature repudiates uniformity. Her beauties everywhere spring from her boundless variety. In morals, minds are not cast in one mould. The consciousness of responsibility precludes anything like uniformity. Essential unity religion will ever secure. Beyond this, her range is entirely free and limitless.

The teaching of King Edward's Prayer Book on baptism is too instructive to be overlooked. The devil was exorcised to go out and enter no more into the baptized. The child (if not weak) was thrice dipped, then anointed, and a chrism, or white coat, put upon it. " Then the priest shall take the childe in his handes, and aske the name; and, namyng the childe, shall dyppe it in the water thrice. Fyrst dypping the right syde; second, the left syde; the thirde time dypping the face toward the font; so it be wisely and discretely done; saying, I baptize, &c. And if the childe be weake, it shall suffice to powre upon it, saying the foresade wordes." In the public baptism a cross was made on the child's

---

* Burnet, Fuller, and Strype give this commission.
† Collier presents us with a long account of them (vol. ii., book iv.)

forehead and breast; the devil was exorcised to go out of him, and enter no more into him. After the triune immersion, he was anointed, and a chrism, or white coat, put upon him.* It may interrupt the narrative for a moment—more so, perhaps, if we made it a note—but the reader may be pleased with the following, as an illustration of the practice of the church, and the opinions of leading men. The Sarum Liturgy was republished in 1541. The whole is too long for insertion here. We borrow the following from Collier:—

"The Time for Baptizing.

"Upon Saturday, Easter-even, is hallowed the font, which is as it were *vestigium*, or a remembrance of baptism, that was used in the primitive church; at which time, and Pentecost, there was used in the church two solemn baptizings, and much concourse of people came unto the same.

"The first was at Easter, because the mystery of baptism agrees well to the time. For like as Christ died and was buried, and rose again the third day, so by *putting into* the water is signified our death to sin, and the immersion betokens our burying and mortification to the same; and the rising again out of the water declares us to be risen to a new life, according to the doctrine of St. Paul (Rom. vi.).

"And the second solemn baptizing, *i. e.*, at Pentecost, was because that then is celebrated the feast of the Holy Ghost, which is the worker of that spiritual regeneration we have in baptism. And therefore the church uses to hallow the font also at that time." †

---

* Collier, vol. ii., p. 256. The author gives an amusing authority for this, and also for praying for the dead, from Tertullian:—"If you demand a text of Scripture for these usages, you will find none. The practice stands on a bottom of tradition; 'tis confirmed by custom, and one generation follows it upon the credit of that which went before." The candid ever acknowledge this. The following lies before us:—"In my book of tradition I said and affirmed, that Christ and his apostles taught and left to the church many things, without writing, which we must both believe stedfastly and also fulfil obediently, under pain of damnation ever to endure." Amongst other instances, this author mentions:—"The hallowing of water in the font, the thrice dipping of the child in the water at the christening, the putting on of the chrism, the consecration of the oil, the anointing of the christened children," &c.—Dr. Smith, Memorials of Cranmer, vol. ii., p. 329.

† Sarum Liturgy, Collier, vol. ii., p. 196.

We select now part of the ceremony, omitting the explanation:—

"When the child is brought, the minister beginneth to make a cross upon the forehead of the child that is offered to be baptized. Then he maketh another cross upon the breast. Prayer is then offered for the removal of all blindness of heart, and to make him apt to receive grace given him in baptism. Hallowed salt is then put into his mouth, to signify the Spirit's real salt, which is the word of God. Then the minister makes the sign of the cross on the child's forehead, adjuring the devil to depart. After this is read the Gospel of Matthew xix. Then the minister putteth his finger into his mouth, daubs with spittle the *nose, thurles,* and ears of him that shall be baptized. After an exhortation to the sponsors, the priest makes the sign of the cross in the right hand of the infant. Taking it by this holy hand, he bids it enter into the church, there to be admitted as one of Christ's flock. Approaching the font, the name of the child is asked. Then follow these questions to the godfathers and godmothers, as representatives of the child.—Forsakest thou the devil? Ans. *I forsake him.*—All his works? Ans. *I forsake them.*—And all his pomps and vanities? Ans. *I forsake them.*—Satisfied with these, the minister then anoints the child with holy oil upon the breast and betwixt the shoulders. Questions to ascertain the orthodoxy of the child are then propounded. Then follows another series: for example, to the child the minister says,—What askest thou? Ans. *Baptism.*—Wilt thou be baptized? Ans. *I will.*—Satisfied with these sage replies, then the minister calls the child by name, baptizes it in the name of the Father, Son, and Holy Ghost (putting it into the water of the font and taking it out again, or else pouring water upon the infant). Then, after his baptism, he is anointed with holy chrism on the head; after that he is clothed in a white vesture, significant of his freedom from the captivity of the devil; and, finally, this superstition is closed by the minister placing in the infant's right hand a lighted candle." *

Tyndale thus refers to the feeling of the people about this:—"If aught be left out, or if the child be not altogether *dipt* in the water, or if, because the child is sick, the priest dare not plunge him into the water, but pours water on his head,—how tremble they! how quake they! 'How say ye, Sir John,' say they, 'is this child christened enough? hath

---

* Collier, vol. ii., pp. 192, 193.—Note A.

it his full christendom?' They believe, verily, that the child is not christened." * " In the Prayer Book of Edward VI., the priest, looking upon the children, was required to say, ' I command thee, unclean spirit, in the name of the Father, of the Son, and of the Holy Ghost, that thou come out, and depart from this infant,' " &c.† "After a fewe things rehearsed, he taketh the child and dippeth it in, but warily and discretely, as it is in the book; upon whose forehead also he shall make a crosse," &c. ‡ Frith, in his Treatise on Baptism, says:—"The signification of baptism is described by Paul, in vi. of the Romans; that, as we are plunged bodily into the water, even so we are dead and buried with Christ from sin; and as we are lifted again out of the water, even so are we risen with Christ from our sins, that we might hereafter walk in a new conversation of life. So that these things—that is, to be plunged into the water, and lift up again—do signify and represent the whole pith and effect of baptism,—that is, the mortification of our old Adam, and the rising up of our new man." §

The influence of the continental Reformers on the Reformation must not be overlooked. From the distance they had watched the early struggle with intense interest. Henry never loved or hated like other men. Luther treated him as an ordinary man, when combating for the truth, and inflicted blows on the chivalric knight of Rome which made him reel more than once. The pride of the monarch was wounded, and the influence of the German Reformers was never very powerful with him. It was not so now, in the period over which we are travelling. Cranmer appears to have consulted them on nearly all occasions; and the correspondence of the great German Reformer with Somerset and

---

* Obedience of a Christian Man, vol. i., p. 310.

† *Vide* Hans L'Estrange (Dinis Affier), p. 243. *Apud* Zurich Liturgy (note), p. 178.   ‡ Troubles at Frankfort (Petherham reprint), p. 32.

§ Works of Tyndale and Frith, vol. iii., p. 289. On the opposite page he refers to the opinions of the Baptists.

others was not unfrequent. More than this: theological chairs in both universities were occupied by some of the most eminent disciples of this illustrious man. Peter Martyr, Bucer, and Fagihus, threw their influence over these seats of learning, and, from the professor's chair, sought to mould the rising theological mind of England with their own views of doctrine and polity. The influence of this was soon perceptible. The archbishop and his intimate colleagues changed their opinions, and from a Lutheran tendency the Calvinian element became more apparent. At this period, too, another individual appears, who occupies no subordinate place on the page of history. Fiery, impassioned, of indomitable courage, and imbued with the love of the truth, John Knox was a fitting instrument for the advancement of the great work. With the concurrence of the Council and Cranmer, the Scottish reformer was engaged. For ten years he devoted himself to itinerant labours. Berwick, Newcastle, and the northern parts, were the chosen fields for his culture. Success was the result, though the Bishop of Durham checked his career in every way he could. Higher honours awaited him. First, a church in the metropolis; and then, the Protector offered to confer upon him the see of Rochester. †

Amidst difficulties of no common kind, Cranmer and his co-workers advanced the Reformation so far, in its doctrines and polity, that the Anglican church, with certain modifications and additions, became what it is at present. They left it far below the ideal which existed in their own mind; tolerating much, confessedly, which has no sanction in the word of God, and the existence of which only impairs the moral beauty of that church, weakens its efficiency, and renders it of necessity, to minds who recognize and implicitly bow to the supreme authority of Christ, a constant source of dissent and divisions.

---

* Collier, vol. ii., p. 304.

† Macrie's Life of Knox, chap. iii. Select Works of the Reformer, with Life, p. 13.

The violent persecutions to which the Baptists were everywhere exposed on the Continent, both in Catholic and Protestant countries, induced many of them to take refuge in this country. Life was precious. They fondly hoped that in quietness and peace they might worship God. Their zeal did not slumber. Their tenets were industriously disseminated, and many converts were made to their views of Christian truth. The highest character was given to these persons, by men religiously opposed to them. To most of our readers the following will be new:—"In general, Anabaptism required that those who came over to it should be possessed of the strict heroic morals of the early Christians, the same contempt for the world and its pleasures and pains, and even its outward forms. By baptism a renunciation was made of the devil, the world, and the flesh; and a vow taken to do nothing but the will of God. Any wilful sin of an Anabaptist would not be pardoned, and entailed on its perpetrator hopeless expulsion from the community, and loss of the grace of God. It was exactly on this account that the heresy was so dangerous, for the greater part of its adherents could appeal to the sanctity of their mode of life." *

But their enemies were sleepless. The mild and gentle Cranmer, Ridley, and others, felt as much, nay, more horror-struck at an Anabaptist heretic than at a dozen Papal advocates. Few, if indeed any, suffered but from this detested sect.† In the spring of 1549 a report was laid before the Council, charging them with the usual errors of the sect. Commissioners, consisting of Cranmer and six other prelates, and divines of a lower order, with various distinguished laymen, among whom the names of Cecil and Sir Thomas Smith are found, were appointed.‡ They were to try to

---

* Dr. Hase (Neue Propheten). *Apud* Madden, Phantasmata, vol. ii., pp. 439–440. † Vaughan's Revolutions of English Hist., vol. iii., p. 393.

‡ "An Ecclesiastical Commission in the beginning of this year was issued out for the examination of the Anabaptists and Arians, that began now to spring up apace and show themselves more openly."—Strype's Life of Sir Thomas Smith, p. 37.

reclaim them, to enjoin them penance, and to give them absolution; or, if they were obstinate, to excommunicate them, and deliver them over to the secular power, to be dealt with in the usual way. *

A singular statement appears in Strype,—an accusation not unfrequent in subsequent writers; it is as follows:— "Whereupon were sent two of their emissaries (Romanists) from Rotterdam unto England, who were to pretend themselves Anabaptists, and preaching against baptizing infants, and preach up rebaptizing and a fifth monarchy upon earth. And besides this, one D. G., authorized by their learned men (the Council of Trent), despatched a letter, written in May, 1549, from Delf in Holland, to two bishops, whereof Winchester was one, signifying the coming of these pretended Anabaptists, and that they should receive them, and cherish them, and take their parts, if they should chance to receive any checks; telling them, that it was left to them to assist in this cause; and to some others, whom they knew to be well affected to the Mother Church." †

In another form, which indeed would always be welcome, the influence of their principles was opposed. That they were widely spread admits of no doubt. The activity of their opponents makes this manifest. Either just before, or following in the wake of the state-paid hunters of heresy, appeared, "*A short Introduction for to Warn all Christian People against the Pestiferous Errors of the Common Sect of Anabaptists.*" This professes to be a translation from some compilations of Calvin, and it is printed by Day.‡ If the Reformer had been content with wielding his pen against them, his character would have stood before us with more brightness and beauty. To him may be traced much of the

---

* Todd's Cranmer, vol. ii., p. 146. Collier gives the commission, vol. ii. (Intro.), p. 12. Bacon, the martyr, condemns "the wicked and ungodly opinions of the Anabaptists."—Todd's Cranmer, vol. ii., p. 351.

† Strype's Cranmer, vol. i., pp. 299, 300.

‡ *Vide* Todd's Cranmer, vol. ii., p. 146.

fierce hostility which our brethren had to encounter. His appeals sustained, if they did not beget, the demon of persecution in the minds of the Council and the Court. The spirit of Antichrist never showed itself more intolerant than in the following:—" These all together do deserve to be well punished by the sword, seeing they do conspire against the king, and against God, who had set him in the royal seat.* It will be said that we must tolerate our neighbour's weakness, that great changes are not easily to be borne. That were to be suffered in worldly affairs, where it is lawful for the one to give place to the others, and to give over his right, thereby to redeem peace; but it is not like in the spiritual rule of Christ,—there we have nothing to do but to obey God. . . . . Thefts, fightings, extortions, are strictly punished, because that men thereby are offended; and the meantime whoredoms, adulteries, and drunkenness, are suffered as things lawful, or of very little importance. That the honour of God be mindful ever to you, punish the crime whereof men are not wont to make any great matter."

Ridley, who filled the episcopal throne of the metropolitan city, was not a whit behind his brethren in efforts for the suppression of this sect. In his first visitation, we believe, early in June, questions were issued on various matters relating to the religious state of his diocese and the conduct of his clergy. Amongst them we may note the following:— "Whether Anabaptists or any other sects held conventicles, preached heterodoxies, or administered the sacraments in a different manner from the public Establishment? Whether baptism was administered contrary to the public Establishment, with respect either to time or language? Whether infant baptism was impugned?"†

These efforts were successful. To escape was all but impossible. Kent supplied the first victim. There is reason

---

* "He advised that Anabaptists and reactionists should be alike put to death."—Froude, vol. v., p. 99.

† Collier, vol. ii., p. 304.

for believing that in this district of the country, and in East Anglia, Anabaptists were numerous. The evidence of this will be supplied presently. Joan* Boucher, or Joan of Kent, was one of the few who suffered martyrdom during the reign of the youthful monarch. The information about this noble-minded woman is only scant, and tradition identifies her with the town of Eythorne, with a small congregation of Baptists there.† Her life was holy, her connections respectable, and her devotedness to the truth of a marked kind. She was intimate with some of the religious leaders of the court of Henry, and was an intimate friend of Ann Askew.‡ To the circulation of Tyndale's New Testament and religious books she gave much time. The heresy with which she was charged was one commonly alleged against the sect at that time. Burnet says that "she denied that Christ was truly incarnate of the Virgin, whose flesh, being sinful, He could take none of it; but the Word, by the consent of the inward man in the Virgin, took flesh of her : these were her words."§ We have adverted to this matter before. ǁ It will again claim the reader's attention under a subsequent reign. Upon this "subtle fancy concerning the incarnation," ¶ a grave and learned theologian disputed with her, but without effect. The trial was again made, but with similar results. Sentence was then passed upon her; and, as an obstinate heretic, she was consigned to the civil power. The church never sheds blood. The butchery is always left to the state. In her

---

* Joan Knell, alias Butcher, often Joan Van Kent, was burnt in Smithfield.—MS. in the archives of the Mennonite Church, Amsterdam.

† Private information. Ashford is mentioned in Historia Der Beroerten van Engelandt, p. 2.

‡ *Vide* Anderson's Ladies of the Reformation : Vaughan's Revolutions of English History, vol. iii., p. 394; Burnet's History of the Reformation, vol. ii., p. 110.

§ "A poor frantic woman, more fit for Bedlam than a stake." Just as true of D. Neal, the utterer of this, as of Joan Boucher.—History of the Puritans, vol. ii., Edward's reign.

ǁ *Vide* p. 54.   ¶ Vaughan, vol. iii., p. 394.

wretched prison she continued for months. Amongst others, she was visited by Mr. Hutchinson and Thomas Lever, who sought to bring her opinions into harmony with the received doctrine. In reply to an argument of the former, she placed beyond all reasonable doubt her faith in the perfect humanity of Jesus. "I deny not Christ is Mary's seed," she said, "or the woman's seed; nor I deny Him not to be a man. But Mary had two seeds—one seed of her faith, and another seed of her flesh and in her body. There is a natural and a corporeal seed, and there is a spiritual and an heavenly seed, as we may gather of St. John, when he saith, '*The seed of God remaineth in him*, and he cannot sin.' And Christ is her seed; but He is become man of the seed of her faith and belief—of spiritual seed, not of natural seed; for her seed was sinful, as the seed and flesh of others." * Before the fiery trial, another attempt was made. Their lordships of London and Ely called her before them. It was the day before her execution. Ridley used all his eloquence with Joan. The attempt was vain. Her confidence in the truth of her opinions was unshaken. "It was not long ago," said the heroic woman, "since you burnt Ann Askew for a piece of bread, yet came yourself to believe the doctrine for which you burnt her;† and now you will burn me for a piece of flesh, and in the end you will believe this also." ‡ To throw the sanction of religion around the final scene, Bishop Scorey was employed to preach, and then Joan submitted to the last trial of her faith, and added another to the list of the Smithfield martyrs.

Burnet says that Edward manifested extreme reluctance to sign Joan's death warrant, and that the archbishop was employed to remove his scruples. "He argued from the law of Moses, by which blasphemers were to be stoned. He

---

* Martyrology, vol. i., p. 350.

† Ann was martyred for rejecting transubstantiation. Cranmer, Ridley, and others, had, before this, repudiated the same.

‡ Strype's Memorials, vol. iii.

told the king he made a great difference between errors in other points of divinity and those which were directly against the Apostles' Creed; that there were impieties against God, which a prince, as God's deputy, ought to punish, as the king's deputies were obliged to punish offences against the king's person." Neither the principles nor the logic of Cranmer satisfied the king; and the narrator adds that he signed his name with tears, and told his spiritual instructor that if it was wrong he should answer for it to God. The friends and the enemies of the archbishop have expended much energy on this. The former have laboured to shield his memory from the guilt of this atrocious act. Judging from the evidence before us, we think that they have been successful. Few, if any, religionists of that age, except the despised sect which felt the consequences of these Antichristian sentiments, would have objected to these principles. The dogma was received as a truth, by universal Christendom, that it was the duty of the state to punish error. It is not on this ground, however, that the vindication of Cranmer can be placed. It is on others widely different. Edward's journal gives no intimation of the scene. The record is as follows:—" May the 2nd.—Joan Boucher, otherwise called Joan of Kent, was burnt for holding that Christ was not incarnate of the Virgin Mary; being condemned the year before, but kept in hope of conversion. And on the 30th of April, the Bishop of London and the Bishop of Ely were to persuade her, but she withstood them, and reviled the preacher at her death." * No tears are shed here. No indication can be gathered from this of a troubled conscience. Yet the opportunity was fitting for a statement of the same, if it had ever transpired. Besides all this, it is certain that Cranmer was not present at the Council when the Lord Chancellor was ordered to make out the writ for consigning Joan to the flames. The memory of

---

* Burnet, vol. ii. (Appendix.)

the archbishop has enough to bear, without imposing upon it what in point of fact has no existence.*

In the examination of Philpot, the following occurs in relation to this victim of episcopal brutality:—"*Riche:* All heretics do boast of the Spirit of God, and every one would have a church by himself, as Joan of Kent and the Anabaptists. I had myself Joan of Kent a fortnight in my house, after the writ was out for her to be burnt, when my Lord of Canterbury and Bishop Ridley resorted almost daily to her. But she was so high in the spirit, that they could do nothing with her for all their learning; but she went wilfully unto the fire, was burnt, and so do you now. *Philpot:* As for Joan of Kent, she was a vain woman (I knew her well), and a heretic indeed, well worthy to be burnt, because she stood against one of the manifest articles of our faith, contrary to the Scripture."† There is also an allusion to Joan in the examination of Thomas Hawkes. We quote it:—"*Chidsey:* Ye die boldly, because ye would glory in your death, as Joan Boucher did. *Hawkes:* What Joan Boucher did, I have nothing to do withal; but I would my part might be to-morrow." ‡

"The day after this woman's condemnation, was one Putts, a tanner, of Colchester, brought before the king's commissioners. He was either of her opinion (Joan of Kent's), or an Anabaptist. For these commissioners were appointed to sit upon inquiry after these sectaries chiefly. But Putts recanted, and bore a fagot at St. Paul's Cross, and after that at Colchester." §

To Kent we must again conduct our readers for a short time. We have intimated before that it was fruitful in the detested Anabaptistical error. "I was sent," says Fox, "from

---

* *Vide* Todd's Life of Cranmer; Vaughan, vol. iii., p. 395. Todd's Defence of Cranmer, pp. 93, 94.
† Philpot's Works (Parker Society), p. 55.
‡ Fox, *apud* Maitland's Essays on the Reformation, p. 507.—Note B.
§ Strype's Memorials of the Reformation, vol. i., part 1, p. 336.

the Council to my lord of Winchester (Gardiner), to exhort him to receive also the true confession of justification. And because he was very refractorious, I said to him, 'Why, my lord, what make you so great a matter herein? You see many Anabaptists rise up against the sacrament of the altar; I pray you, my lord, be diligent in confounding of them.' For at that time my lord of Winchester and I had to do with two Anabaptists in Kent. In this sense I willed my lord to be stiff in the defence of the Sacraments against the detestable errors of the Anabaptists," &c.* Other evidence presents itself. Knox had thrown the whole weight of his influence into the reform movement. Into the spirit of Geneva he had not yet been immersed. Nor did "black prelacy" appear so baleful to him. His sympathies were strong with the doctrine and polity of the Anglicans; and his aid had been solicited in the revision of the Prayer Book. That high preferment had been offered him, admits of no doubt. His biographers suppose the Council proposed to form a new bishopric at Newcastle; but a letter from Northumberland to Cecil mentions Rochester as the place. One of his reasons for this appointment will interest our readers:—" I would to God it might please the king to appoint Mr. Knocks to the office of Rochester bishopric; which, for three purposes, would do well. The first, he would not only be a whetstone, to quicken and sharpen the Bishop of Canterbury, whereof he hath need; but also he would be a great confounder of the Anabaptists lately springing up in Kent." We need not give his other reasons; and only add his entreaty to Cecil: —"Herein I pray you desire my Lord Chamberlain and Mr. Vice-Chamberlain to help towards this good act, both for God's service and the king's." † From what cause this singular reason did not prevail with the Reformers, we know not. Other letters from the earl manifestly indicate that his respect for Knox had undergone a considerable modifi-

---

* Fox. Ridley's Works (Parker Society), pp. 264, 265.
† Macrie's Life of Knox, Note D., p. 354.

cation. At a later period he dipped his pen in gall, and wrote in extreme bitterness against the Baptists.* In this work he warns his countrymen against their approach, and the pernicious influence of their doctrines.

"Sectaries appeared now in Essex and Kent, sheltering themselves under the profession of the Gospel, of whom complaint was made to the Council. These were the first that made separation from the reformed Church of England, having gathered congregations of their own. The congregation in Essex was mentioned to be at Bocking; that in Kent at Feversham, as I have from an old register. From whence I also collect, that they held the opinions of the Anabaptists and Palagians; that there were contributions made among them for the better maintaining of their congregations; that the members of the congregations in Kent went over to the congregation in Essex, to instruct and to join with them; and that they had their meetings in Kent in divers places besides Feversham. The names of the chiefs of these sectaries in Kent were, Henry Hart, Cole of Feversham, George Brobridge, Humphrey Middleton (who were their teachers, as it seems), William Greneland, John Gray, William Forstal, Edmund Morris, Laurence Ramsey, Thomas Broke, Roger Linsey, Richard Dimeslake, Clarke, Nicoles Yong, John Plumer of Lenehame, and Cole of Maidstone. Their teachers and divers of these were taken up, and found sureties for their appearance, and at length brought into the Ecclesiastical Court, when they were examined in forty-six articles or more. Many of those before-named being deposed upon the said articles, confessed them to be some sayings and tenets amongst them: 'That the doctrine of predestination was meeter for devils than for Christian men; that children were not born in original sin,' which were Cole's assertions. These that follow were

---

* A notice of his work will appear in another part of this volume; we content ourselves here by referring the reader to Macrie's Life, pp. 119, 120.

taught by Hart: 'That there was no man so chosen but that he might damn himself; neither any man so reprobate but that he might keep God's commands, and be saved; that St. Paul might have damned himself, if he listed,'" &c.*

We gather a little more information of these men in another work of this writer. "In January 27th," says Strype, "a number of persons, a sort of Anabaptists, about sixty, met in a house on a Sunday, in the parish of Bocking, in Essex, where arose among them a great dispute, 'Whether it were necessary to stand or kneel, bare-headed or covered, at prayers? And they concluded the ceremony not to be material, but that the heart before God was required, and nothing else.' Such other like warm disputes there were about Scripture. There were, likewise, such assemblies now in Kent. These were looked upon as dangerous to Church and State; and two of the company were therefore committed to the Marshallsea, and orders were sent to apprehend the rest."†

Of Hart‡ and his companions we know but little. There is a letter of his now lying before us, to which we shall have occasion to refer again. Hart and his brethren sought the propagation of their religious views amongst their fellow-prisoners. Bradford, if not other confessors, engaged in the conflict.§ Strype has preserved two letters, no doubt from parties more or less interested in it. One is, "A pious letter

---

* Strype's Memorials of Reformers. Oxford: vol. i, book i., pp. 369, 370. Strype's Life of Parker, vol. i., pp. 54, 55. *Vide* vol. iii., p. 413.

† Memorials of Cranmer, vol. i., p. 337. Poor Strype knew nothing of the anxiety of a tender conscience to know the will of God. He had been taught to swallow wholesale the creeds and formularies of others, and thought he could afford to sneer at the solicitude of others to be right.

‡ He was the principal of the *Free Willers Men*, so they were termed by the Predestinators. This man drew up thirteen articles to be observed among his company; and there came none into their brotherhood, except they were sworn.—Strype's E. Memorials (Mary), c. 53.

§ Bradford's Works (Religious Tract Society), p. 45. "He was the chief maintainer of man's free will, and enemy to God's free grace."—Letters of the Martyrs.

against complying with the idolatrous worship in Queen Mary's days, by a Free Will Man." The other is, "A letter to a congregation of Free Willers, by one that had been of that persuasion, but came off, and now a prisoner for religion." We quote a sentence from it: "And although I thought I should lose many friends, yet it hath pleased God to raise up many friends for me. And I thank God that they, whom I thought would have been mine enemies, are become my friends in the truth; as in sample by our brethren Ledlay and Cole, and such like."*

These matters will claim attention in another part of our work.

To stamp the character and principles of these troublers of the commonwealth, the legislature, in closing its session in 1551, exempted the Baptists from the pardon which was granted to those who had taken a part in the late rebellion. Dissent from the dogmas of the church was a crime of deeper dye than rebellion against the state.

In 1552 a letter from the Council ordered Cranmer to examine a new sect lately sprung up in this country. Information had been lodged against them by some of those reptiles who are ever creeping into houses and insinuating themselves into the confidence of the simple-minded. Cranmer was at home in the work. The examination of this new sect was one of the businesses the archbishop was employed in while he was in his retirement at his house near Canterbury. Strype says:—"What this sect was, appeareth not. It may be they were of the Family of Love, or David George sect, who made himself sometime Christ and sometime the Holy Ghost." † He favours us, in another work, with a

---

* Strype's E. Memorials, vol. vii. A Catalogue of Originals, p. 172.

† Strype's Memorials of Cranmer, vol. i., p. 421. Todd says that Henry Nicholas, the founder of the Family of Love, is represented by Rogers as making his followers disclaim the doctrines of the Anabaptists. *Vide* his Displaying of the Secte of the Family of Love.—Life of Cranmer, vol. ii., p. 351.—No doubt of this. That they were Baptists is often affirmed, but without the shadow of proof.

somewhat different account. "A commission was directed this year, dated October, to the Archbishop of Canterbury and the Bishop of London, and other worshipful persons in Kent, to make inquiry after sundry heresies lately sprung up; and for the examination and punishment of erroneous opinions, as it seem, of the Anabaptists and Arians, of which sort some now, notwithstanding former severities, showed their heads."*

One of the last acts in this painful drama was now to be performed. The victim was a Dutchman, of the name of George Van Pare.† He practised as a surgeon, and was a man of unblemished character. The names of the commissioners before whom he appeared ought to be preserved in this record. We select a few. Archbishop Cranmer, Bishop Ridley, Miles Coverdale, &c. Before these ghostly lords the foreigner pleaded, through the medium of an interpreter. The charge, as reported by his enemies, was, "That God the Father is only God, and that Christ is not very God is not heresy. And being asked, through an interpreter, whether he would abjure the said opinions, he answered, 'No!'"‡ Unmoved by the threats of his merciless persecutors, and strong in the moral consciousness of the truth which he professed, he prepared for the fiery trial. "He suffered with great constancy of mind, and kissed the stake and fagots that were to burn him. Of this Pare I find a Papist wrote, saying, that he was a man of a most wonderful strict life; that he used not to eat above once in two days; and before he did eat, would lie sometimes in his devotions prostrate on the ground." §

---

* Strype's E. Memorials, Edward VI., b. ii., c. xv.

† Vaughan calls him Paris, vol. iii., p. 394.

‡ We had doubts about his Arian tendencies; but since writing the above, we gather the following statements from MSS. which have just reached us from Amsterdam:—"Anno 1551, the 24th of April, Jovis Van Pavis, one Dutchman, was burnt in Smithfield : was one Arian."

§ Burnet, vol. ii., part i., p. 232; part ii., p. 239 (Oxford edition).

Archdeacon Todd says a full account of the opinions held by this class may be found in the proceedings against Giles Van Bellan, another Dutchman, who abjured them about this time. His recantation has not been published. From a copy now before us we select the following :—

"I have diverse and sundry times affirmed, said, taught, defended, and holden, in the parish of Worksop, of the said diocese, that there is no priest but God only; and that no priest hath power to consecrate the very body of Christ, as he was here reigning on earth, for the apostles had no power to consecrate the body of Christ; and that no priest had power to take away man's sin.

"*Item:* That the Sacrament of the altar is but bread, except it be received by faith, and in the name of Jesus. *Item:* That God doth not dwell in temples or churches made by man's hands, but in a faithful ——*a* man to God. *Item:* That no man can make any water holier than God makes it; therefore, the water in the font, nor the holy water in the church, is holier than the water in the river; for the water in the river is as holy as the water in the fonts, if a man be baptized in it, and the words of baptism be spoken over him. *Item:* That every ——*b* man may baptize in water as well as a priest. *Item:* That no bishop can make no ground holier than another. That no man is bound to fast. That no man ought to keep any holy day but the Sunday. That prayer made to saints is of no value. That no man ought to go on pilgrimage. That a man may be confessed of another man as well as of a priest. That there is no purgatory."*

The feeling excited by these cruelties told with fearful effect on the bishops. In the discussion of a bill for enforcing ecclesiastical laws, in 1567, it is said, "All the bishops joined in a complaint to the Lords, that they were much despised by the common people; that vice and disorder much abounded; and that they durst not punish any sin, by reason that some late proclamations had almost totally deprived them of any jurisdiction, so that they could not oblige any person to appear before them, or observe the order of the church."†

(*a*) A word we cannot make out. (*b*) The same word as before.
* Note C.
† Parl. History, vol. i., p. 591.

The power which these men had so shamefully abused was soon to be taken away. The death of the young monarch soon followed; and though plans had been formed for the exclusion of the rightful heir to the throne and the election of Lady Jane Grey, yet the rapid and successful efforts of Mary to secure her rights, exposed them not only to the vindictiveness of the professors of the old faith when restored to power, but to the penalties of treason against the state. The fabric which they raised by the hand of cruelty, and cemented by the blood of harmless and truth-loving men, was soon to crumble to dust. The measure which they had meted out to others would be meted out to them again. Justice seldom sleeps in the presence of wrong. The cry of suffering innocence was heard; and, by a death similar to that of their victims, were many of the leading inquisitors removed from the world. But the narrative of these events will claim our attention in another chapter.

CHAPTER IV.

MARY.

No doubt Mary's accession to the throne was welcomed by the majority of the nation.* The plot for her exclusion and the enthronement of Jane exploded at once, and placed the innocent and the guilty alike at her mercy. There were causes which contributed to her success. Into a full detail of these we cannot enter. The merest outline must

---

* "I have seen the most sudden change that could have been believed among mankind; and I think that Heaven alone has conducted the work, and caused such innumerable people to be moved to the greatest affection which has ever been seen amongst subjects." "About 35,000 or 40,000 men, foot and horse, armed at her devotion."—Noailles, *apud* Turner, vol. iii., p. 379.

suffice for the present. We have already seen that more than three-fourths of the population were attached to the Romish —perhaps more correctly the Anglican, in contradistinction to the ultra-Protestant—faith, though opposed, unmistakably, to the Papal supremacy.* Their king, in his will, had recognised the claim of the daughter of Catherine; and both houses of the legislature had most deliberately owned it. Northumberland, petted by the Reformers, the "Joshua"† of his time, under the mask of the loftiest pretensions to sanctity, was without moral principle. His tyranny and selfishness, and that of his creatures, had concentrated the hatred of the community on him. His plotting against Somerset—a weaker, but far better man,—and finally the Protector's death in violation of justice, had never been forgiven; whilst the supposed poisoning of the lamented Edward had filled to overflowing the cup of public indignation. Reform, too, had been carried on in a spirit which had awakened the hostility of thousands. Force, not suasion; punishment, not love; imprisonment, not the recognition of the rights of conscience,—had been the weapons with which these mistaken Reformers had worked. Scenes which were a disgrace to morality had been exhibited. One spiritual tyranny, clothed with all the sacredness of antiquity, and sanctioned by the public religious sentiments of the civilized world, had been thrown off, only to give place to another which violated the moral training of many, and robbed them of sources of daily pleasure and gain. Vicious, selfish, hypocritical men, under the guise of piety, had made a perfect onslaught on all holy things. Holy roods, holy images, holy vessels, holy bread and water, holy candles,‡ holy beads, had been

---

* The Pope felt "that she had obtained her throne by the favour of those who, for the most part, *hated to death the Holy See.*"

† So called by Sandys, afterward Archbishop of York.

‡ Father Latimer, in his own way, explains the use of these:—"Now there was an old cousin of mine, which, after the man was dead, gave me a wax candle in my hand, and commanded me to make certain + + + over

swept away; and above all, the wealth of the church had been seized to gratify their ambition and their lust for power.* Thousands of wretched monks were wanderers. Thousands, who had been allowed to fill vacant cures, retained the fullest sympathy with their early religious training. Over a wide circle their power extended. It could not be otherwise. No religious movement which is not the result of individual consciousness, can be genuine. Politicians, for their own worldly interest, may force the outward man; civil power may compel an external obedience,—but they leave the heart untouched. Germany, Scotland, and England, are standing proofs of the misery

---

him that was dead; for she thought the devil should run away by and by. So I took the candle, but I could not + him, as she would have me to do, for I had never seen it before. Now she, perceiving that I could not do it, with a great anger took the candle out of my hand, saying," &c.—Sermons, vol. i., p. 543.

* Complaints of the spoliation of the church by the lay lords, and the poverty of the church dignitaries, meet you everywhere. It may be so. Large portions of property had been abstracted from ecclesiastical affluence. Their wretchedness may be gathered from an item or two from the records of the spoil which his enemies carried away from the castles at Battersea and Cawood, palatial residences of Holgate, the Archbishop of York. "From Battersea they carried £300 in gold; in specialties and good debts, £400 more; in plate gilt and parcels gilt, 1,600 ounces; a mitre of fine gold, with two pendants, set about the sides and nindit with very fine diamonds, sapphires, and bailists, and all the plain with very good stones and pearls, and the pendants in like manner, weighing 125 ounces; six or seven great rings of fine gold, with stones in them, whereof were three fine blue torquoise and a diamond; a serpent's tongue, set in a standard of silver, gilt and graven; the Archbishop's seal, in silver; his signet; an old antique, in gold. From Cawood and other places, £900; two mitres; in plate and parcel gilt, 770 ounces; gilt plate, 1,157 ounces; one broken + of silver gilt, weighing forty-six ounces." Substantials, as well as the ornamental, were carried away. "2,500 sheep, 100 beasts, 200 quarters of wheat, 500 of malt, sixty of oats, and five or six tons of wine." (Strype's Cranmer, vol. ii., pp. 8, 9.) These are only a few of the good things of this life which were found in the stores of the Archbishop. Yet Cranmer, in a note to Cecil, says,—"If I knew of any bishop who was covetous, I would surely admonish him, but I know none; but all beggared, except it be one, and he I deem will say he is not very rich."—*Ibid*, vol. ii., p. 405.

and failure of moral changes effected by such instrumentality. Difficult we know it is to form anything like an accurate conception of the state of the rural mind at this time. The data from which we could draw our conclusions are very limited. But it must not be forgotten, that thought and intelligence had more power and play in the great hives of industry and commerce than in the sparsely populated districts of the country. The cities and great towns were the Reformers' strongholds. *

To the rustic mind there was a charm about the old form of worship. It appealed to the senses, if it did not affect the mind. The eye and the ear were gratified, as the one gazed on the splendours of art and decorative effect in the awful mysteries of the altar, and the other drank in the rolling notes of the organ or the plaintive strains of the officiating staff of priests, although the heart might be immersed in all its moral pollution. Compared with the baldness of the new, the auxiliaries of the old faith were most telling. Besides, Mary had pledged her word that there should be no changes. The ecclesiastical polity, the doctrinal formularies of her father's reign, were to be the great standards of the national faith. She herself had consented to them. The imprisoned bishops, likely to wield the most powerful influence under her reign, had worked them out from the mass of corruption with which they had been surrounded. Hence, Protestants were as loud in their welcome as Catholics. The reason is here: both had confidence in the sincerity of the queen; both hoped that their claims would be respected. Toleration had been promised. These

---

* "In London alone there were 15,000 French, Flemish, and German refugees, most of them headstrong and ungovernable enthusiasts."—Froude, vol. vi., p. 43. Many of them, we have no doubt, were Flemish Baptists—men who believed truth to be a reality, and could afford to keep a conscience, at the risk of everything else.

"The city of London is a whirlpool and sink of all evil humours, where they be bred, and from thence spread into all parts of the world."—Gardiner. Fox, book i., Mary's Reign.

expectations were well grounded; whilst the mass of the people were ready to hail any change which would gratify their senses or improve their social state. Heaven, too, was regarded as deeply interested in this conflict. Prodigies of no common order were interpreted in Mary's favour.* Let the reader give but ordinary weight to these concurrent circumstances, and the facility with which the eldest born of Henry ascended the throne will be no longer a mystery.

"The path of honour, of comfort, and of national peace and prosperity, was never more straight and perceptible—never more easy and certain to any sovereign, than that which opened before Mary." † The past in her history warranted, to some extent, if not entirely, the confidence of the nation. Her conduct during the reigns of her father and brother, though firm, and unfolding many of the Tudor elements of her nature, had given no ground, even to conjecture, that the fearful scenes which marked her short and unhappy reign could by any possibility transpire. Amiable, cultivating in her retirement an acquaintance with the noblest productions of past ages, conscientious in the highest degree,‡ and standing out as a lonely royal and suffering maiden, she enlisted the sympathies of the people, and warranted the hope that her rule would be marked by a wise and tolerant policy, and be followed by all the elements of prosperity and national wealth. Besides, for a time, the promise she had so distinctly given to her East-Anglican supporters remained intact. Whilst doubt and uncertainty

---

* Froude, vol. vi., chap. 1. "Therefore, no marvel why God fought against them, seeing they were hypocrites, and under the cloak of the Gospel would have debarred the queen's highness of her rights; but God would not so cloak them."—Bradford's Works, p. 324.

† Turner, vol. iii., p. 395.

‡ "My soul is God's," she said to her brother; "my faith I will not change; my opinions I will not dissemble. I therefore desire your highness rather to take my life than to restrain me from hearing mass."—Soame's Reformation, vol. iii., p. 615.

as to certain final issues—whilst dangers, more or less, marked her pathway, she not only did not violate her word, but breathed the spirit of conciliation; and though she would indulge her own religious convictions, and devoutly conform to the rites and ceremonies of her own faith, still no embargo should be laid on the consciences of others. More than this. The rabid zeal of her co-religionists speedily manifested itself. In more places than one, the mass, in violation of the law, was publicly celebrated. At Paul's Cross, a canon of the metropolitan church so aroused the indignation of his audience by his intemperate eulogies on the hated Bonner and the dogmas of the old faith, that, but for the protection of Bradford, his life would have been sacrificed by the excited multitude.* Against these untimely and unexpected outbreaks, the lord mayor complained to the queen. The calm was ruffled, and the deep wide sea was agitated, and it might be lashed into terrific fury. "Go tell them," was the reply to his lordship, "in the best words the mayor and recorder can devise, that albeit her grace's conscience is stayed in matters of religion, yet she meaneth graciously not to compel and constrain other men's consciences, otherwise than God shall put in their hearts a persuasion of the truth that she is in, through the opening of his word unto them by godly, virtuous, and learned preachers."

The better qualities of her nature were speedily eradicated. Into all the arts of duplicity she was very soon

---

* A spectator of the scene thus describes the excitement :—"Others, more excited than the rest, began to climb up the pulpit, to pull him down. Such an uproar began, such shouting at the sermon, such casting up of caps, that a bystander, who kept a journal of the events of the day, affirmed that the people seemed to be mad, and much mischief would have been done if the mayor and his brethren had not been present."—Life and Defence of Bonner, p. 156. Collier, vol. ii., p. 345. Mary was present at this scene, accompanied by sixty guards, besides the attendants of the nobles who accompanied her.—Howard's Lady Jane Grey, pp. 303, 304.

indoctrinated; and her progress was rapid. Before she had been three weeks on the throne, she had received a secret messenger from the Vatican, and had opened a correspondence with the Pope.* She stands before us, in the page of history, as a fearful, and, indeed, terrific example of the power of superstition and priestly tyranny to convert a nature which might have unfolded all the elements of moral and political greatness, into one which the Moral Governor of the Universe—happily for man, at far distant periods— sends as the ministers of justice to correct nations for their transgressions. True it is, the seeds of her cruel tyranny were there—deep hidden in her nature; but her youth, and the first acts of her reign, gave the promise of a different harvest. Like the vast primeval forests of the New World, which have beneath the wide-spreading roots of their magnificent trees the seeds of other forms of vegetable life: till the former are removed, the latter cannot vegetate.

Liberated from the Tower, restored to his see, and invested with the highest legal, and probably at this time the highest political authority in the kingdom, Gardiner soon made his influence felt in every department of the state.† Ambitious, vindictive, regardless in a great measure of high-toned moral principle, he was "in wit crafty and subtle; towards his superiors flattering and fair-spoken; to his inferiors fierce; against his equals stout and envious." Thoroughly familiar, from early and long practice, with every diplomatic art, more than with theological science, he was one of those men, by no means rare in his age, who

---

* *Vide* Froude, vol. vi., p. 83.

† "Winchester shows already, in the opinion of many, that he will not be less arrogant and violent in the administration of affairs than others who have had this authority; and we may see that he has forgotten nothing, in his seven years' prison, of his accustomed manner." (The French Ambassador to his Court.)—Turner, vol. iii., p. 381.

"Gardiner," said Mary, "was obstinate, and would listen to no one; she herself was helpless and miserable."—Froude, vol. vi., p. 221.

regarded the possession of power as more than justifying the means by which their boundless lust of dominion was gratified. Extremes centred in the bishop. There was much that was noble and commanding, blended with a reptile meanness which stamps his character with features which, as a whole, are ever repulsive. *

To men of the chancellor's spirit revenge was sweet; to triumph over a foe his highest glory; to gaze on his sufferings, and to aid in augmenting them, was no very limited source of enjoyment.

Gardiner had felt the power of Cranmer and his reforming brethren during the former reign. In his conflict with the archbishop his overthrow was signal. Deprived of his bishopric, stripped of all his authority, he had cherished in the solitude of his cell the spirit of revenge. His hour was now come; and in the agony and blood of his martyred foes the plenitude of his vengeance was satisfied. Nor was this all. The bishop, in the fulness of his zeal, during the reign of Henry, had published a work in defence of the monarch. It now supplied his opponents with strong defensive armour. They galled the apostate prelate with arrows snatched from his quiver. His work against the Papal supremacy, and his

---

* The following is Bishop Ponet's description of him:—"The dóctor hath a smart colour, hanging look, frowning brows, eyes an inch within his head, a nose hooked like a buzzard's; nostrils like a horse, ever snuffing in the wind; a sparrow mouth, great paws like the devil, talons on his feet like the grife, two inches longer than the natural toes, and so tied with sinews that he cannot abide to be touched." Ponet hated Gardiner. —Froude, vol. vi., pp. 105, 197, 295, 395.

Lloyd says, "His reservedness was such, that he never did what he aimed at, never aimed at what he intended, never intended what he said, and never said what he thought; whereby he carried it so, that others should do his business when they opposed it, and should undermine theirs when he seemed to promote it. A man that was to be traced like the fox, and read, like Hebrew, backward. If you would know what he did, you must observe what he did not; that, whilst intending one thing, he professed to aim at the very opposite; that he never intended what he said, and never said what he intended."—Lodge's Illustrations, vol. i., p. 126.

ready concurrence in the divorce, had been republished. It was considered the best defence of the king's divorce, and the most unanswerable attack on the Pope's supremacy, which had hitherto appeared. To this work a preface had been written by Bonner.* Again and again his own sentiments were quoted by the prisoners at his bar, and the protection of his opinion was invoked by thousands of dissidents from Popery. Renegades always feel this deeply.† To trample on their own principles in the madness of their rage, to heap insult and calumny on those who retain them, is the highest proof they can give of the sincerity of their conversion and the reality of their faith. To rescue their discarded opinions from neglect, to lay them in all their breadth and importance before the nation, to show that interest, not principle—selfishness, not the love of the truth, may fairly be recognized as the cause of the change, is, beyond all dispute, the deadliest blow which can be inflicted on an opponent. This was the doom of the unhappy chancellor. His holy anger could only be quenched in the blood of his enemies.

Far less public for a time, though not less potent, was the influence of another councillor. Renard, the ambassador from Spain, was early admitted to the confidence of Mary. He was a thorough diplomatist. The end with him always justified the means. Spanish interests were paramount with him. At these he ever aimed. The supremacy of the

---

* The Life and Defence of Bishop Bonner, by a Tractarian British Critic. London, 1842. A work of great interest and equal clearness.

"Gardiner's spite was at this time much impelled by the reprinting of his book on True Obedience, which was done at Strasburg, and sent over. In it he called King Henry's marriage with Queen Catherine incestuous, and had justified his divorce, and his second marriage with his 'most godly and virtuous wife, Queen Anne.'"—Burnet.

† He had thus spoken also: "The king's majesty hath, by the inspiration of the Holy Ghost, composed all matter of religion, which uniformity, I pray God, it may in that, and all other things, be extended unto us."—Address to the University of Cambridge, in Strype's Ecclesiastical Memorials, vol. vi. *Apud* 243.

queen's uncle in the English Council was the end of his mission. Moral restraint was unknown when these were to be secured.* The union of the two crowns was the triumph of his skill. Mary was fascinated by this unprincipled minister. In the solitude of midnight, and in the loneliness of the royal closet, he poured his insidious advice into her willing ear. Gradually her whole heart was laid open before him. Intensely hating the reformed doctrines, feeling that nothing but the entire destruction of its abettors would give security to his master's policy, he urged the death of the unfortunate Lady Jane Grey and her friends. And only the dread of a nation's rising prevented his infatuated mistress from listening to his pernicious counsels, and offering her sister as a victim to his malignant nature.† His was a dark spirit of evil, rejoicing only in the agony and suffering of his fellow men.‡

The influence of these two men, till the arrival of Pole, was all-powerful; yet, in many respects, their line of policy was divergent, and the ends they sought to secure very

---

* The emperor and his clerical advisers had promised to prevent Mary either from attempting innovations in religion without their consent, or marrying against the approbation of her subjects. Mary herself had authorised Renard to assure the Council that she had no thought of marrying a stranger. And yet Turner says,—"On the 30th of October Mary sent for the Spanish ambassador by night, and in the seclusion of her own room, prostrate on her knees before the most sacred object of her faith, and after repeating the *Veni Creator*, she solemnly vowed to him that none other than Philip would she take for her husband. I take the substance of this from Renard's despatch."—Turner, vol. iii., p. 392. Duplicity marked her character from the first.

† "With Elizabeth," he said to Charles, "there will be religious revolution. The clergy will be put down, the Catholics persecuted, and there will be such revenge for the present proceedings as the world has never seen."—(Renard to the Emperor.) *Apud* Froude, vol. vi., p. 355.

‡ "If England should be ruled by such a councillor, woe, woe, to England! for then it would come to ruin and destruction; and them that favour God's Word would be in worse case than those that were in the time of Sodom and Gomorrah."—Sir P. Hoby to Cecil. Burleigh State Papers, vol. i. *Apud* Froude, vol. v., p. 488. Hoby in this case was all but prophetic.

opposite. One in their intense hatred to the reformed,—hesitating at no means to annihilate the friends of the new doctrine,—yet the one was the Spaniard, seeking to subordinate England to the politics of Spain; the other the Englishman, not less anxious for the independence and greatness of his country, and the union of the queen with an English noble. Renard triumphed, and Philip was declared king.

For the political events which led to the sacrifice of Lady Jane Grey upon the scaffold,*—for the various means employed for the restoration of the old faith and the supremacy of the Papal power,—for the history of the rebellion excited by the intended marriage with Philip, and the hostility of the people to the restoration of the ancient rites,—for the account of the martyrdom of some of the best, the noblest, and the most enlightened of England's sons at that time, and the suffering and the misery which followed, we must refer our readers to other sources of information. Ours is not a history of Mary's reign. It is not a martyrology. Only to these can we refer so far as it may place before our readers the design of this volume.

The first year of her reign had not closed before the reconciliation to Rome was complete, and the Cardinal Legate invested with full power. The joy of the Romanists was full.† The prospects of an heir to the throne made them all but delirious. She was another Mary favoured of heaven, to give birth to another son who should save the church. Gratitude was demanded for all this. Mary and her Council were ready. Spanish gold had done

---

* *Vide* Howard's Life of Lady Jane Grey.

† "Then you might have seen those which had been bishops, who had been displaced by the young King Edward and his late father Henry, coming in great joy and magnificence about the town, mounted on mules and little pompous horses, dressed in great gowns of black camlet, over which were beautiful surplices, their heads covered with satin hoods like those worn by the monks, being joyous on account of the queen's victory."—Howard's Lady Jane Grey, p. 302.

much,* and the promise of undisturbed possession of church lands more, with her councillors and senate. The past presented them with precedents. The times of Moses, the Judges, and the Kings, were full of examples which they might imitate. Agreements, and great national festivities, were marked by sacrifice. That with Rome demanded one. Completeness without it would be wanting. Their sincerity would be questioned if the land, once more restored to the unity of the church, was not cleansed from the hated and polluting presence of the heretics. The Cardinal Legate demanded it. "Bring forth," said he, "fruits meet for repentance. Here is another point that you must show worthy of a repentant mind: that whereas you have sore offended God by giving favour to heretics, now transfer your favour under such manner, that if you can count them by any means unto the unity of the church, then do it, for it is a great work of mercy. But if ye cannot, and ye suffer or favour them, there cannot be a work of greater cruelty against the commonwealth than to nourish or favour any such. For be ye assured, there is no kind of men so pernicious to the commonwealth as they be; there are no thieves, no murderers, no adulterers, nor no kind of treason, to be compared to theirs, who, as it were, undermining the chief foundations of all commonwealth, which is religion, maketh an entry to all kinds of vice in the most heinous manner."† To the senate, as it knelt before the proud priest, he had given

---

* Gardiner "suggested that without great remittances of money to gain the principal nobility and leading men, the next parliament would be as troublesome as the last." £400,000 was employed in this business.—*Vide* Collier, vol. ii., p. 353. "Upon Tuesday, the 2nd of October, there came to the Tower in 20 cartes made for the show, accompanied with certain Spaniards of the king's guard, iv. xx. xvii. little chests, of a yeard long and iiii. inches broad, of silver, which will make by estimation L. thousand pound."—The Chronicle of Queens Jane and Mary, p. 83 (Camden Society). Stowe makes it 27 chests. Fox says it was matted about with mats, &c.

† Cardinal Pole's Address to the Citizens of London.—Appendix to Strype's Ecclesiastical Memorials.

similar advice. Philip and Mary responded to the call. It was a glorious work. The merits would be enormous. The Divine favour would rest on the land. A son would be given, and the power of His Holiness consolidated in the nation. In Bonner, an officiating high-priest was found. His qualifications were of the highest order. Others of the episcopal bench were ready to aid in the pleasant work; while subordinate Levites, in almost countless numbers, were ready to discharge the inferior duties in this great national holocaust. But caution was necessary. The elements of danger existed. Rebellion had already threatened Mary's existence. The old forms of faith were preferred, no doubt, by the mass of the people, but not the Papal supremacy.*

Early in her reign articles were sent to the bishops to aid them in their godly work. One or two will illustrate their design :—

"*Item:* That every bishop, and all other persons aforesaid, do diligently travel† for the repression of heresies and notable crimes, especially in the clergy, duly correcting and punishing the same.

---

* "Yet they did not (the parliament) gladly hear of the abolishing specially of that law, that gave the title of the supremacy of the church in the realm to the crown; suspecting that to be an introduction to the Pope's authority into the realm, which they cannot gladly hear of; and for this cause cannot gladly hear of my legation in the Pope's name. Whereupon her Grace, in the same letter, doth exhort me to stay my voyage until a more opportune time; and asketh my counsel, in case the lower house make resistance in renouncing the title of supremacy, what her Grace were best to do, and what way she had best to take." (Cardinal Pole.)—Memorials of Cranmer, vol. ii., 414.

Anxious that our readers should have full evidence on this point, we select a sentence or two from an appeal to the Council by the prisoners for the Gospel :—"So that there was not one parish in all England that ever desired again to have the Romish superstition and vain services, which is now by the popish, proud, covetous, clergy placed again, in contempt not only of God, all heaven, and all the Holy Ghost's lessons in the blessed Bible; but also against the honour of the said two most noble kings, against your own country, fore-agreement, and against all the godly consciousness within this realm of England and elsewhere."—*Ibid,* vol. ii., p. 442. † Labour.

"*Item:* That every bishop, and all other persons aforesaid, do likewise travel for the condemning and repressing of corrupt and haughty opinions, unlawful books, ballads, and other pernicious and hurtful devices, engendering hatred amongst the people and discord amongst the same. And the schoolmasters, preachers, and teachers, do exercise and use their offices and duties, without teaching, preaching, or setting forth any evil and corrupt doctrine; and that doing the contrary, they may be by the bishop and his said officers punished and removed.

"*Item:* That by the bishop of the diocese an uniform doctrine be set forth by homilies, or otherwise, for the good instruction of all people; and that the said bishop, and other persons aforesaid, do compel the parishioners to come to their several churches, and there devoutly to hear divine service, as of reason they ought." *

The chief magistrate of the metropolis was a fitting instrument for this work. His name was Blackwall. In obedience to the mandate of the queen, he issued his orders to the several wards, commanding them to assemble "all and every the said householders, that both in their own persons, and also their wives, children, and servants, being of the age of twelve years and upwards, and every of them, do at all and every time and times henceforth, and namely at the holy time of Easter now approaching, honestly, quietly, and catholickly, use and behave themselves like good and faithful Christian people," &c. They are then to see that the admonitions of Bonner "to all parsons, vicars, and curates" are executed; "that they and every of them do truly, without delay, advertize you of the names and surnames of all and every person and persons, that they or any of them can or may at any time hereafter know, perceive, or understand to transgress or offend in any point or article concerning the premises, at their utmost peril." †

To facilitate her ends, and to check the Protestant heresy, Mary laid the pulpit under an interdict. Little need there was for such a step in relation to her friends. Romanists never liked it. Letters were sent to the bishops, command-

---

* Fox (Madden's edition), Mary's reign, book i., p. 22. † *Ibid*, p. 22.

ing them not to suffer any person in their diocese, either priest or deacon, or otherwise distinguished, to preach or expound the Scriptures openly in any church, chapel, or other place, without special license from the queen. By this exercise of regal power she hoped to arrest the progress of the Reformation. Vain hope! The rising tide is not thrown back by barriers of sand.*

We have seen already that vast multitudes of the people, some from self-interest, others from fear, and various other motives, had outwardly conformed to the new order of things during Edward's reign.† Upon this class the measures of the government, and the zeal of the episcopate in carrying them out, told with speedy effect. Many of the clergy that were forward men under King Edward, now, by the terror of the times, recanted and subscribed. "And these were of two sorts. Some out of weakness did it, but persisted not in it, but, as soon as they could, revoked their subscriptions and recantations; and after their release and escape out of prison made a sorrowful confession in public of their fall."‡ Others conformed, soothing their consciences with the delusion "that their bodies might be there so long as their spirits did not consent."§ Bradford, in one of his letters, says "that not the tenth person abode in God's ways; and that the more did part stakes with the Papist and Protestant, &c. For they pretended Popery outwardly, going to mass with the Papists, and tarrying with them personally at their antichristian and idolatrous service;

---

* *Vide* Collier, vol. ii., p. 345; Records, p. 68.

† "The use of the old religion is forbidden by law," said Pagit to Somerset, "and the use of the new is not yet printed; printed in the stomachs of nearly eleven out of every twelve parts of the realm; what countenance soever men make outwardly to please those in whom they see the power resteth." July, 1549.—Strype's Eccle. Memorials. *Apud* Soame's History of the Reformation, vol. iii., p. 391.

‡ Strype's Cranmer, vol. ii., p. 88. Jewel and others belonged to this class.

§ Strype's Cranmer, vol. ii., p. 90.

but with their hearts they said, and with their spirits they served the Lord."* Many fled to the continent, and found refuge amongst the various religious communities in Switzerland, Holland, &c.†

It would give additional interest to our narrative, we feel persuaded, to narrate the sufferings and martyrdom of those illustrious servants of our common Lord—Bradford, Philpot, Saunders, Ridley, Hooper, Latimer, Cranmer, and others; but our space forbids this. They were victims upon whom Bonner and Gardiner soon laid their hands. Their zeal was kindled by their deadly hatred to the men, and they rested not till the martyr's fire had removed them from their path. Gardiner "thought no argument would operate so strongly as penalties, and that the terror of fire and faggots, in some cases, were the best methods of conviction; that when people were incorrigible, they ought to be capitally punished."‡ The pages of Fox are rich in details. In this glorious cloud of witnesses some of our fathers are found. The extent of their sufferings we cannot accurately estimate. The martyrologist is not sufficiently explicit. Internal evidence would justify the conclusion that they were far more than his positive and clear statements warrant. Intense as the hatred to the Reformers was, it did not diminish in intensity when it hunted Anabaptists from their seclusion. Nowhere were they safe. Spies everywhere haunted their steps. "For now a man can go to no place, but malicious busybodies curiously search out his deeds, mark his words, and if he agree not with them in despising God's Word, then will they spitefully and hatefully cavil against him and it, calling

---

* Works, p. 106 (Religious Tract Society). "They never came to the Gospel but for commodity and gain's sake, and even for gain they leave it."—P. 325.

† *Vide* The Troubles at Frankfort (Petherham ed. ; London, A.D. 1846). Collier states that about 12,000 of the clergy were turned out of their livings for being married.—See vol. ii., p. 366.

‡ Collier, vol. ii., p. 378.

it error and heresy, and the professors thereof heretics and schismatics; and with other odious and spiteful names, as traitors and not the Queen's friends."*

Amidst other means for supressing the heretics, an order was issued to the justices of Norfolk, May the 27th. We select a few sentences from it to show its spirit. They were, " I. To divide themselves into several districtions. II. To assist such preachers as should be sent. III. To lay special weight for teachers of heresies, and procurers of secret meetings to that purpose. V. To procure one or more of every parish, secretly instructed, to give information of the behaviour of the inhabitants. VI. To charge the constable, and four or more Catholic inhabitants of every parish, to give account of idle vagabonds and suspected persons, and the retainers of such persons. To observe hue and cry; and to look after the watches in every parish."† These men were willing tools of the royal tyrants. Men were base enough, though sworn to judge with equity, to examine the accused on secret information, and without the knowledge of their accusers. Norfolk had many individuals who thought they were doing God service, by hunting the heretics from their hiding places.

In articles concerning archdeacons, issued this year, occurs the following :—"Whether there be any that will not suffer the priest to dip the child three times in the font, being yet strong and able to abide and suffer it in the judgment and opinion of discreet and expert persons, but will needs have the child in the clothes, and only be sprinkled with a few drops of water?"‡

In 1554, Pole ordered a visitation to be held throughout the whole country. A book was to be kept, in which the names of conformists were to be entered, and the separatists

---

* Norfolk Petition to the Queen. Fox, book ii.
† Strype's Cranmer, vol. ii. pp. 93-94.
‡ Collier, vol. ii. (Records, p. 87.)

were to be reported, and proceeded against with the utmost severity of the law."*

Kent supplied a large number of Christian heroes. Many of them, no doubt, were Baptists. It is clear from Fox, that many dissidents from the State Church resided here, and met in separate congregations; and the principles they held, though imperfectly stated by the martyrologist, are decidedly Anabaptistical. Of their existence in the former reign we have already placed evidence before our readers. Cranmer and his brethren did not convert them. Persecution never extinguished them. Their influence had grown. About the following there can be no doubt :—In Maidstone resided John Denby, described as a gentleman, and John Newman, by trade a peuterer, the progenitor of him of Oriel College, Oxford, and now a brother of the Oratory.† Visiting some friends in Essex, not unlikely some of their Baptist brethren, they were accosted by a bitter persecutor, who was returning from an *auto-da-fé*, either at Raleigh or Rochford. "Even as I saw them, I suspected them; and then I did examine and search them, and found about them certain letters, which I have sent you, and also a certain writing in paper what their faith was. And they confessed to me that they had forsaken and fled out of their country for religion's sake." They had visited other countries. The papers found on Denby were simply certain notes collected and gathered out of the Scriptures, with a confession of his faith touching the Sacrament of Christ's body and blood. Fox has given this simple and Scriptural confession. It would secure Denby's condemnation. It is more than probable that it was prepared for the satisfaction of some perplexed one. Its clearness and simplicity admirably fitted it for such an end.

---

* *Vide* Froude, vol. vi., p. 314.

† "I am sure that the opinions of John Newman, who was burnt, on transubstantiation, are further from the doctrine of the Church of Rome, and, I must say, more intelligible, than the opinions of Oriel John Newman, lately published."—Life of Bonner, p. 273.

To the palace of Bonner we now transfer our readers. With Denby and Newman we find one Patrick Packingham arraigned before his Lordship. Upon their confession they were examined; the bishop "objecting also unto them certain other articles of his own: to which they all answered in effect one thing, although Denby answered more largely than the others, and, therefore, I thought his answer sufficient to lay down as containing the substance of all the rest."* From his examination by Bonner it will be enough, from the eleven articles which were objected against him, to select the seventh:—"*That the said Denby hath believed, and doth believe, that the christening of children, as it is now used in the Church of England, is not good, nor allowable by God's Word, but against it; likewise confirming of children, giving of orders, saying of matins and even-song, anointing of persons, making of holy bread and holy water, with the rest of the church.*" His reply to this was as follows:— "To the seventh article I answer, that as touching the christening, the sacrament of baptism, which is the christening of children, it is altered and changed; for St. John used nothing but the preaching of the Word and water, as it doth appear when Christ required to be baptized of him, and others also, who came to John to be baptized of him, as it appeareth in Matthew iii., Mark i., Luke iii., and Acts i. The chamberlain said, 'See, here is water; what doth hinder me to be baptized?' It appeareth here that Philip had preached unto him; for he said, 'Here is water.' We do not read that he asked for any cream, oil, or spittle, or conjured water, or conjured wax, no croysom, or salt, for it seemeth that Philip had preached no such things unto him; for he would as well have asked for them as for water; and the water was not conjured, but even as it was before. Also Acts x.: 'Then answered Peter, Can any man forbid water, that these should not be baptized?' Acts xvi.: 'And Paul and Silas preached unto him the Word of the

---

* Fox. Mary's reign, book ii.

Lord, and to all that were in his house; and he took them the same hour of the night, and washed their wounds; and so was he baptized, and all them of his household straitway;' where you see nothing but preaching the Word and water."

Denby was finally condemned, and burnt at Uxbridge on the 8th of August. In the midst of his sufferings he gave utterance to the joy of his soul in a Psalm. Fox tells us that the " cruel Dr. Story commanded one of the tormentors to throw a faggot at him, wherewith being so hurt that his face bled, he left singing, and clapt both his hands upon his face. 'Truly,' quoth Dr. Story to him that hurled the faggot, 'thou hast marred a good old song.'* Only momentary was this effect. Stretching his hands abroad, and whilst the flames were licking off the skin and flesh, he burst into another song, and then resigned his soul into the hands of God, through Jesus Christ."†

The examination of Newman follows, and also his confession of faith. In the former, the usual points in discussion are urged on his attention, whilst the latter is a clear and manly exhibition of the great Christian verities. On transubstantiation, Fox gives us, in a separate form, four of his arguments. We quote the last :—"When remembrance is of a thing, there is imported the absence thereof. Remembrance of Christ's body is in the Sacrament,—' Do this in remembrance of me;' *ergo*, Christ's body then is imported to be absent."

"Packingham was charged by Bonner for his behaviour in the bishop's chapel, who at the mass time, then standing, would not pull off his cap, which was taken for a heinous offence. Packingham being much persuaded by Bonner to recant, protested in these words to the bishop : 'That the

---

* "An earwig was singing a Psalm at the stake at Uxbridge; but I cut him short; for I threw a faggot in his face and a bush of thorns at his feet."—Soame's Reformation, vol. iv., p. 660. Strype's Annals, vol. i., p. 115.   † Fox, book ii.

church which he believed was no Catholic church, but was the church of Satan, and, therefore, he would never turn to it.'"* Packingham suffered on the 28th of the same month, and in the same town, as Denby; and Newman was burnt at Saffron Walden on the last day of the same month.

Later in the same year, another large contribution to the noble army of martyrs was supplied by our brethren. We are indebted to Fox for the information. He mentions the martyrdom of ten persons in the year 1555. Their names merit a transference to our pages. We give them in the order in which they occur in the pages of the Martyrology :—

ELIZTH. WARNE.	WILLIAM HALE.
GEORGE TANKERFIELD.	THOS. LEYES.
ROBT. SMITH.	GEORGE KING.
STEPHEN HARWOOD.	JOHN WADE.
THOS. FUST.	JOAN LASHWOOD.

Reference again and again is made to Bow churchyard, as a place where these early Nonconformists were accustomed to meet. Fox is not clear as to the whole, but certainly Elizth. Warne, whose husband had already passed to the martyr's home, was apprehended on the first of January, in a house in Bow churchyard, as they were gathered together in prayer. Most, if not all of them, were resident in the city or its neighbourhood. A letter from the commissioner consigned these "Sacramentarians" to the tender mercies of Bonner. His lordship was never slow in the discharge of these pleasurable duties. Smith appears to have been a man of influence, if not a teacher. He was acquainted with Denby,† and was probably a fellow labourer with him. The examinations were long and frequent. Smith's was the

---

* Fox, book ii., pp. 278-280.

† "We were baited by my lord's band of servants almost all the day, until our keeper, seeing their misorder, shut us all up in a handsome chamber, while my lord went into his synagogue to condemn Mr. Denby and John Newman."—R. Smith.

most protracted, or at least it is reported at greater length by Fox. It is full of noble sentiments, and discovers a spirit of genuine moral heroism. The bishop and his colleagues are like children in the hands of a giant.* The whole would fill many pages of this volume, if given in full. Only a portion can be selected, in part illustrative of his Baptismal views, and the holy confidence in the truth of God which supported him in the fiery conflict. The colloquy on the former will not be uninteresting to our readers :—†

"*Bonner.*—Why is God's order changed in baptism? In what point do us differ from the word of God?

"*Smith.*—In hallowing your water; in conjuring of the scenes; in baptizing children with anointing and spitting in their mouths, mingled with salt; and many other lewd ceremonies, of which not one point is able to be proved by God's order.

"*Bonner.*—By the mass! this is the most unshamefaced heretic that ever I heard speak!

"*Smith.*—Well sworn, my lord; ye keep a good watch.

"*Bonner.*—Well, Mr. Controller, ye catch me at my words; but I will watch thee as well, I warrant thee.

"By my troth, my lord, said Sir John Mordant, I never heard the like in all my life. But I pray you, my lord, mark well his answer for baptism. He disalloweth therein holy ointment, salt, and such other laudable ceremonies, which no Christian man will deny.

"*Smith.*—That is a shameful blasphemy against Christ, so to use any mingle-mangle in baptizing of young infants.

"*Bonner.*—*I believe, I tell thee, that if they die before they be baptized, they be damned.*

"*Smith.*—Ye shall never be saved by that belief. But I pray you, my lord, show me, are we saved by water or by Christ?

"*Bonner.*—By both.

"*Smith.*—Then the water died for our sins; and so must ye say, that the water hath life, and it being our servant, and created for us, is our Saviour. This, my lord, is a good doctrine, is it not?

---

* "He was smart and quick in conversation, and fervent in religion, wherein he was confirmed by the preaching of Mr. Turner, Canon of Windsor, and others."—Strype's Life of Sir T. Smith, p. 51.

† "Thou art weary of painting, and hast studied divinity, and so hast fallen, through thy departing from thy vocation, into heresy, said Bonner to R. Smith, a yeoman of the guard at Windsor."—Life of Bonner, p. 266.

"*Bonner.*—Why, how understandest thou the Scriptures? 'Except a man is born of water,' &c., &c. And again, 'Suffer (saith our Saviour) these children to come unto me:' and if thou wilt not suffer them to be baptized after this laudable order, then thou hinderest them to come unto Christ.

"*Smith.*—When ye allege St. John, 'Except a man be born,' &c., and will thereby prove the water to save, and so the deed or work to put away sins, I will send you to St. Paul, which asketh of the Galatians, 'Whether they received the Spirit by the deeds of the law, or by the preaching of faith,' and then concludeth that the Holy Ghost accompanieth the preaching of faith, and with the Word entereth into the heart. So now if baptism preach to me the washing in the blood, so doth the Holy Ghost accompany it, and it is unto me as a preacher and not a Saviour. And when you say I hinder the children from coming to Christ, it is manifest by our Saviour's words that ye hinder them to come, that will not suffer them to come unto him without the necessity of water. For he saith, 'Suffer them to come unto *me*,' and not unto water; and, therefore, if ye condemn them, ye condemn both the merit and the words of Christ. For our Saviour saith, '*Except* ye turn, and become as children, ye cannot enter into the kingdom of God.' And so brought I out many other examples, to make manifest that Christ hath cleansed original sin, bringing examples out of the Scriptures for the same.

"*Bonner.*—Then thou makest the water of non-effect; then put away the water.

"*Smith.*—'It is not,' saith St. Peter, 'the washing away the filth of the flesh, but in that a good conscience consenteth unto God.' And to prove that water only bringeth not the Holy Ghost, it is written in the eighth of the Acts, that Simon received water, but would have received the Holy Ghost for money. Also that the Holy Ghost hath come before baptism: it is written that John had the Holy Ghost in his mother's womb. Cornelius, Paul, and the queen Candace's servant, with many others, received the Holy Ghost before baptism. Yea, and although your generation have set at naught the Word of God, and, like swine, have turned his words upside down, yet must his church keep the same order which he left them, which his church dare not break; and to judge children damned that be not baptized, it is wicked.

"*Mordant.*—By our lady, sir, but I believe that if any child die without water, he is damned.

"*Bonner.*—Yea, and so do I, and all Catholic men, good Mordant.

"*Smith.*—Well, my lord, such Catholic, such salvation."*

---

* "He calls the oyl, salt, &c., used in baptism, blasphemies, and denies

On the spiritual character of Christ's church, Smith's views were also expressed, notwithstanding he was fully conscious of the danger to which the avowal would expose him. "I believe," said he, in reply to his wily examiner, "that there is one Catholic church or faithful congregation, which, as the apostle saith, is built upon the prophets and apostles, Christ being the head corner-stone; which in all her words and works maintaineth the Word, and bringeth the same for her authority, and without doth nothing, nor ought to do; of which I am afraid I am by grace a member." Equally distinct and manly is the following: "I told you whereon the true church is built, and I affirm that in England to be the true congregation of God, and also in *omnem terram;* as it is written, 'Their sound is gone forth into all lands;' and this is the afflicted and persecuted church which ye cease not to imprison, slay, and kill. And in Corinth was not all the congregations of God, but a number of those holy and elect people of God? For neither Paul nor Peter were present at Corinth when they wrote, and yet were they of the church of God, as many thousands more which also communicate in that Holy Spirit."

During his imprisonment, he not only sought to confirm his companions in suffering in Christ's truth, but his pen was not idle. Fox has given us several of his letters and pastoral effusions. Those to his wife are full of tenderness. Addressing his brethren, he said, "Mistrust not God; be of good comfort; rejoice in the Lord; hold fast your faith, and continue to the end. Deny the world, and take up your cross, and follow him who is your leader, and is gone before. If you suffer with him you shall reign with him. What way can you glorify the name of our heavenly Father better than by suffering death for his Son's sake? What a spectacle shall it be to the world,

---

the necessity of water baptism to children. Fox overlooks these failings and mistakes, and gives him commendation without abatement; which undistinguished regard is by no means serviceable to the reader."—Collier, vol. ii., p. 381.

to behold so goodly a fellowship as you servants of God, in so just a quarrel as the Gospel of Christ is, with so pure a conscience, so strong a faith, and so lively a hope, to offer yourselves to suffer so cruel torments at the hands of God's enemies, and so to end your days in peace, to receive in the resurrection of the righteous life everlasting."

"Robert Smith, to all the faithful servants of Christ, exhorting them to be strong under persecution," is a poetical effusion. Whatever defects the reader may discern in the loftiness and beauty of the muse, he will find none in the subject of her notes:—

> "Content thyself with patience,
> With Christ to bare the cross of pain,
> Which can and will thee recompence
> A thousand-fold with joys again.
>   Let nothing cause thy heart to quail,—
>   Launch out thy boat, hale up thy sail,—
>   Put from the shore;
> And be thou sure thou shalt attain
> Unto the port that shall remain
>   For evermore."

His noble spirit triumphed over the terrors of death. Uxbridge was the place of martyrdom. The 8th of August was the day of sacrifice. At the stake, and from the midst of the fire, he addressed the people. His zeal only expired with life. Half burnt, and all black with fire, clustered together as in a lump like a black coal, all men thinking him for dead, suddenly he rose up right before the people, lifting up the stumps of his arms, and clapping the same together, and declaring a rejoicing heart unto them. And so bending down again, and hanging over the fire, slept in the Lord, and ended this mortal life."*

Short but interesting accounts are given by Fox of Smith's companions also. Elizth. Warne was burnt at Stratford; Tankerfield, at St. Alban's; Harwood and Fust were burnt,

---

* In some editions of Fox there is an engraving of these moral heroes, holding, evidently, a meeting for worship in the prison. Smith is in the act of teaching. The sacred volume is before him.

one at Stratford, the other at Ware; W. Hale at Barnet. The remainder, from their suffering in Lollards Tower, fell sick and died. Heretics have no right to the burial of Christians. Their dead bodies were cast into the open fields, and in the darkness of midnight interred by some of the faithful.*

The imprisonment and sufferings of these heroic men in their gloomy prisons, instead of quenching their love of the truth, rather intensified it. More and more solicitous they became to know the mind of their Lord. No part of it was insignificant. No means within their reach were neglected, which would realize this end. In their intercourse with each other, as well as from the "lively oracles," they sought instruction, and the interchange of thought. As we have already seen, Predestination, Grace, Liberty,—the Calvinian and Pelagian views of truth,—had been discussed. The Anabaptists were not indifferent to the discussion. Against their views most of the leading prisoners protested. Their whole influence was wielded against them. The baptismal question was rife, and Philpot employed his pen in defence of the ceremony on which State churches are based; and from which, if he had calmly traced effects to their cause, the whole of the cruel sufferings to which he and his fellow prisoners were exposed had sprung. We select the following from a letter which this confessedly eminent servant of Christ addressed to a fellow prisoner, who if not a Baptist, had most serious doubts about infant baptism. The following shows him to be a dissident, and probably he was one of the Kent or Essex brethren :—"Hitherto I have showed you," says Philpot, "(good brother), my judgment generally of that you stand in doubt and dissent from others, to which I wish you, as mine own heart, to be conformable, and then, doubtless, you cannot err, but boldly may be glad in your troubles, and triumph at the hour of your death, that you shall die in the church of God, a faithful martyr, and receive the crown of eternal glory."

---

* *Vide* Fox. Mary's reign, book ii.

The ignorance of Philpot and the spirit of the martyr are alike unfolded in the following. Gentleness, and even sanctified meekness, were aroused by the hated principles of the Anabaptist heretics. "Aurentius, one of the Arian sect, with his adherents, was one of the first that denied the baptism of children, and next after him, Pelagias, the heretic, and some others that were in St. Bernard's time, as it doth appear by his writings, *and in our days the Anabaptists, an inordinate kind of men, stirred up by the devil to the destruction of the Gospel.*"

We will only add a sample of the reasoning of this holy man. It must have excited the pity, if not the contempt, of all intelligent Baptists.

"Now will I prove, with manifold arguments, that children ought to be baptized, and that the apostles of Christ did baptize children. The Lord commanded his apostles to baptize all nations: therefore all children ought to be baptized, for they are comprehended under this word, all nations.

"Further, when God doth account among the faithful, they are faithful, for it was said to Peter, 'That thing which God hath purified, thou shalt not say to be common or unclean.' But God doth repute children among the faithful. *Ergo*, they be faithful, except we had rather to resist God, and seem stronger and wiser than he.

"And without doubt, the apostles baptized those which Christ commanded; but he commanded the faithful to be baptized, among which infants be reckoned; the apostles then baptized infants."

We need add no more. It was a mercy for the martyr that godliness and logic are not identical.*

Smith was not the only Anabaptist in the court at Windsor. Strype gives an account of another, and the

---

* Works of Philpot (Parker Society). Fox records the whole letter. Vol. ii. A.D. 1555, p. 606.

opinions held by him. Though not in exact chronological order, our readers will not object to it :—

"The Anabaptists of these days were generally infected also with Pelagianism and other heresies; they were also very confident and disputatious. One of this sort was now crept into the court, namely, Robert Cooke. He was a person of very courteous, fair deportment, of some learning, and particularly well-skilled in music. When Parkhurst (he that afterwards was Bishop of Norwich) was preacher to Queen Katharin Par, at the court, he was keeper of the wine cellar. Here he came acquainted with the said Parkhurst, and also with Coverdale and Dr. Turner, and other learned men, in their attendances at the court. This man, besides that he was against the baptism of infants, denied original sin, and concerning the Lord's Supper he dispersed divers odd things. The said Dr. Turner wrote a book against him, in which he confuted his opinion of original sin. He often created trouble to Parkhurst and Coverdale, about these controversies, so that they were tired with him; for he was a man full of words. When Jewel, and other learned men, his friends, came sometimes to court to visit Parkhurst, Cooke would presently begin a dispute with them, and would never make an end. This man seems to have been among the exiles under Queen Mary, and became then known to the learned Rudulph Gaulter, of Zuric; who afterwards, in his correspondence with the said Parkhurst, then Bishop of Norwich, enquired after him; which was in the year 1573. He was then alive, and still in the court, being one of the gentlemen of the queen's chapel. And for his opinions, which he still retained, had sometime before been like to have been discharged of his place. But he made a recantation, and so continued still in his room at the chapel."*

East Anglia was rich in confessors and martyrs to the faith of Jesus. On one occasion, whilst Hopton, Bishop of Norwich, was engaged in his work of extirpation, at Ipswich, Dunning, his chancellor, ran up to the ecclesiastical tribunal to announce to his lordship the glad tidings that a number of heretics had just arrived. Baxford and Lanham, and what Fox calls the cloth county, had supplied this corps of the sacrificial hosts. It was maddening to hear them, the chancellor declared. There were among them many heretics and Anabaptists.†

---

* Ecclesiastical Memorials, vol. ii., p. 71. † Fox, Book ii., p. 545.

Two years later we get another fact or two from the pages of the venerable martyrologist. He mentions the examinations of three men and two women, by Bonner, on March 6th, 1557. The proceedings of the bishop varied very little. A string of questions was always ready. It embraced the true church, the sacrament, the real presence, &c. It is evident, from the charges brought against them, that they were not only Nonconformists, but that the chief of them had taught in some part of the city and diocese of London, "that the faith, religion, and ecclesiastical service here observed and kept, as it is in the realm of England, is not a true and a laudable faith, religion," &c.

These departures from the State religion embraced thirteen distinct articles. It is only necessary to select one:—

"8 *Item*. Thou hast thought, &c., that the fashion and manner of christening of infants is not agreeable to God's Word, and that none can be effectually baptized, and thereby saved, except he have years of discretion to believe himself, and so willingly accept or refuse baptism at his pleasure."

Their answers to these charges are given by Fox, apparently in his own words, and not theirs. In one case, three of them are grouped together, and in general terms denied. The eighth is one of these. The threats of the bishop availed not. Their confidence in the truth which they had professed was unshaken, and in April of the same year another fiery spectacle was exhibited in Smithfield, to the multitude which crowded that open space.*

For no crime did these men suffer. Against them no charge of rebellion, conspiracy, or disloyalty, was ever urged. Their secret meetings had no hostile design against their cruel oppressors. They stand before us untainted by any civil crimes. Their bitterest foes are silent on these matters. They are "fanatics," detested, the enemies of the church;

---

* *Vide* Fox, book iii., pp. 576-7.

their principles are subversive of all ecclesiastical rule, and the fruits of Satanic influence; their destruction would be a blessing to the church and the nation,—phrases like these, and opinions kindred to them, may be found in abundance; but even Bonner and his harpies never allege other charges. They were disloyal to Rome, but not to England's queen. They claimed the right to think and judge for themselves on the great matters of the present and the future life. From this circle they excluded all influence. Monarchs, popes, councils, bishops, were not allowed to speak. Only One voice was heard, only One authority was recognized. To catch the voice of Jesus, to bow implicitly and reverently to his authority, was the great business of their life. Boldly they avowed this. Collision with Rome was inevitable. With the spiritual despot they grappled. Against his usurped power they swore eternal hostility, and by their teaching and patience in death they inoculated the public mind with the only true principles of civil and spiritual freedom. To this comparatively small and hidden spring we must trace back the deep and expanding stream of freedom which we now enjoy.

Heresy was easily tested. Bonner and his companions in blood had no difficulty. Their scent was keen, and their means ample and varied for the detection of heretical pravity.

Fox, referring to certain charges against some persons, says, "What their articles and answer were, I need not here recite, seeing all they in the time of queen Mary commonly suffered for one manner of cause, that is, for holding against the seven Sacraments, against the reality of Christ being in his Supper, for speaking against the Church of Rome, and determination of the same against images set up and worshipped in the church, for not coming to church," &c.

Rising in importance and magnitude above all other dogmas, were the Sacrament of the Mass and the unity of the Romish Church. Against these dogmas the Reformers exhausted their strength, and Gardiner and his friends stood forth in their defence. "The said Darnley hath believed, and doth believe, that the mass now used in this realm of England, is naught, and full of idolatry and evil, and plain against God's Word, and therefore, he, the said Darnley, hath not heard it, nor will hear it."* "I do believe, that the mass now used in this realm of England, is naught, and abominable idolatry and blasphemy against God's holy Word; for he, in his holy Supper, instituted the sacrament of bread and wine, to be eaten together in remembrance of his death, till he come, and not to have them worshipped, and made an idol of them. . . . I pray, what do you call kneeling down, holding up the hands, knocking of the breast, putting off the cap, and making curtsey, and other kind of superstition? You would make men to be so blind as to think that this is no worshipping."† Assent to these dogmas of the Romanist would cover a multitude of sins. Attendance at the mass secured a toleration for innumerable iniquities. No moral excellence, no virtue, no social rank, no mental culture, could shield the possessor from the vengeance of the church, if this absurd and revolting dogma were denied. In the one case, it changed vice into virtue; in the other, it converted the loftiest virtues into vices so repulsive and so dangerous to social order and the salvation of souls, that to scent out a heretic was a virtue, but to condemn him to the stake was an act the most benignant to man, and the most acceptable to the God of peace and love.

The holy anger of the Episcopate being kindled, the subordinates emulated their superiors in vindictiveness, and exhausted all the means within their reach to gratify it. But excesses sooner or later produce a rebound. The first intimation of the restoration of the Papal supremacy excited tumults. Every fresh step deepened the hatred of the people. The sufferings and patience of the martyrs

---

* Articles objected by Bonner against Darnley, &c.—Fox, vol. ii.
† *Ibid.*

augmented it. No art was neglected to weaken this. Every means were employed to blacken the character of the Protestants. The restraints of moral principles were thrown aside, and the pulpit became the vehicle for the grossest violation of truth. "And so, my lord," said Gratwick, in his examination by Gardiner, "you standing there in the pulpit, in the meantime seduced your tongue to slander us poor prisoners, being then present in iron-bands, burdening us with the sect of Arians, and with the sect of Herodians, and with the sect of Anabaptists, and with the sect of Sacramentarians, and with the sect of Pelagians."* Thousands gathered round the fiery pile. It is computed that not less than 20,000 gazed on the execution of thirteen persons at Stratford.† Indignation, rage, execrations against the ruling powers—admiration, veneration, for the patient sufferers, became the feeling of many. Of the deep hatred of the citizens of the metropolis to the triumphs of the "bloody Bonner" and his colleagues over inspired innocence and moral excellency, Pole complains in his address to the citizens :—"But wherefore cometh this, then, that when any heretic shall go to

---

* *Vide* Fox, book iii., p. 580.

† Strype's Ecc. Memorials, vol. iii., p. 494. Dr. Maitland (*a*) labours hard to prove the mildness of this bishop, and to wash away the filthy calumnies which till now have been heaped upon him. The following occurs in a letter to some friends on his restoration. It was written the day after he heard of it. "By this sentence, my usurper, Dr. Ridley, is utterly repulsed: so that I would ye did order all things at Kidmerly and Bushley at your pleasure, not suffering Sheepshead or Shipsside to be any meddler there, or to sell or carry anything away from thence; and, I trust, at your coming up now at the parliament, I shall so handle both the said Sheepshead and the other Calveshead, that they shall perceive their sweets shall not be without sour sauce."—Letter from Bonner. Burnet's Reformation, vol. ii., p. 248. The cardinal was far less severe than the bishop. The latter complains that the former had been angry at his proceedings, and asks his advice as to the way in which he should deal with the heretics.

(*a*) Essays on Subjects Connected with the Reformation, by S. R. Maitland, D.D.—Essay xx. The Doctor admits that 119 were burnt by Bonner's orders.—P. 5, 75-80.

execution, he shall lack no comforting of you and encouragement to die in his perverse opinions, given by those that come out of your house, 'when he shall be put in prison, he shall have more cherishing: what sign is this?'"*

The same fact is indicated by Gardiner:—"For the last day when thou wast before me, upon Sunday, in St. Mary Overy's Church, thou there reprovest my sermon, and hadst a thousand by thee, at least, to bid God strengthen thee," &c.

Bonner, in a letter to Pole, complains of the attention of the populace to twenty-two heretics, and says that "They would come no way but through Cheapside, so that they were brought to my house with about a thousand persons—which thing I took very strange, and spake to Sir John Grassam, these being with me, to tell the mayor and the sheriffs that this thing was not well suffered in the city. These naughty heretics, all the way they came through Cheapside, both exhorted the people to their part, and had much comfort from the promiscuous multitude."† Earlier on the Lords of the Council had written to the Earl of Shrewsbury as follows:—"Whereas, we have been lately informed that certain lewd persons, to the number of six or seven in a company, . . . have wandered about these north parts, and represented certain plays and interludes, containing very naughty and seditious matter, touching the king and queen's majesties, and the state of the realm, and to the slander of Christ's true and Catholic religion, contrary to all good order, and to the manifest contempt of Almighty God, and dangerous example to others," &c.‡

Deeper and broader these sympathies became. Every fresh victim augmented the hatred to Rome. We get a

---

* Strype's Ecc. Memorials, vol. vii., p. 355. *Cat.*
† Fox, vol. ii.
‡ Lodge's Illustrations, vol. i., pp. 260-1.

glimpse of this from a speaker in the next reign :—"And as for the dealings in Queen Mary's days, they much misliked them; calling the bishops bloodsuckers, and bade "fie" on these tormentors that delighted in nothing else but in the death of innocents; that threatened the whole realm with their fire and faggots; murderers; that they were worse than Caiaphas, worse than Judas, worse than the traitors that put to death," &c.* The contrast between the sufferers and the persecutors told with uncommon effect on the public mind. Repression was impossible. The government put forth all its power to effect it.† Orders in Council were issued to the civic authorities, commanding them to keep the apprentices and the younger members of their families at home during the procession of the heretics to Smithfield. The bishops warned, threatened; many imprisoned the sympathizers, but in vain. Romanism received shocks which prepared the nation during the next reign for its easy and final overthrow.

That Mary, under the influence of Spanish and Italian advisers, sanctioned, nay, stimulated, these proceedings, can admit of no doubt. Apologies are vain. They violate the plainest historic truth. The removal of Gardiner,‡ who

---

* Speech of John Atkinson on the Supremacy Act. Parliamentary History, vol. i., p. 691.

† The lord mayor received a letter from the queen and Council early in January, 1556, commanding him "to give substantial orders, that when any be delivered to be bound, there be a good number of officers and others appointed to be at the executions; who may be charged to apprehend, and to commit to ward, all such as shall comfort, aid, or praise those that are executed. And to charge all householders not to suffer any of their servants to be abroad then, other than such as they will answer for."—Strype's Ecc. Memorials, vol. iii., p. 470. *Apud* Soame's Reformation, vol iv., p. 555.

‡ Gardiner died on the 12th of November, 1555. On the 16th of October, Ridley and Latimer were committed to the flames. On the day of their death, or three days after, Gardiner is said to have anxiously expected the news of their execution, and to have rejoiced, before he died, that the reconciliation with Rome was strengthened by this additional splendid sacrifice. That day "the dart of death struck his body, and the

though hating with intense hatred the Protestant leaders, yet was by no means favourable to Spain, gave full play to the spirit of persecution. His death is thus mentioned by a contemporary:—"My Lord of Winchester, whose soul God pardon, is departed; and his bowels were buried at St. Mary Overy's, Southwark, but his body, as the saying is, shall be carried to Winchester, to be buried there. What time he departed is not yet certainly known, but most men say he died on Tuesday, at night, being the 12th day of this instant (1555), about two o'clock after midnight, at Westminster, and was brought in his barge thence to Southwark."*

Deep, intense, religious convictions swayed the mind of Mary. No duty was so binding—no obligation so solemn—as the purging of the land from the presence and pollution of heretical pravity. So thoroughly was this unhappy woman prostrated by the power of superstition, that, when mistaking disease for fertility, she said, "that she could never be happily brought to bed, nor succeed well in any other of her affairs, unless she caused all the heretics she had in prison to be burnt, without sparing so much as one."†

But all this was in vain. Disappointment and vexation only resulted from her course. Upon her perjured and bloody proceedings, heaven's deepest, darkest frown appeared to rest. She had violated her word to her people, she had corrupted her nobles and counsellors with gold, and risked civil war for the match with the heir of Charles, and soon found that the sombre mind of Philip regarded her with

---

excruciating pains he endured were longer in duration, and possibly not altogether less intense in their agony, than those of his brother bishops at the stake." "Do not open that gap," said the wretched, wealthy, successful persecutor, to one who spoke to him of the justification of the sinner by the blood of Jesus. "He found no comfort in that doctrine, and no words of faith, or hope, or confidence, are reported of his bed of death."—Life of Bonner, p. 288. Fox, vol. ii. Soame makes no allusion to it.

* Letter to Lord Shrewsbury. Lodge's Illustrations of English History, vol. i., p. 258.

† Memorials of Cranmer, vol. ii., p. 165.

perfect indifference,* and that he exhausted his affections, or rather gratified his passions, with others.† Her nights were spent in sorrow and her days in gloom. With broken repose, from the night's visions which haunted her, she pictured to her superstitious mind a thousand horrors. In her agony of disappointment, she offered fresh hecatombs of human victims to appease the wrath of the holy ones. But peace came not. In the splendid, varied, and imposing ceremonies of the church, relief was now sought. The Episcopate exhausted its resources. Processions were planned, which she dignified with her presence. Bishops in gilt slippers and splendid robes, with banners flying and priests chanting, with sermons and masses, intermingled with fasts and sharp penances, and all the various religious services which marked her favourite church, occupied no inconsiderable portion of her time. Still relief came not. The promised heir came not. Philip was still a truant, and wandered far away from her. Disaster abroad and discontent at home preyed upon her spirit, and gradually consumed her life. The Virgin and all the saints were angry. Her hatred to the detested heretics was not sufficiently intensified. Many still lived. The efforts of the bishops in town and country had not yet freed the land from these pollutions. Peace with heaven was incompatible with their toleration; and, encouraged and sustained by her Papist

---

* Philip had entreated his father to give him a wife younger than himself, and not eleven years older.—*Vide* Strickland's Queens of England, vol. v., p. 318.

† Henry of France, in a letter to his ambassador, thus expresses his opinion of the match between Philip and Mary :—"The unfortunate queen will learn the truth at last. She will wake too late, in misery and remorse, to know that she has filled the realm with blood for an object which, when she has gained it, will bring nothing but affliction to herself or to her people."—Froude, vol. vi. p. 229. We will only add that, if any one wishes to see the craft of the politician, the power of superstition, hypocrisy in cruelty, intensified to the highest degree, let him study the character of Philip and Granville, in the pages of Motley. The sketch of Prescott is that of a master, but it wants the fulness, the shade, the Rembrandt touches of Motley.—*Vide* The Rise of the Dutch Republic.

counsellors, she inflicted afresh her indignation on the Nonconformists of the land.*

Happily for humanity, her reign was short. Disease, the desertion of her husband, threatened insurrection at home, the fear of invasion from abroad, with the absorbing consciousness that by thousands her memory would be execrated, and that her life was not safe, filled her mind with torturing anxiety, and rendered her latter days very unhappy. Thousands suffered the loss of all that was dear to them. From all the circles of social life the victims of her heartless cruelty had been snatched, but chiefly from the lower walks of society. Old men and maidens, the matron and the child, the tradesman from his shop, the mechanic from his bench, and the husbandman from the field, had swelled the number of sufferers. But revolting to all the sensibilities of our nature, and detestable, as these cruelties were, there were redeeming elements. Popery stood before the nation in all its unveiled loathsomeness, and in its hostility to every right view of the character of the God of truth and love. Admit the plea of Mary's apologists. Grant, and we are prepared to concede the fact, that from disease, superstition, and slighted passion, her mind was not always sane. You do not diminish the difficulty. The spirit of the Papacy must be visited with a heavier curse. Sane or insane, never was a governor so entirely in the hands of her spiritual advisers. Gardiner and the Spaniards, then Pole and his Italians, swayed her mind on all ecclesiastical matters. The supreme power was in their hands. Bonner and his colleagues, bloodthirsty and vindictive as they were, only executed the behests of these men. A word from the cardinal would have quenched the martyr's fire, and opened the dungeons to the multitudes who perished in these living tombs from want and disease, engendered by their confinement. But the legate knew

---

* It was reported that she had spoken of herself as a virgin sent from God to ride and tame the people of England.—Strype's Cranmer. Soame, vol. iv., p. 81.

nothing of such tolerance. He was impelled by the consciousness of a sacred duty. Heretics were far worse than thieves and murderers. The latter only affected the present and the temporal: the former were destructive to all that was vital to the spiritual and the eternal. The history of the past, the teaching of the theologians, the decisions of councils, all influenced by the Holy Ghost, taught this prince of the church that the extirpation of the heretics was a sacred duty. Success in England would invest him with a glory far more bright than the triple crown.

Both Mary and Pole lay on the bed of death at the same time,* both, too, with the conviction, that, after all the cruelty they had inflicted, and the blood they had shed in restoring and building up the old faith, in a few months, it was more than probable, the edifice would crumble to dust, and their memory would be loaded with execration in the country and on the spot where their dark deeds had been perpetrated.† Justice is sometimes slow, but always sure. Her verdict may not come with haste, but when uttered it is irrevocable. So here. Her pen, whilst recording the martyrdom of 288 victims,‡ not for disloyalty to the civil ruler, but for the assertion of man's

---

* Mary died on the 17th of November, 1558, deserted by her whole court.—Miss Strickland, vol. v., p. 443. Pole died a few hours later.

† "Dying, to be spared a second exile, and the wretchedness of seeing with his eyes the dissolution of the phantom-fabric which he had given the labours of his life to build."—Froude, vol. vi., p. 526.

‡ Anno $\begin{cases} 1555—71 \\ 1556—89 \\ 1557—88 \\ 1558—40 \end{cases}$ making 288.—Besides those who died of famine in sundry prisons.—Strype's Ecc. Memorials, vol. vii., p. 419. Maitland, from Fox, gives a list of martyrs amounting to 739.—Essays, p. 582. Lord Burghley says:—"In the time of Queen Mary, there were, by imprisonment, torment, famine and fire, of men, women, maidens, and children, almost the number of 400, and of that number above twenty that were archbishops, bishops, and principal prelates or officers in the church, lamentably destroyed; of women above sixty, and of children above forty; and amongst the women some great with child, out of whose bodies the child, by fire, was expelled alive," &c.—Execution of Justice in England. *Apud* Soame's Reformation, vol. iv., p. 588.

inalienable rights, his liberty to think, and to worship God according to the teachings of the Divine word, has written a sentence which succeeding generations will never revoke. History will ever inscribe on her monument, "THE BLOODY QUEEN MARY."

CHAPTER V.

ELIZABETH.

JUST as some traveller, benighted in some distant land, fearful of danger every moment, would hail the dawn of the morning with gladsome feelings, as he discovered the pathway along which he could journey without exposure to peril, so did the nation regard the removal of Mary and the accession of Elizabeth to the throne. Amidst the execrations of thousands, and the deepening dissatisfaction of a much greater number, the spirit of the infatuated Mary passed to the tribunal of One, whose loving servants she had offered as a "burnt sacrifice" to His Majesty. Either truly or not, hitherto her name has been associated with deeds of cruelty and blood, and the transactions of her reign have been regarded as violating all the principles of law, humanity, and religion.

On Elizabeth the hopes and fears of both parties in the state now centred. Intensely hated by her sister, who could never love the child of her mother's detested rival, her life was in constant danger. This was no secret. In all the courts of Europe the feeling was known. Nothing was neglected which could by any means implicate her in the various plots which marked her sister's unhappy rule. Bribes were offered to the unprincipled. Life was promised to imprisoned rebels, if only they would implicate the royal maiden in their lawless enterprises. If Mary's power, and that of her most trusted advisers, had been equal to their will, the claim of Elizabeth as the heir apparent to the crown would have been cut off. Depriving her of liberty for a time, her steps tracked and her movements watched by some veiled villain, she was subjected to the most humiliating state, and compelled, at the risk of the most fearful peril, to violate her conscience, and outwardly conform to the rites of the Romish faith. Mary exhausted her vindictiveness on this favourite of the people.

Gardiner and Renard, the governors of the queen, as we have already seen, till Pole bowed her to his will, felt that the death of Elizabeth was essential to the success of their enterprise, and to the stability of the restored authority of the Holy See. Again and again they urged it on their not unwilling mistress.* This fact is placed beyond the region of doubt. Every art which cunning could employ, every motive which policy could suggest, every reason which selfishness, combined with the most powerful superstition, could supply, were laid before their mistress. They secured her warmest sympathies. No sisterly affection restrained her blind devotion to her spiritual guides. Her hand was ready to inflict the fatal blow, but a power, invisible but supreme, held her back, and saved the maiden from the butcher's knife.

In the eyes of the increasing number of Elizabeth's admirers, hers was a charmed life.† Her enemies had not

---

* Bishop Gardiner remarked, "that as long as Elizabeth lived there was no hope of the kingdom being tranquillized; and if any one went to work soundly as he did, things would go on better." "It was of the utmost consequence," said the Spaniard, "that the trial and execution of the criminals, and especially of Courtney and the lady Elizabeth, should take place before the arrival of his highness the prince of Spain."—Tytler's Edward and Mary, vol. ii., p. 365. Strickland's Queens of England, vol. v., p. 372. Turner supplies abundant proof of the truth of the text, vol. iii., pp. 376-77.

† "Commendone had perceived and understood that the sister, both

done these deeds in a corner. Heaven was her protection. As months rolled over, many of the young, the ardent, the liberty-loving of England's noblest blood,—thousands of England's bold yeomen, and the commercial classes—now rising as a power in the state—were ready to shed their blood and risk all that is dear to men, in her defence. The nation's love, the nation's sympathies, became the body-guard of the insulted and injured princess, and compelled even Philip to warn his creatures against the invincible power.

The reign of Elizabeth forms a proud era in our nation's history. It is the "golden," the Augustan age of the nation's literature; commerce, science, and religion shed their light and beautiful charms upon it. Poets, statesmen, historians, have exhausted their genius in eulogy and narrative. We would not detract an atom from its glory. Still we think the true estimate of the character of the queen and her reign has yet to be formed. Nor have the times yet come for this. The magic influence of those events which so largely contributed to the material splendour of her era, still hides her enormous moral obliquity, and the crushing spiritual despotism which she exercised on those men whose lofty principles and unflinching integrity laid the foundations of our liberties. Higher, and still higher, the moral tone of the historian must rise,—deeper and stronger must be his appreciation of those men who braved her fiercest wrath rather than sacrifice their allegiance to God,—with a steadier hand must he unveil the surpliced tyrants who filled the Episcopate,—before he can portray the character and reign of the Virgin Queen as truth will one day demand.

To trace the political movements of this age, to unfold the plots which marked it,—the growth of the commerce, the material prosperity of the nation, during the reign of this

---

heretical and schismatical, who had been substituted for the present queen by her father, was then in the heart and mouth of every one."—Turner gives the original of this, vol. iii., p. 403.

monarch, and the triumph of her arms over her various and numerous foes,—is not compatible with our design. We have to deal with loftier principles,—to unfold their working in laying the foundation of a moral change which laughed to scorn the imperious wrath of the sovereign, and treated with contempt the more rabid rage of the Episcopate, and the efforts of which have from year to year been affecting the character and policy of this great empire. Principles to which we may trace up, with a distinctness which silences controversy, and with a clearness which excludes all doubt, all that is great and distinctive of us as a nation. To understand the character of the Early Baptists aright, a glance at some of them becomes imperative.

It is very difficult to form anything like a correct estimate of the moral state of the church, still more of that of the mass of the community. Pole had tried to check the prevailing corruptions, and to pare down those things which heretofore had done violence to ordinarily virtuous minds. But the evil was deep-seated. Gentle means could only touch the surface—they failed in reaching the core.

"The monks were put into all the small benefices in the king's gift. So that the greatest part of the clergy were such as had been formerly monks and friars; very ignorant for most part, and generally addicted to their former superstition, though otherwise men that would comply with anything rather than forfeit their livings."*

They luxuriated in their power, and aided in every way to deepen the hold of superstition on the minds of the people. The great hives of industry and commerce were, to some extent, exceptions. There other influences operated. Mind was there far from stagnant. Through these channels voices from the continent were heard, wakening to efforts and encouraging the faithful. By Christian merchants, the Bible and other books were smuggled,—yes! that

---

* Burnet's Reformation, vol. ii. Preface.

is the only word which can be used truthfully,—into the country.* But in the rural districts of the nation the influence of Rome was supreme. Virtue never rises above the standard with which men are familiar. Moral excellence never can flourish when the only element of its nutriment is withdrawn. Some of the exiles write in strong language.

"Turn thine eyes," says one, "to thy counsel, England; how fierce tygers, how cruel wolves, how ravening beares, how lecherous goats, how wilie foxes, or to speak plainly without figure, what perjured traitors, to God and thee! What murderers, what oppressors of the poor, what voluptuous Sardanapales, what adulterers, how vile flatterers, shalt thou finde amonge them! It were a small fault, and a very peccadillo in them, to dissemble the truth of religion. They rail on it, they toss it with scoffs and mocks, they bloodily and tyrannically persecute it. It might be winked at if they took bribes only to oppress the cause of a few poor men: they take bribes to betray the cause of the whole realm. It might be passed over with silence if they had murdered but one man apiece: the blood of innumerable saints crieth up to heaven against them, and the groanings of many thousands of oppressed are heard everywhere. It might, perchance, be pardoned if they spent but some weeks in pleasure; they wallow continually in vile voluptuousness and wanton dalliance, or waste all their unhappie daies in beastlie delites; neither can change of women, nor women only, satisfie their filthie, abominable desires."† "For what idolatry, what pride, what covetousness, what cruelty, what lechery, what sodomy, was ever heard of in any ages, that they have not far exceeded? Thou canst not name a bishop, but thou

---

* "It is said that there are diverse evil books cast by night into the city, conveyed from beyond the seas; but I have not seen any of these yet."—Lodge, vol. i., p. 260.

† Traheron's Warning to England. *Apud* Maitland's Essays, pp. 136–7.

shalt see his tongue swollen with blasphemy, his fingers dripping with the blood of innocents, his body shattered with most filthy villainy; and the rest of thy Egyptian shaulings strive which shall pass others farthest in all kinds of beastly abomination."* Bale gives us rather a curious glimpse of some of the social habits of the age :—" My lord bishop hath a sum of money of the priests for doing his part so well. My lord abbot and master doctor have had pheasants, plovers, and partridges, pigs, geese, and capon, for disputing their matters so valiantly. Master parson hath been commended for scolding, and Sir Saunder Smell Smock (one given to love women), one parish priest for bearing false witness."†

The seats of learning,—Oxford, and not less the sister university,—were the strongholds of Papal influence. Into all offices, Pole and his colleagues had placed men of like spirit with themselves. On the young mind of England, or the future hereditary and elective statesmen of the nation, and the rising ministry, they sought to stamp their own image, and to control their thoughts and moral training. Success in one was realized. Oxford has always been noted for its leaning that way. " Our universities are so depressed and ruined, that at Oxford there are scarcely two individuals who think with us; and even they are so dejected and broken in spirit that they can do nothing. That despicable friar, Soto, and another Spanish monk, I know not who, have so torn up by the roots all that P. Martyr had planted, that they have reduced the vineyard of the Lord into a wilderness."‡

---

* Traheron's Warning to England, p. 84.

† Bale's Image of the Two Churches (Parker Society), p. 395. "I do not know who this Paul was," said the cruel Nix, Bishop of Norwich, "but sure I am his writings smell of the faggot."—Life of Bonner, p. 38.

"I am content with my breviary and pontifical," said the enlightened Bishop of Dunkeld, "and know neither the Old or New Testament, and yet thou seest I have come on indifferently well."—Tytler's Scotland, vol. v., p. 225.

‡ Jewel. Zurich Letters (Parker Society). Letter xxxiii.

Strype gives us a fuller account of this.* He tells us that Ormaneto, one of Pole's creatures, displaced every heretic and all suspected of heresy, and placed over it Peter Soto, a Dominican, who had been confessor to Charles V., and eight others of the same order, who restored the solid scholastic theology, and abolished the affected elegance of words with which the heretics were enchanting their hearers. Soto was a Spaniard, and Garcia, another of his countrymen, was made professor of theology at Oxford. Gardiner fully sympathized with these men, and thought that lectures on the old Magistrum Scientiarum were much preferable to those Hebrew lectures which had been given by their predecessors.†

Nor was the devotion of the students on the banks of the Cam less papal. Perhaps the following may be as much rhetoric as fact; still it is suggestive :—" The most reverend father in Christ, Cardinal Pole," said the Public Orator, on the occasion of the Commission visiting that seat of learning, January 11th, 1557, "legate, who had restored oppressed religion, supported the views of this country, brought back from exile our lares,—he, I say, that English Pole, and our town mostly, was the author of our visitation, from whose excellent visitor many blessings have redounded to all parts of his country."‡

The labours of the godly bishops ceased not. Within five weeks of Mary's death, five persons were immolated on the burning pile. Necessity alone checked them. Their power was broken, not their will. The accession of the new monarch filled them with the most conflicting anxiety, and the reception of Bonner excited the worst fears of the hierarchy.

No sooner was Elizabeth quietly seated on the throne, than she threw off the disguise which, to say the least, had veiled

---

* *Vide* Annals, vol. i., p. 195.
† *Vide* Turner, vol. iii., p. 462.   ‡ Fox's Mary.

her conduct more or less during part of her sister's reign,* and sought to effect another of those revolutions which, as our readers have marked, followed each other through the whole of the Tudor dynasty. In Henry's time, we have seen the state religion, at the bidding of the sovereign, assume simply an anti-Papal aspect, and its claims enforced by exile or death. During the reign of his youthful successor, at the command of his Council, the Papal aspect changes, and a Protestant phase now challenges the conscientious regards of the nation. "The young Josiah" dies, and his sister, by her royal will, in violation, too, of her sacred promise, denounces the leading teachers of her brother's religion as worse than the most abandoned of their fellow-men, the destroyers of souls, and burns them as an offering to the Papal power,† and bids her people that they must give up their religious convictions and be reconciled to a church which they had been taught to consider the very seat and throne of Antichrist, on pain of burning here and of eternal damnation hereafter.‡ The turbulent,§ and happily for the nation, short reign of this devotee to the Vicar of Christ, was followed by a young and reputed Virgin Queen; and she issues her mandate, as sole arbitress of all spiritual matters, that her subjects up to such a day might remain in the

---

* She heard divine service after the Romish religion, and was often confessed, yet at the rigorous solicitation of Cardinal Pole, professed herself, for fear of death, a Roman Catholic.—So says Camden's Life of Elizabeth, p. 9. The reader will find more proof in Turner, vol. iii., pp. 416–17.

† Strickland's Queens of England, vol. v., pp. 305–5.

‡ "This day was performed the confirmation of the alliance between the Pope and this king," said the French ambassador, "by a public and solemn sacrifice of a preaching doctor, named Rogevus, who has been burnt alive for being a Lutheran." "All heretics, who hold or teach otherwise than the Roman Church believes and holds, damnantur et anathematizantur."—Cardinal Pole.

§ The same writer says, "She travels with 1500 horse, as a guard to protect her." "She has twenty-five or thirty gentlemen to sleep in the hall of the presence, near her apartment. Twice every night they make their rounds and visit all the palace."

Antichristian Church of Rome, but ever after that time, on pain of her imperial displeasure, they must mould their religious convictions according to her will, through the teaching of those whom she, as female head of the church, might place over them as their religious guides.*

The rapidity and cruelty of these changes is not the only thing which strikes us. There are principles underlying them, of the greatest and profoundest kind, principles which clothe the chief actors in these startling revolutions with the most aggravated impiety, or exhibit them as profoundly ignorant of the great laws of our moral nature, as well as of the spirituality and majestic simplicity of the religion of the Son of God. We must not in these matters confound things which differ, nor allow the prejudices, to use a very mild phrase, of writers of a certain class, to blind us to the nature of things. Only in a very modified and inferior sense must we regard these as religious movements. There was as much of the political as the spiritual element in them. Perhaps more of the spirit of earth than of heaven. The sovereign found in existence, on his advent to power, a great, wealthy, compact, influential hierarchy, the growth of ages, often the rival of the imperial power, which on all political grounds it was thought desirable he should subordinate to his will. Ages had taught that one was essential to the other. The full and safe development of the one was very dependent on the other. The contract expressed or understood was, "Throw your influence," said the secular power, "around

---

* "Indeed, the Church of England hath the advantage of us, and, as I suppose, of all the churches in the world, for monstrous speedy growth and increase; for from that of a synagogue of Satan, consisting of Popish idolaters, and cruel murderers of the saints, it grew from top to toe into a true and entire body of Christ, of a sudden, and before the greatest part of it so much as heard the Gospel preached in any measure for their conversion."—Robinson, vol. ii., pp. 65, 66, 318, and 319.

"This profane multitude, without any profession of faith and repentance, were forced and compelled by human authority, in the beginning of Queen Elizabeth's reign, to be members of their church."—J. Canne's Necessity of Separation.

the monarchy, and the exclusive right to teach religion and punish conscience shall be yours; and the rich and ample emoluments, which fear or superstition will surrender, shall be your reward." How any intelligent mind, with any apprehension or right conceptions of the nature of the religion of Jesus, and with the Sacred Oracles in his hand,—the only authority to which we should implicitly bow,—should recognize these sectarian, not national, movements, in any other light, is one of those profound moral mysteries of this life which we cannot solve. In this last case, as we shall presently see, the change was marked by an amount of individual and social suffering which has scarcely a parallel in the world's history, and which only lost its power of continued mischief by the presence and growing power of those principles for which so many victims, during Elizabeth's reign, suffered either at the stake, on the tree, or in the prison.*

The change now was one of no small magnitude, and its accomplishment was marked by extraordinary difficulties. It touched so many interests purely selfish, and it involved consequences which perilled the throne of Elizabeth, and even her life. The worst passions of human nature would be stirred to their very depth. Beyond all comparison, religious strife, in its intenseness, exceeds every other strife. Only a mind animated by a love of the truth which nothing could impair, or influenced by a lust of power which could bear no co-ordinate authority within the same realm, could dare it. We have no deep impression that the former was a very potent agent; the latter, we think, was more so. Elizabeth had witnessed the power of the priesthood over the late sovereign, its annihilation of all sisterly affection, the suffering which the recognition of a

---

* "Much has been said of the excellence of the form of worship by them established; but little, alas! of moral or religious merit can be awarded by the verdict of impartial history to the motives or the conduct of the heroine of Protestantism, in a transaction so momentous and so memorable."—Miss Aikins's Elizabeth, vol. i., p. 320.

foreign potentate within the realm, "speaking like a lamb," but over-topping the imperial authority, had inflicted on the people. Above all, her own exposure to death, and the cunning and deadly hate of Gardiner and his associates against her, could not be forgotten. With such experience of the spiritual powers, it excites no surprise that Elizabeth, and her trusted counsellors, should be anxious to subordinate the Church to the State, as in Henry and Edward's times.

Within her own realm numerous and powerful elements of danger existed. Her treasury was exhausted. The nation was at war with France. Scotland was in no pleasant mood, its sovereign proclaiming Elizabeth as illegitimate and an usurper of the crown, and giving signs of a determination to expel her. Ireland was under a chronic disease, relieving itself now and then by a rebellion, and was at present very strong in its blind attachment to Rome. Much of the spiritual power of the kingdom was against her. Bishops and priests had given signal proofs of their attachment to the old faith; and the fear of punishment, if any change took place, made them naturally cling closer to it; the majority of her counsellors were men of the same class; while no doubt can be entertained that the majority of the people, certainly in the northern counties and in the rural districts, preferred the showy and sensuous form of the old religion. Beyond, "the Bishop of Rome will be incensed," said Cecil; "he will excommunicate the queen, interdict the realm, and give it a prey to all princes who will enter upon it, and stir them up to it by all manner of means."[*] The extirpation of heresy was a glorious work. The great Catholic powers of Europe felt it to be so; and "all means," as Cecil says, "would be used to incite them to put down the Islanders, and maintain the Papal

---

[*] "There be not in all this country," said Sadlior later on, "ten gentlemen that do favour and allow of her majesty's proceedings in the cause of religion; and the common people be ignorant, full of superstition, and altogether blinded with the old Popish doctrine," &c., &c.—State Papers. vol. ii., p. 55. Edinbro', 1809.

power." Francis the First marked the latter part of his reign by entire subserviency to the priesthood.* The all-powerful Guises religiously and politically detested Elizabeth, and sought to combine Roman Christendom in a deadly war against the Protestant faith.† Such were some of the evils which stood before the queen as she entered upon her work.‡

Persecution, at least in the horrid form in which it appeared during the late reign, ceased at once. Light was poured into the gloomy cells of the gate-houses, the coal-cellars, and other dungeons; and many confessors were permitted to revisit their desolate homes and suffering families.§ From all places of trust and influence the zealots of Rome were gradually removed. The punishment of fine and imprisonment was suspended over them. Plied with these telling arguments, no pardon was to be granted without entire submission and conformity to the sovereign's will.|| Men of known attachment to Protestant principles were called to fill subordinate, but still important, places in various

---

* Burnet, vol. ii., who gives Cecil's able letter on the difficulties. Cecil, we fear, had no principle. He had passed through all the religious changes of his time.

"The names of all them that dwelleth in the parish of Umbleton (Wimbleton) that were confessed and received the Sacrament of the altar:—my master Sir W. Cecil, and my Lady Mildred his wife."—Tytler's Edward and Mary, vol. ii., p. 435. 1556.

† "We desire that all heresies should be extirpated from our kingdom, and the heretics, and those who instruct them."—Edict of France, May 18th, 1533.

‡ "That the Pope, the emperors, and the kings of Spain and France, should band together to reduce again the most part of Europe to the Roman Catholic religion; and to pursue and punish with fire and sword all heretics that would not willingly condescend to the same."—Melville's Memoirs, pp. 76-7. Turner, vol. iii., p. 541, where more evidence will be found.

§ Collier, vol. ii., pp. 410-11. Soame, vol. iv., p. 606.

|| "The premunire must be played upon them; and when once they are in misericordia, they are not to be pardoned without entire submission and conformity; and by hampering them well, and pressing the laws close, her majesty's occasion for money may be somewhat supplied."—Collier, vol. ii., p. 414. Soame, vol. iv., p. 611.

parts of the country. The return of the exiles, who had fled before the burning zeal of Mary, greatly augmented the swelling tide of popular indignation against the old faith. Many of them were men of rich and varied culture. More valuable still, at this crisis, than even their profound erudition, was their power as ministers of God's Word.* It was their forte. Practice had given them a power their advocates had failed to secure. These and other signs awakened suspicions and alarm in some, and kindled hope in the minds of others. Both parties felt that the conflict would be severe and final. The pulpit echoed with the war cry. Upon all the points of difference between the two churches, both parties exhausted their bitterest local and patriotic resources. Passions were inflamed and prejudice excited. The Papist, on principle, from interest and fear, hated the Protestant, as a man infamous, detested of God, as a moral pestilence in every circle in which he was found : the Protestant, as a matter of duty, declared exterminating war against the Papist as a limb of Antichrist, an idolater, one whose toleration as a religionist was inconsistent with the well-being of the commonwealth and the salvation of men. Society was shaken to its centre by these combatants. Against the Philistines, men who had hidden themselves in caves and dens came out to give them battle, in the name of the Lord of Hosts. The civil power interposed to calm the tumult. All preaching for a time was suspended, till the mind of the country could be expressed through its constituted representatives in the senate of the nation.†

An Act was passed for restoring the supremacy to the crown. Its provisions are worthy the attention of the reader. It provides that all "such jurisdiction, privileges, superiority and pre-eminence, spiritual and ecclesiastical, as

---

* They were men of great and diversified experience, of practical habits, of energy and zeal, and above all, of fervent and exalted piety."—Marsden's Early Puritans, p. 16.

† Collier, vol. ii., p. 411. Strype's Ann., vol. i., pp. 58-9.

by any spiritual or ecclesiastical power or authority hath heretofore been, or may lawfully be, exercised or used, for the visitation of the ecclesiastical state and persons, and for reformation, order and correction of the same; and of all manner of errors, heresies, schisms, abuses, offences, contempts, and enormities, shall for ever, by authority of this present Parliament, be united and annexed to the imperial crown of this realm."*

By this act of the senate the authority of the Pope was thrown off, and the independence of the English Church clearly defined. Subsequently most of the persecuting laws were abolished, and others for the security of the throne passed.

Policy, if not fairness, prompted Elizabeth to proceed with caution. A disputation on important points of difference between the Papists and the Reformed was proposed. In the abbey church of Westminster the combatants were to engage. Heath of York was authorized to select the champions on the one side: the choicest of the returned exiles were nominated for the other. The discussion fixed the attention of multitudes. The members of the Privy Council, most of the nobility and the courtiers, with many of the Lower House, crowded the venerable structure. Over this august assembly, and on an occasion so mighty, the Lord Chief Justice Bacon presided. Like many others, this proved abortive. Expectations so raised were only disappointed. The Romanists, on some plea of informality, withdrew from the hopeless contest. Victory, not truth, is too often the object of public disputations.

The points for discussion were,—the service in the English tongue, the authority of every church to set aside or modify ceremonies, and the doctrines of the mass. The latter was abolished for the administration of the Lord's Supper in both kinds; and the use of Edward the Sixth's second Prayer Book, with some modifications, was authorised.† Images

---
* Collier, vol. ii., p. 420.
† The extent to which alterations were made may be seen in Collier, vol. ii. Records, lxxviii.

were removed from the churches, and many of the objects of idolatrous worship were speedily committed to the flames.* Subsequently the articles were reduced to their present number.†

Partial as these changes were, they touched some members of the old faith. Not a few of these dignitaries had rejected the authority of the Pope before, in one or other of the former reigns, and in that of Mary had again sworn obedience to him as the head of the universal church; but coercion or shame interposed now. One of their own friends gives the following as the result:—" Fourteen bishops, besides three bishops elect, the abbot of Westminster, four priors, twelve deacons, fourteen archdeacons, sixty canons, not so few as 100 priests of good preferment, fifteen heads of colleges, and about twenty proctors."‡ More than 10,000 parishes existed at this time in the kingdom, so that only about 243 out of the great body of the spiritual men refused to submit to the change. The vacancies were filled up, chiefly from the men who had been in exile for the truth's sake during the reign of Mary.

The principle which influenced Elizabeth in remodelling the English Church, was to give as little annoyance to her Romish subjects as possible.§ Opposed on many grounds

---

* Camden's Elizabeth, pp. 30–1.

† In Elizabeth's Prayer Book the following occurs on baptism:—"Then the priest shall take the child in his hands, and ask the name; and naming the child, shall dip it in the water, so it be discreetly and warily done," &c.—Liturgical Service of Elizabeth, p. 203 (Parker Society).

‡ "In one of the volumes of the Cotton Library (which volume seemeth once to have belonged to Camden), the whole number of the deprived ecclesiastics is digested in this catalogue: bishops, 14; deans, 13; archdeacons, 14; heads of colleges, 15; prebendaries, 50; rectors of churches, 80; abbots, priors, &c., 6;—in all, 192."—Strype's Ann., vol. i., p. 106.

§ " Though connected, by her position, with the doctrines of the Reformation, Elizabeth had, in common with the Catholic clergy, a strong taste for pomp and authority. Her first regulations in regard to religious matters were consequently of such a character that most of the Catholics felt no repugnance to attend the divine worship with which the

as she was, politically as well as religiously, to the Papal authority, she yet loved the magnificence of the Romish Church. It accorded with her taste and gratified her love of display. Many of the gorgeous accessories to this worship were left untouched by her. "It was with great difficulty, and not without a protestation from the bishops, that her majesty consented to have so many monuments of idolatry removed out of churches: but she would not part with her altar or crucifix out of her own chapel. The gentlemen and children appeared there in their surplices, and the priests in their copes; the altar was furnished with rich plate, with two gilt candlesticks, with lighted candles, and a massive crucifix in the midst; the service was sung, not only with the sound of organ, but with the artificial music of cornets, sackbuts, &c., on solemn festivals. The ceremonies observed by the Knights of the Garter, in their adoration towards the altar, which had been abolished by King Edward, and renewed by Queen Mary, had been retained. In short, the service of the queen's chapel, and in sundry cathedrals, was so splendid and showy, that foreigners could not distinguish it from Roman, except that it was performed in the English tongue. By this method most of the Popish laity were deceived into conformity, and came regularly to church for nine or ten years, till the Pope, being out of all hopes of an accommodation, forbade them, by excommunicating the queen and laying the kingdom under an interdict."* Her majesty must always approach God as a queen, and not as a poor

---

Reformers were satisfied; and the establishment of the Anglican Church, which was entrusted to the hands of the existing clergy, met with very little resistance, and at the same time very little encouragement, from the general body of ecclesiastics. Religion continued to be regarded by a great many persons as a mere political matter."—Guizot's Life, &c., of Shakspeare, pp. 14, 15.

* Neal, vol. i., p. 95: "The doctrine is everywhere most pure; but as to ceremonies and maskings, there is a little too much foolery. That silver cross of ill-omened origin still maintains its place in the queen's chapel. Wretched me! This thing will be drawn into a precedent."

sinner. With the same end, as indicated above, she would have the clause in the Litany, to be *delivered from the Bishop of Rome, and all his detestable enormities*, expunged.* We will only add, that she completed her work of reforming, for the present, by a legislative enactment which entailed an amount of misery on thousands of the holiest, noblest, and most loyal of her subjects, which is almost without a parallel; and presented the hierarchy in a light which, the more the truth and power of Christ are spread, will expose it to the scorn and condemnation of the wise and good, as a spiritual tyranny which no well regulated commonwealth should ever tolerate. The Act of Uniformity was passed in 1559, June 24th. It aimed at a hopeless task. It insisted on all minds conforming to her majesty's religious notions, and conforming to her splendid pageantry in Christian worship, on pain of her imperial displeasure; and, worse still, though that was bad enough, of that of a higher and holier authority. No language is too strong in denouncing the folly,—yea, the madness, the very aggravated wickedness,—of these attempts. They involve an invasion of the rights of our moral nature; a daring rebellion against the authority of the Son of God.

From another source we gather that "there is yet a general prohibition of preaching; and still a crucifix on the altar at court, with lights burning before it. Though by the queen's order, images are removed out of the churches all over the kingdom; yet the people rejoice to see that this is

---

Jewel (Zurich Letters), p. 55. "And yet is sche that now reigneth over thame, neither gude Protestant nor yet resolute Papist, let the world judge Quhilk is the third."—J. Knox. Macrie, p. 255.

* In the Litany of Henry VIII., and after in those of Edward, this prayer was inserted: "*From the tyranny and all the detestable enormities of the Bishop of Rome.*" Elizabeth would have it expunged. The sacramental bread was made round, like the wafer of the Romanist. A table was also placed where the altar formerly stood, and many of the old festivals retained in the church, &c. *Vide* Ward's Reformation, canto ii., pp. 283–4. Note Heylin, p. 203. Soame, vol. iii. &c.

still kept in the queen's chapel. Three bishops officiate at the altar; one as priest, another as deacon, and a third as sub-deacon, all in rich copes before the idol; and there is sacrament without sermon. Injunctions are sent to preachers not to use freedom in reproving vice."*

It is not compatible with the design of these pages even to glance at some of those events which agitated Elizabeth's government, but which invest her reign with all its material brilliancy. We cannot now dwell on the conspiracy of the Pope and the Catholic States of Europe to assassinate Elizabeth, and uproot the Protestant faith;† on the Northern rebellion, for the restoration of the Papal power;‡ or on the armada of the sombre-minded Philip, and its providential defeat; whilst the bitter hostility of the bishops to holy, conscientious men, will claim attention hereafter: but on another topic we must touch, as bearing powerfully on early Baptist history.

The Act of Uniformity brought into full play some of those

---

* Burnet, iii., p. 292. Congregational Magazine, 1840, p. 89. "After I had written this, lo! good news was brought me, namely, that the crucifix and candlesticks in the queen's chapel are broken in pieces, and, as some one has brought word, reduced to ashes."—Parkhurst, Bishop of Norwich. Zurich Letters, p. 122, Aug., 1562. "I wrote you word that the Christmas candles and candlesticks had been removed from the queen's chapel; but they were shortly after brought back again, to the great grief of the godly."—*Ibid*, April 26th, 1563.

† The reader will find ample details of this in Turner, vol. iv.

‡ That this was purely a religious rebellion admits of no doubt. The Bowes MS. supplies a large amount of information. We give an extract: "The mass of the people were in favour of the old superstition. There was no part of the British empire where the first pale and struggling ray of the Reformation broke with more vermilion lustre." "All the gentlemen, save a few in the East-Riding of York, remained neuter in the contest; but either their sons and heirs, or second sons, are with the rebels." "Bibles and Prayer Books were everywhere burnt, and altars and the mass everywhere restored." "With tears and entreaties the Countess of Westmoreland induced her reluctant husband to enter on the war."— Memorials of the Rebellion of 1596, from the Bowes MS., pp. 10, 41, 76, 252, 261. London, Nichols and Son, 1840.

great and everliving principles, the existence of which we have already indicated; which, whilst they have checked the pride and persecuting power of the hierarchy, have kept the holy fire burning on the church's altars, and contributed beyond anything else to the moral and social greatness of the nation. The great Puritan controversy forms one of those grand national epochs, the results of which are endless. It stands before us in all its commanding majesty, curbing tyranny in the State and the Church, and opening a thousand channels through which the most benignant influences can flow to elevate the commonwealth. Its ability to benefit is not impaired. Over a wider and still wider circle it is multiplying its triumphs. Every year presents us with fresh proofs of its vitalizing energy in this and in other lands. To overlook this would be a sin against the truth, and an injury to our readers.

For more than thirty years the battle about copes, surplices, &c., raged. It had mainly to do with "the ceremonial of religion, not with the purity of its doctrine, but with its external fabric." Priestly vestments, the cross in baptism, the use of the ring in marriage, baptism by women, kneeling or sitting at the Supper, the use of organ music in divine services, pluralities, and the wealth and display of the bishops,*—these were the great subjects of controversy. Upon religious dogmas, the nature of the sacraments, and

---

* In an age of state and pageantry, Archbishop Parker exhibited a model of almost regal magnificence. Whitgift, shortly afterwards raised to the primacy on the death of Grindal, surpassed even Parker in stateliness. It is recorded of him by one of his biographers, that he travelled with a retinue of a hundred servants, including forty gentlemen with chains of gold. And that nothing might be wanting, he kept a good armoury for the exercise of military discipline, and a fair stable of horses, insomuch that he was able at all times to equip both horse and foot, and frequently mustered a hundred of the former and fifty of the latter, his own servants trained and mounted. No wonder that prelacy, with its pomp and pride, was the favourite mark of the keen shafts of the Puritans.—Marsden, p. 86. Certainly the church was very militant at this time, and its chiefs needed this protection.

the constitution of the church, opinions were uniform.* Into the grounds of these objections we enter not. The Puritans regard these things "as masks of the heart," "rags of Antichrist," "the gear of the apostate church." In similar robes "the massing priests" performed their idolatrous services. They were Jewish in their origin, and marred the simplicity of Christian worship. "If we are bound," said one, "to wear Popish apparel when commanded, we may be obliged to have shaven crowns, and to use oil and cream and spittle, with all the rest of the Papistical additions to the ordinances of Christ." Again and again their removal was implored. Against their imposition the plea of conscience was heard. The queen, the prelates, the senate, the lord treasurer, were memorialized, but in vain. The loyalty of the Puritans was unimpeached; their attachment to the church, as constituted, strong. But the episcopate was immovable. Parker, once an exile, then meek and gentle, after a doubtful consecration now reigned at Lambeth. His government, sustained by Aylmer, another exile, but now renegade to his former principles, was exceedingly severe. Elizabeth, sustained and incited by her spiritual advisers, was inexorable. Her imperious Tudor temper could brook no opposition. She was jealous of her spiritual, as of her temporal power.† Burnet says: "Men opposed to the improvements suggested by the leading Puritans, demonstrated to her that these new models would certainly bring with them a great abatement of her prerogative; since if the concern of religion came into popular hands, there would be a power set up distinct from hers, over which she could have no authority. This she perceived well, and therefore resolved to maintain the ancient government in the church; but by this means it became a matter of interest, and so those differences which

---

* Marsden, c. viii.
† "She was so proud of her ecclesiastical power that she condemned the Commons for ordering a public fast without her authority."—Lord Campbell's Chief Justices, vol. i., p. 186.

might have been more easily reconciled before grew more into formal factions."* Or, as one of the most illustrious of living writers records : "To allow churches with contrary rules and ceremonies (said Elizabeth), were nothing else but to sow discord out of religion; to distract good men's minds, to cherish factious men's humours, to disturb religion and commonwealth, and mingle divine and human things, which were a thing indeed evil; to our own subjects hurtful, and to themselves to whom it is granted neither greatly commodious, nor yet at all safe."†

Jewel, one of the best, as certainly he was one of the ablest of the brotherhood, thus complains to his Swiss correspondent : "The bishops are a great hindrance to us; for being, as you know, among the nobility and leading men in the Upper House, and having none there on our side to expose their artifices or confute their falsehoods, they reign as sole monarchs in the midst of ignorant and weak men, and easily overreach our little party. The queen, meanwhile, though she openly favours our cause, yet is wonderfully afraid of allowing any innovations; this is owing, partly, to her own friends, by whose advice everything is carried on," &c.‡

Upon two results arising from this unholy and impolitic conduct of Elizabeth and her bishops, we would detain the reader's attention for a moment. The injury it inflicted on the State Church was irreparable. Sooner or later this result always follows. Facts place this beyond all doubt. We select two classes. The first we gather from the confidential utterances of private friendships. Most of the exiles who had been elevated to dignified positions in the

---

* Burnet, vol. ii., preface. "The queen valued her ecclesiastical supremacy more than any part of her prerogative. Next to the succession to the crown, it was the point she could least endure to be touched."—Hallam's Con. History, vol. i., p. 253.
† Motley's Dutch Republic, vol. i., p. 26.
‡ Jewel. Zurich Letters, p. 10.

church, kept up an intimate correspondence with Bullinger, Gaulter, and others.

Bishop Cox, whose spirit was chafed by the Puritan controversy, says in a letter to R. Gaulter, in no very respectful tone, that "many obstinately refuse to enter our churches, either to baptize their children, or to partake of the Lord's Supper, or to hear sermons. They are entirely separated both from us and from those good brethren of ours: they seek bye-paths; they establish a private religion, and assemble in private houses, and there perform their sacred rites, as the Donatists of old, and the Anabaptists now," &c.*
"Many of the parishes," writes Lever, "have no clergymen, and some dioceses are without a bishop. And out of the very small number who administer the sacrament throughout this great country, there is hardly one in a hundred who is both able and willing to preach the Word of God, but all persons are obliged to read what is prescribed in books."†

From another source we gather fresh proofs. Bishop Sandys, writing of his metropolitan city, says, "The city (London) will never be quiet till these authors of sedition, who are now esteemed as gods, as Field, Wilcox, Cartwright, and others, be far removed from the city. The people resort unto them, as in Popery they were wont to run on pilgrimage. If these idols, who are honoured as saints, and greatly enriched with gifts, were removed from hence, their honour would fall into the dust; they would be taken for blocks, as they be. There be some aldermen and some wealthy citizens who give them great and stout countenance, and persuade

---

* Zurich Letters, p. 237.
† Lever to Bullinger. Zurich Letters (Parker Society). Letter lxxxv.

"Let it be remembered that there existed few books of divinity in English; that all books were, comparatively to the value of money, far dearer than at present; that the majority of the clergy were nearly illiterate, and many of them addicted to drunkenness and low vices; above all, that they had no means of supplying their deficiencies by preaching the discourses of others."—Hallam's Con. History, vol. ii., p. 200, note.

what they can, that others may do the like. A sharp letter from her majesty would cut the courage of these men."*

"Our (bishops') estimation is weak; our authority is less; so that we are become contemptible in the eyes of the baser sort of the people. How or by what means, or who is in the fault, I will not dispute, but leave to the Searcher of all hearts to judge."†

The influence on the people was deplorable. We take one illustration from opposite parts of the empire. In a petition to parliament from Cornwall, the inhabitants say: "We have about 160 churches, the greatest part of which are supplied by men who are guilty of the grossest sins; some fornicators, some adulterers, some felons, bearing the marks in their hands for the said offence; some drunkards, gamesters on the Sabbath day," &c. "There were 140, scarcely any of whom could preach a sermon, and most of whom were pluralists and non-residents."‡

Ministerial destitution in Suffolk in 1567 is thus described in a letter to the primate, asking for the restoration of Mr. Lawrance to his ministry. The petitioners say "there is not one preacher within a circuit of twenty miles, in which circuit he was wont to preach."§ "It appears from an impartial survey of all the counties in England, that there were only 2,000 preachers to serve nearly 10,000 parishes, only 416 ministers in the county of Norfolk, and 457 in the Lincoln, who could not preach," &c.|| Yet Aylmer and his

---

* Letter to Burghley, Congregational Magazine, 1840, p. 222.

† *Ibid*, p. 225. Other instances from Parker occur on p. 155. "I am hated like a dog, and even called the oppressor of the children of God." —*Ibid*, p. 370.

‡ Brooke's Puritans, vol. i., Introduction, p. 41.

§ *Ibid*, vol. i. p. 237.

|| *Ibid*, vol. i., p. 49. Neal, and even Marsden, supply the most painful facts on these points. The latter says, "Many there are that hear not a sermon in seven years; I might say in seventeen." Only two preachers were found in the whole diocese of Bangor. In Cornwall, Neal tells us,

brethren persecuted godly and well-qualified ministers, and ejected them from their livings, because they could not wear a certain garment, &c., in their ministry.

Only one other instance. The Lords of the Privy Council, in a letter of rebuke to Whitgift and Aylmer, say, "That they had lately received information that great numbers of zealous and learned preachers were suspended from their cures: that there was no preaching, prayer, nor sacraments in vacant places; that in some cases, the persons appointed to succeed them had neither good learning nor good name, but were drunkards and of filthy life;* and that, in other places, a great number of persons occupying cures were notoriously unfit; some for lack of learning, and others charged with enormous crimes; as drunkenness, filthiness of life, gaming at cards, and haunting of alehouses, against whom they heard of no proceedings," &c.†

That the moral state of the people was low, admits of no doubt. Hitherto the glorious Reformation had shed but little light on them. We catch a glimpse of their state in some injunctions issued by Grindal in 1570. We select the following from them:—"That no pedlar shall be admitted to sell his wares in the church porch in divine service; that parish clerks shall be able to read; that no lord of misrule, or summer lords and ladies, or any disguised persons, or morris-dancers, or others, shall come irreverently into the church, or play any unseemly parts with scoffs, jests, wanton gestures, or ribald talk, in the time of divine service."‡

The other great results touched the interests of the non-

---

there was not a single preacher capable of preaching a sermon. Oxford had three, but they were all chief men amongst the Puritans.—*Vide* Marsden, pp. 100–1.

* "In the diocese of Bangor it was usual for the clergy, some years after Elizabeth's accession, to pay the bishop for a license to keep a concubine."—Hallam, vol. i., p. 176.

† Strype's Whitgift, pp. 165–6. Congregational Magazine, 1840, p. 525. *Vide* Letter from Knollys to Burghley.—*Ibid*, pp. 734–5.

‡ Biog. Britt., vol. vii., Sup., p. 73. Brooke, vol. i., p. 256.

conforming body. Multitudes were forbidden to preach, and were exposed to suffering in every form. The great martyrologist passed his old age in poverty and shame. He complains even of want of clothes. His words to Dr. Humphreys are touching: " I still wear the same clothes, and remain in the same sordid condition, that England received me in when I first came home from Germany; nor do I change my degree or order, which is that of the mendicant; or, if you will, of the friar preacher."* Coverdale, the venerable translator of the Bible, and formerly Bishop of Exeter, was brought with sorrow to the grave. Sampson, Lever, and others, the equals of Parker in mental power and scholarly attainments, in all the elements of moral greatness his superiors, suffered greatly. Littleness was enthroned in high places, and wielding a power, the accident of its position, sought to make the great and the noble conform to its tyrannical will. A dark and painful history is that of the treatment of these holy men.

The intercourse of the exiles with the Swiss and German reformers has been indicated before. We have, in part, noticed its influence, but its full power only now began to unfold itself. From the externals in Christian worship the Puritans now aimed at a more radical change, and sought a more distinctive alteration in the constitution of the national church. The pomp of the bishops, their cruelty in persecutions, the hatred of the people, the teaching and influence of Knox and his brethren in Scotland, forced the question on public attention: Are bishops necessary to the church of Christ? Under various forms it presented itself: Are not all Christian ministers on an equality? Does not the New Testament warrant this? Is not all the evidence which the primitive church supplies, in its favour? Is not the practice of all other Protestant churches in favour of this? Or, if there be anything exceptional to this, is it anything more than that which accident or moral worth would

---

* Neal, vol. ii., chap. iv.

supply? Cranmer, and many of the early reformers in Edward's time, fully agreed with the Swiss pastors as to the constitution of the church.

The elements of Presbyterianism were wrapt in these guises. Their advocacy followed. Cartwright, the most able and sturdy champion, early demanded "that bishops, priests, and deacons ought to be reduced to the apostolical institutions (meaning that bishops, as a third order in the church, should be abolished), and that presbyters only should remain to preach the Word of God and pray: and deacons be employed in taking care of the poor. That every church ought to be governed by its ministers and presbyters; that no man ought to solicit, or be a candidate for, the ministry; and that ministers ought to be openly and fairly chosen by the people."* The alterations involved here were vital. Cartwright would overthrow Prelacy, and fix instead of it the Presbyterian power.† Around these grave questions the champions exhausted their great powers. Long and angry was the contest between Whitgift on the one side, and Cartwright on the other. The discussion was exhaustive. Old Thomas Fuller remarks "that if Cartwright had the better of his adversary in learning, Whitgift had more power to back his argument; and by this he not only kept the field, but gained the victory." Just so; no one can study the controversy impartially without rising up with the conviction that truth was on the one side and the civil power on the other.‡ God's Word sustained the one, the

---

* Marsden, pp. 76–7. In a letter from Hooper to Bullinger, he says that "the archbishop of Canterbury, the bishops of Rochester, Ely, St. David's, Lincoln, and Bath, were sincerely bent on advancing the purity of doctrine, agreeing in all things with the Helvetic Church." Cranmer avowed his conviction that "bishops and presbyters had but one office in the beginning of Christ's religion." He proposed to establish church courts and synods, like those afterwards introduced by Knox into Scotland.—*Vide* a large body of evidence in Chrichton's edition of Knox.

† "In 1572 a Presbyterian church was formed, and a meeting-house erected at Wandsworth, in January."—Marsden, p. 61.

‡ "The queen was for laying hold of all opportunities to suppress a

imperious will of the monarch was the shield of protection for the other.* Cartwright, Field, and Wilcox, though they had not the clear conceptions of the true constitution of Christ's church which the despised Anabaptists held, yet were noble explorers in the field of truth, and have laid posterity under a vast debt of obligation. Much as we admire these spiritual heroes, it has its limits; and we cannot dismiss them without a word more on the matters for which they contended. Neal says, "Both parties agreed too well in asserting the necessity of uniformity of public worship, and of calling in the sword of the magistrate for the support and defence of the several principles, which they made an ill use of in their turns, as they could grasp the power into their hands. The standard of uniformity, according to the bishops, was the queen's supremacy and the law of the land; according to the Puritans, the decrees of provincial and national synods, allowed and enforced by the civil magistrate; but neither party were for admitting that liberty of conscience and freedom of profession which is every man's right, as far as is consistent with the peace of the government he lives under." †

But other men appeared with clearer views and wider aims. The question naturally arose, Can the tree be good, the fruit of which was so essentially bitter and destructive ?

---

number of conscientious men, whom, she would often say, *she hated more than the Papists.*"—Neal, vol. i., ch. v.

"A sharpe letter from her magesty," said his lordship of London, " would cut the courage of these men. Good my lord, for the love you bear to the church of Christ, resist the tumultuous enterprises of these new-fangled fellows."—*Ibid*, vol. i., ch. v.

* Sandys, another exile in Mary's time, says, "The matter is merely temporal, fittest for temporal men to deal with. It is not convenient that men of my calling deal with matters of conscience, and to send men to the Tower and torture. As your lordship well remembered, in your last letter to me, we should rather be *feeders* than punishers."—Letter to Burghley, Congregational Magazine, 1840, p. 225. Quite right, though, for a successor of the apostles to excite others to send men to the Tower and torture!   † Neal's Elizabeth, vol. i., p. 147. *Apud* Hallam.

The Baptists had always been Separatists. Their views of the nature of Christ's church were now embraced by others. Robert Brown enunciated the principles of Congregationalism from the pulpit and the press. Brown was a minister of the State Church, and a relative of Cecil. For some years he laboured to diffuse his newly-discovered principles;—they spread, disciples increased; but after long and severe suffering, he died in comparative obscurity, a minister of the church upon which he had flung every malediction, and whose very foundation he had laboured to upturn. The Church of England and her ministers he held to be unchristian; its discipline was Popish, and its ordinances and sacraments invalid. Separation was to be entire. Truth cannot perish. These great principles are more potent, after the test of centuries, than ever. Barrow, Greenwood, and others, men of the loftiest principles and of heroic spirit, embraced and preached them. Their homage to these verities was entire; their love to them quenchless; whilst a life of suffering and the martyr's death, proclaimed the intenseness of Episcopal hate and dread of freedom of thought and the rights of conscience. But their history is not within the design of this work.* It is quite time the attention of the reader was fixed on other men and their doings.

Not only the existence, but the wide spread of Baptist principles, during the reign of the "royal Tudor lioness," is acknowledged on all hands. One of the latest, and we are bound to say, one of the calmest and most candid writers on the Puritanic history, says: "But the Anabaptists were the most numerous, and for some time by far the most formidable, opponents of the church. They are said to have existed in England since the early days of the Lollards, but their chief strength was more abroad," &c.† "You must not be grieved, my Gaulter," wrote Bishop Cox, "that sectaries are showing themselves to be mischievous and

---

* The reader is referred to Neal, Brooke, and Fletcher's histories.
† Marsden, p. 144.

wicked interpreters of your most just opinion. For it cannot be otherwise but that tares must grow in the Lord's field, and that in no small quantity. Of this kind are the Anabaptists, Donatists, Arians, Papists, and all the good-for-nothing tribe of Sectaries."* Approximation to some of their distinctive principles was growing, but love to the professors of them existed not. The writer already quoted truthfully says: "In the judgment of the church party, and of not a few of the Puritans, Anabaptists were heretics of the worst kind, and those who denied the necessity or validity of infant baptism, however orthodox on other points, are constantly classed by writers of that period, with Donatists, infidels, and atheists," &c.† This is true: eminently so with some of the bishops. Aylmer's malice was intense. The following more than justifies the opinion:—"The Anabaptists, with infinite other swarms of Satanistes, do you think that every pulpit may wyll be hable to aunswer them? I pray God there may be many that can."‡ "And in these latter daies, the old festered sores newly broke out, as the Anabaptists, the free-willers, or rather the forward-willers, with infinite other swarms of God's enemies. These 'vgglie monsters,' 'brodes of the devvil's brotherhood.'" §

In Dr. Parker's letter declining the Archbishopric of Canterbury, the following occurs: "They say that the realm is full of Anabaptists, Arians, libertines, free-will men, &c., against whom I only thought ministers should have need to fight in unity of doctrine." ||

Jewel, in his correspondence with the Swiss divines, utters the same complaint: "We found, at the beginning of the reign of Elizabeth, large and inauspicious crops of Arians, Anabaptists, and other pests, which, I know not

---

* Bishop Cox to Gaulter, 1575. Zurich Letters, 285.

† Marsden, p. 65. "I am not an Anabaptist, thank God," said Greenwood.—Brooke's Puritans, vol. ii., p. 36.

‡ Bishop Aylmer's Harborough for Faithful Subjects. Maitland, p. 216.

§ *Ibid*, p. 205. || Burnet's Reformation, vol. ii., p. 359.

how, but as mushrooms spring up in the night and in darkness, so these sprung up in that darkness and unhappy night of the Marian times. These, I am informed, and hope it is the fact, have retreated before the light of pure doctrines, like owls at the light of the sun, and are nowhere to be found."*

Two causes may account for the number of our brethren in this country at this time. Protection had been given to Dutch and French refugees. Churches had been given to them in which divine worship, according to their own views, could be conducted. The state of the Netherlands supplies another cause. England appeared the land of freedom under the rule of the Protestant queen, and the liberty granted to others many hoped to find here, partial liberty of conscience. These hopes were only temporary. No rest could be found for their weary spirits. The animus of the government soon manifested itself.† Burghley, Knolleys, Leicester, and others, threw the shield of their protection around the Puritans and Brownists, and frequently employed their great powers in checking the fury of the bishops, delivering their victims from their iron grasp. But whoever found mercy, the Baptists had none. As we have seen, detested by all, obnoxious to the government, and hated by all religionists, they were "hunted like a partridge on the mountains."

In the fourth year of her reign a proclamation was issued by the queen, commanding "the Anabaptists and such like heretics, which had flocked to the coast towns of England, from the parts beyond the seas, under colour of shunning persecution, and had spread the poison of their sects in England, to depart the realm within twenty days, whether they were natural-born people of the land or foreigners,

---

* Zurich Letters, 92.

† Elizabeth said, "That it was not with safety, honour, and credit, to permit diversity of opinion in a kingdom where none but she and her Council governed."—Foxes and Firebrands, part iii. *Apud* Strype's Annals, vol. i., p. 128.

upon pain of imprisonment and loss of goods."* Many were forced to wander in other lands, and probably fell victims to the persecuting power. Collier says, "Several secured themselves with their Protestancy, and joined the French and Dutch congregations, both in London and the coast towns. And here, by venting some of their dotages, they occasioned such warm contentions that P. Martyr found it necessary to interpose his interest for bringing them to more temper." An example of these "warm commotions" is given us by Strype: "In the year 1560 one of their ministers, of the Dutch Church, Austin Friars, namely, Hamstedius, was convened before the said bishop (Grindal), judicially, for favouring some Dutch Anabaptists that desired to be received into his church, and had supplicated the bishop to be admitted. He had asserted in their behalf concerning that heresy of theirs (viz., that Christ took not his flesh of the Virgin Mary, but brought it from heaven), that the doctrine of the incarnation of Christ, and his partaking of our nature, was not a foundation (*i.e.*, a fundamental doctrine), but a circumstance only of the foundation; and that children and distracted persons were saved without faith. But the bishop required him to renounce these and other like errors; which he refused to do, and continuing obstinate in them, was excommunicated by the bishop, and so was declared next Sunday in the Dutch Church." The annalist adds: "Soon after Hamstedius retired beyond the sea. And in the year 1564 there happened again an earnest contention in the church, concerning baptizing infants, which was finally referred to the Bishop of London, their superintendent, to decide."†

---

* Camden's Elizabeth, p. 47 : "Some of these were German Anabaptists, and others propagated opinions of a very dangerous tendency; and thus misbelief gains ground, and some of the ignorant natives were miserably misled."—Collier, vol. ii., p. 471.

† Annals, vol. i., p. 176. In another volume he gives an account, extending over several pages, of a disturbance in the same church, by one

The year 1575 was marked by one of those events which stamp the character of this reign with many of its dark spots. Macintosh says:—"This was the first blood spilt by Elizabeth for religion, after a reign of fourteen years; and it forms, in the eye of posterity, a dark spot upon a government, hitherto distinguished, beyond that of any other European community, by a religious administration which, if not unstained, was bloodless."* True, it witnessed the martyrdom of servants of Christ; it was blood-shedding by the fires of Smithfield. We have but an imperfect narrative at command, but from the various sources within our reach we shall give as much completeness to it as we can.

It was the morning of Easter-day, a season of joy and festivity, at this time, to the whole church, when some of the bishop's creatures discovered a body of Flemish Baptists, who had assembled in a house in Aldgate, to commemorate the triumph of their risen Lord. Their number is variously reported, but the best authority gives thirty.† They were hurried to prison. Grindal at this time filled the metropolitan chair. He was one of the exiles, and had tasted the bitterness of persecution under the former reign. Into his court the prisoners were conducted. His lordship was aided in this Christian affair by "Master Joris, James de Koninck, John de Rode-Maker, two members of the Council, and a French clergyman. We were placed before these lords and their servants, who propounded four questions to us, to which we were to give either an affirmative or negative." The questions which were put by these inquisitors were the following:—"1. Whether Christ did

---

Velsius. He calls him sometimes an enthusiast, at others a madman, and, of course an Anabaptist. He was finally banished the kingdom by Elizabeth.—*Ibid*, vol. ii., c. xxxiv. Strype professes to draw his accounts from Dutch MSS. These, we believe, still exist, and yet unpublished. Their publication is much to be desired.

* History of England, vol. iii., p. 170.
† Collier, Fuller, and Wall only give twenty-seven.

not assume his flesh from the body of Mary? We replied that he is the Son of the living God. 2. Whether infants should not be baptized? We cannot understand matters so, for we read nothing of it in the Scriptures. 3. Whether it was lawful for a Christian to attend to or discharge the duties of a magistrate's officer? We replied that our conscience would not suffer us to do so; *but we consider the magistracy as a minister of God* for the protection of the servants of God. 4. Whether a Christian was allowed to take an oath? We again replied, our conscience would not even allow us to do so, for Christ said, 'Let your communications be yea, yea, and nay, nay.' We then kept silent. The bishop said that our misdeeds were very gross, and we could not inherit the kingdom of God. Oh, Lord! avenge not. The bishop then remanded us to prison. A young brother, who was first interrogated, boldly confessed the truth; and on that account was sorely accused, and led to Westminster, where he was imprisoned by himself. This caused us much grief." From the same document we get a further glimpse of the proceeding. During this first interview, as one of the prisoners appeared to take the lead in the conversation, the judges said :—" 'This is the captain; you shall no longer scatter your baneful seed in our country;' and they secured him immediately. The bishop then showed them a letter, and said to them in a very surly tone, that the court had agreed that all the strangers should subscribe the above four questions. The one that would do so should be at perfect liberty in the country; but all who should refuse should be punished with death; 'therefore, you may now choose.' This cruel and unchristian ordinance alarmed some, so that on account of the weakness of the flesh, five of them fell from the truth, and refused to offer their bodies for the name of Christ." During the interval between their first and second examinations, means were employed to seduce them from the truth. Master Jovis visited them in prison. In the name of his episcopal chief, he promised them freedom from bonds on condition that they would join the church. The voice of the tempter was powerless. Their attachment to the faith was unwavering. It was on the morning of another great festival, when the church commemorates the effusion of the Divine Spirit, that these confessors were again led from their prisons before the lords. They were chained two and two like the worst malefactors of the land. The narrative is brief and touching:—"When we were brought before them they presented the same four questions, urging us to subscribe them; but we told them that we would abide by the Word of the Lord. We were then remanded to prison, fettered as before: the women were confined at Newgate, together with a young brother, but they were all released and transported. The young man, however, was tied to a cart and scourged, and afterwards whipped out of town. We were in the midst of thieves and malefactors. These the bishop and a preacher worried, lest they might be corrupted by us and deceived."

We have a clear view of the charges brought against them and the nature of their replies, in one or two letters written by the martyrs during their imprisonment:—

"We poor and despised strangers, who are persecuted for the testimony of Jesus, desire that God may grant all mankind peace, so that they may live together in all godliness, to the praise of the Lord and to the advancement of their souls' salvation. Since so many, both by writing and verbal statements, do us great injustice, accusing and charging lies upon us, I am constrained to present our belief very summarily.

"They do not speak to us, and do not in a mild manner inquire of us what our religious views are, as the Scriptures teach, but they speak all manner of evil of us, so that they may increase our miseries and sufferings; and besides, they have no compassion either on our distressed wives or helpless children. We had to forsake our friends, our country, and our possessions, on account of tyranny, and fled as lambs from a wolf, only because of the pure evangelical truth of Christ, and not for uproar or faction's sake, like those of Munster, whose views are an abomination, of which we have been slanderously accused.

"Who would like to be persecuted in a strange country, when he is already wretched and poor? Therefore, says Christ, 'Whatsoever ye would that men should do unto you, do ye even so to them; this is the law and the prophets.' Oh, that they would thus treat us! How soon persecutions would cease! Christ and his followers never persecuted any one, but, on the contrary, taught that we should 'love those who hate us, and pray for those who despitefully use us, that we may be the children of our Father in heaven, who lets his sun shine over the righteous and the wicked.

"We seek no salvation in our works, as it is reported we do, but we hope to be saved alone through the merits of our Lord Jesus Christ. Nor do we boast that we are without sin, but we always confess ourselves sinners before God. But we have to refrain from voluntary sins if we would be saved, such as adultery, fornication, sorcery, sedition, bloodshed, cursing and swearing, lying and cheating, pride and drunkenness, hatred, envy: these are the sins which the Scriptures declare, who do them shall not inherit the kingdom of God.

"They also say, we refuse to hear the Word of God, because we do not go to hear the preaching of the church. To this charge we would say, that why we do not hear the preacher, is, that the Word of God constrains us so to do; because they are people not fit to attend to the sacred callings of a Gospel preacher; for Paul teaches Timothy, and says:—'The things which thou hast heard of me, among many witnesses, the same commit thou to faithful men, who shall be able to teach others; because if a man undertakes to teach or reprove another, he must be blameless himself.' Now if the preachers were such as the apostles required, we should cheerfully hear them,—we would be the first and the last in the church.

"We are also accused of not being subject to the magistrates, because we do not baptize our infants. To this we reply, we desire to submit to the magistracy, in all things not contrary to the Word of God. That we do not suffer our children to be baptized by the priests, is not done out of temerity, but we do it out of fear to God, for Christ commands believers to be baptized; for Christ's apostles did not baptize infants, but adults only, and those on their faith and confession of their sins. . . . If it had been the will of God that infants should be baptized, he would have commanded it to be done. Christ would have been baptized in his infancy, as well as circumcised; but as it is not the will of God, therefore did he teach them differently, and received baptism differently himself.

"But they have stretched considerably in bringing charges against us, saying there are many thousands of us. Our belief has not been so generally embraced; we are not treated so kindly as to induce the crowd to adopt our views. True, here and there you may find some secluded family, like the lily among the thorns,—as the apple-tree among the trees of the woods, bringing forth good fruit."*

These are noble words, and worthy of the martyr's spirit. Of these thirty, five recanted, five were imprisoned, and the remainder were banished from the country.† The narrative from which we gather these facts, says:—"Instead of honouring the five apostates, they were scandalized and exposed at St. Paul's Cross, and were branded as having been deceived, and had to confess that it was the truth; and then to enter bail that they would unite themselves to the German Church, and then become brethren." Crosby has preserved the form of renunciation which was imposed on these weak brethren. The document is curious, and we fear no censure in transferring it to our pages:—

"Whereas, we being seduced by the devil, the spirit of error, and by false teachers, have fallen into those most damnable and detestable errors:—that Christ took not flesh of the Virgin Mary; that the infants of the faithful ought not to be baptized; that a Christian man may not be a magistrate, or bear the sword and office of authority; and that it is not lawful for a Christian man to take an oath. Now, by the grace of God, and by the assistance of good and learned ministers of Christ's church, I understand the same to be most damnable and detestable heresies: and do ask God, before his church, mercy for my said former errors, and do forsake, recant, and renounce them; and I abjure, from the bottom of my heart, protesting I certainly believe the contrary. And further, I confess that the whole doctrine established and published in the Church of England, and also that as received in the Dutch Church, in London, is found true and according to God's Word: whereunto in all things I submit myself, and will be most gladly a member of the said Dutch Church, from henceforth utterly abandoning and forsaking all and every Anabaptistical error."‡

Poor men! But life is sweet! This scene, more humiliating to those who imposed it than to the unfortunate ones so prominent in it, took place in the Dutch Church, Austin

---

* References to Origen, Luther, and others, in support of these views, are omitted here.

† Crosby states four. ‡ Collier, vol. ii., p. 549.

Friars, in the presence of De Laune, one of the ministers of that community.*

The condition of the incarcerated excited much sympathy. Even those who dissented from their religious views greatly compassionated their state. Petitions and a confession of their faith were laid before the imperious monarch. Fox, who had recorded with touching interest and graphic power the martyrology of the past, in a Latin letter pleaded with the queen on their behalf. But all was in vain. Submission or death was the alternative.† Fox's letter is a noble specimen of enlightened piety. We give a sentence or two. This act of brotherly kindness should be embalmed in every Baptist memorial of this age:—

"I understand there are some here in England, though not English, but come here from Holland, I suppose both men and women, who, having been tried according to law, publicly declared their repentance, are happily reclaimed. Many others are condemned to exile; a right sentence, in my opinion. But I hear there is one or two of these who are appointed to the most severe punishment, viz., burning, except your clemency forbid. Now in this one affair I conceive there are two things to be considered; the one is the wickedness of their errors, the other the sharpness of their punishment. As to the errors, indeed, no man of sense can deny that they are most absurd; and I wonder that such monstrous opinions could come into the mind of any Christian; but such is the state of human weakness, if we are left ever so little awhile destitute of the Divine life, whither is it we do not fall? and we have good reason to give God thanks on this account, that I hear not of any Englishman that is inclined to this madness. As to these fanatical sects, therefore, it is certain they are by no means to be countenanced in a commonwealth, but, in my opinion, ought to be suppressed by proper correction. But to roast alive the

---

* Crosby, vol. i., p. 69.

† "She was of a proud and imperious spirit, and usually carried things with a very high hand, expecting all to bow to her will and pleasure. Her own clergy felt it. On one occasion, Dr. Nowell, the Dean of St. Paul's and one of her chaplains, spoke less reverently of the cross, in a sermon he was preaching before her, when, from the closet window, her voice was heard, forbidding his ungodly digressions, and commanding him to return to his text."—*Vide* Haylin's Reformation, p. 124, Ed. 1670. Brooke, vol. i., p. 208.

bodies of poor wretches that offend rather through blindness of judgment than perverseness of will, in fire and flames, raging with pitch and brimstone, is a hard-hearted thing, and more agreeable to the practice of Romanists than the customs of the Gospeller. . . . Wherefore, if I may be so bold with the majesty of so great a princess, I humbly beg of your royal highness, for the sake of Christ, who was consecrated to suffer for the lives of many, this favour at my request, which even the Divine clemency would engage you to, that if it may be—and what cannot your authority do in these cases? —these miserable wretches may be spared; at least, that a stop may be put to the horror by changing their punishment into some other kind. . . . This one thing I most earnestly beg, that the piles and flames of Smithfield, so long ago extinguished by your happy government, may not more be revived."

Warmly did these sufferers for Christ feel the kindness of the venerable man. Their gratitude was ardent; and in a letter, from which we extract a sentence or two, they gave utterance in language, which if we had no other evidence, would give them a high place in our Christian regards, as they deserved. After recognizing his personal kindness and his efforts on their behalf with the queen, and noticing the advice of some to give up their peculiar views, they say :—

"We confess that the flesh of Christ is not a phantasm, or ethereal, but true human flesh, like unto us in all things, sin excepted; that he is the true seed of the woman, the son of David, and the fruit of the body of Mary. Finally, we believe all which the Holy Scriptures further testify concerning him, and we place our salvation, whether in our life or our death, not in our own works or holiness, but alone in his death and resurrection. If men would only be content with this, and not wish to constrain us to confess that Christ assumed his humanity from the flesh of Mary, which we can neither comprehend or believe, because the word humanity is not expressed in the Scripture. Hence it is inferred against us that we teach that Christ is not very man, and in general that we deny our salvation; whereas on the contrary, the inference should be even as charity teaches us. That when we say that Christ had flesh, as truly as our first parent Adam had before the fall, even as we at the same time confess that he is a true man and our Saviour, we make specific confession of this in express terms. But if you say that you discover little or no difference between your faith and ours, except in the phrase, 'humanity of the woman' (wesen des weibes), and that we ought not obstinately to reject it on this account, our reply on the other hand is, that we ought not to be constrained thereto by violence, but our weakness in this part ought to be borne with, inasmuch as we are not otherwise convinced in our conscience, and would commit a great sin against God, if we would speak contrary to the testimony of our conscience. Wherefore, if we are delivered to death (the contrary of which we hope from her majesty's clemency), we testify before God that we do not die for this or that article (which we would willingly accept if they could only convince us with solid arguments) but for conscience sake; for, if we would act contrary thereto, even if we did right, yet we would do amiss, and bear testimony against ourselves, which you, by your learning, are better able to understand than we common and illiterate people. Finally, we are men, and what is further, unlearned men, who are liable to err. Hence, we are willing to submit to the instruction of all those who are able to prove to us, by the Scriptures, something that is better; but that men should constrain us with fire and sword, appears to us to be vain, and to militate against reason— for it is possible to constrain us, through fear of death, to speak differently from what we understand; but that we should understand differently from our belief, you are well aware is an impossibility."

Two of these, Von Byler and Von Straatam, after much suffering in their dreary prison, were liberated; Kemels, another of the martyrs, died in prison. Pieters and Terwoort finished their course in Smithfield, and thus "became the proto-martyrs under the reign of Elizabeth."

The following is a copy of the writ issued by the queen for the execution of these men:—

"ELIZABETH, by the grace of God, Queen of England, France, and Ireland, Defender of the Faith, unto our righteously and right well-beloved Councillor, Sir Nich. Bacon, knight, Lord Keeper of our great Seal of England, greeting:—

"When the Reverend Fathers in God, Edwin, Bishop of London, Edmund, Bishop of Rochester, and our right trusty and well-beloved Sir W. Cordell, knight, Master of the Rolls, Roger Manhood, and Robert Mounson, two of the Justices of our Common Pleas, with other Commissioners sufficiently authorised by our Commission, under our great Seal of England, have travelled upon the examination, hearing, and determination of John Pieters and Henry Terwoort, being Flemings born, and now living in this our realm, concerning their false opinions, and sects of Anabaptists, holden and averred by them, wherein they have, before the said Reverend Father, and others, our said Commissioners, maintained their said most perilous and dangerous opinions, for the which they are by definite sentences, declared by the said Reverend Father, the Bishop of London, with the consent of others, our said Commissioners, justly adjudged and declared to be heretics; and therefore, as corrupt members, to be cut off from the rest of the flock of Christ, lest they should infect others professing the true Christian faith, and are by them left under the sentence of the great excommunication, to be by our secular power and authority punished as heretics, as by the significavit of the said Reverend Father in God, the Bishop of London, with the assent of our said Commissioners, remaining in our Court of Chancery, more at large appeareth; and although the said Anabaptists have, since the said sentence pronounced against them, been often and very charitably travelled with, as well by the ministers of the Dutch Church in the city of London, as by other godly and learned men, to dissuade, revoke, and remove them from their Anabaptistical and heretical opinions, yet they arrogantly and wilfully persist and continue in the same.

"We, therefore, according to our regal functions and office, vindicating the execution of justice in this behalf, and to give example to others, lest they should attempt the like hereafter, have determined, by the assent of our Council, to will and require you, the said Lord Keeper, immediately on the receipt hereof, to award and make out our writ of execution, according to the tenor in these presents ensuing, and these our letters signed with our hand shall be your sufficient warrant for the same."*

Long as this narrative is, we cannot even now close it without appending to it a beautiful letter, written by one of their countrymen to his mother, then resident at Ghent. Both appear to have been members of the Dutch Church. Besides, it contains additional particulars of great interest.

"BELOVED MOTHER,—This has reference to the peculiar circumstances attending the execution of the Anabaptists, though I have not the least doubt but you have already received from others much information relative thereto, even as it is with extreme reluctance that I write upon a subject of which you cannot even think, without emotions of the deepest distress. But, as you desire, and it is probable that I am better acquainted with the circumstances than the generality of people, inasmuch as I have had frequent intercourse with them, and

---

* Collier, vol. ii., p. 15.

have received information from all of them; so I cannot forbear giving such an account of it as accords with the extent of my information in reference to the matter. In connection with which I send you a copy of their confession, on account of which some died, and others are retained in prison; and a petition was presented by them to her majesty, but which was not accepted by her.

"It happened on Easter, the 3rd of April, A.D. 1575, that thirty Anabaptists of both sexes had assembled together in a house near Alligator, on the road leading to Spiegelzhof, for the purpose of mutual exhortation and prayer; but being detected by the neighbours they were nearly all taken then to prison, by so small a guard that some could easily have escaped, if they could have felt liberty of conscience to do so. Having fallen into the hands of the magistracy, they were conducted to the house of the Bishop of London, in order to be examined by him concerning their faith, which examination had to be conducted through the medium of a German and a French preacher, because the bishop did not understand the language.

"Their confession of faith was Scriptural, and drawn up in such a manner that I would be free to subscribe to every tenet, with the exception of the article concerning oaths, in which they publicly confessed their belief that men should 'Swear not at all.'

"The bishop, not satisfied with this confession, presented four articles to be subscribed, with the provision that if any remained obstinate, they should be burned alive; adding that such charge was imposed upon him by the court.

"These articles were the same as those which have been mentioned before.

"They replied that they were conscientious in regard to these matters, and maintained the principles set forth in their first profession; so they were reconducted to prison. But on their way thither, ten or twelve of them made their escape, as they were aware of the danger to which they were exposed, and perceived the fine opportunity of escape that presented itself, the guard consisted of but one or two individuals. The whole of them, however, in the course of two or three days, returned to the prison, partly in order to acquit their bail, who were bound in the sum of one hundred pounds, and partly because the bishop, as a man of honour, promised with an oath that he would set them all at liberty in the course of five or six days, if they would return; but if not, the rest should remain in prison till Candlemass. Immediately after this, five of the men were converted (through much disputation with these Netherlanders, who belonged to the church) before they were condemned as heretics, nevertheless, they were placed upon a rostrum in St. Paul's churchyard, in a large assembly of some thousands of Englishmen, and a bundle of faggots was laid upon each one's shoulder, as a sign that they deserved to be burnt; in addition to which, they inflicted many other injuries and much ignominy upon them, though the bishop had promised that he would set them at liberty without any incumbrances if they would only sign *the four articles;* but the event proved to the contrary. This transpired on the 25th of May, A.D. 1575. In the course of a few days, the bishop perceiving that the rest would not apostatize from their faith, sentenced them all to death, in the ecclesiastical court-room, in St. Paul's Church (as was customary with the Papistical bishops during Queen Mary's reign, who were wont to condemn the Christians to death), and deliver them into the hands of the civil judge; then they bound the women hand to hand, and conducted them to Newgate,—the prison for capital convicts,—together with one of the men, which was considered the youngest and most innocent among them; but the rest of the men were conducted to their old episcopal prison, for which reason it was supposed that the women would be executed first, even as persons came daily to threaten them, and to present death to them, unless they would apostatize. Hence they suffered great anguish and temptation for five or six days, supposing every day that they would be burnt,—nay, on the very day that the sentence of their banishment came from the court, for the bailiff came with his servants at ten in the evening into the prison to take an inventory of all their property, informing them, in addition, that they should prepare for death the next day. This he did in order to see whether any of them would apostatize through fear; but perceiving that they all remained steadfast, he informed them that it was the queen's pleasure to be gracious to them, and merely to banish them from the country, and have the young man whipped behind a cart. Accordingly, in the course of five or six days, about fourteen women were conveyed from the prison, which is situated in the space between St. Martin's Church and St. Catherine's, to the ship, by the apparitors; but the young man was whipped behind a cart, which moved on before him. Thus they were all banished from the country, on pain of imprisonment, and reside for the present in Holland and Zealand. A few days after, the five men that remained in the bishop's prison, were likewise sentenced to death by the bishop, and conveyed to Newgate, where one of them died of wretchedness and of a load of chains, and the rest were apprehensive that they would inflict extreme punishment upon them, because they had exercised so much severity towards the women. They were also informed that the queen and her whole Council were so highly offended at them that no person would venture to present a petition for them, since an evil report arose that they denied God and Christ, and rejected all government, and all respect for the magistrates and civil power, as ungodly and unchristian. Therefore they sent a petition to her majesty, together with their confession concerning the four articles, which had been presented to them; a copy of which I send enclosed. But she was so exasperated at them that she refused to accept it, but severely reprimanded the Staats who presented it to her, as they informed those who handed in the petition to them. When they perceived this they delivered the articles, together with the petition, which was somewhat altered, to Lord Bodley [or Burghley], who having laid the matter before the bishop, answered them on the succeeding day, that he was very much distressed on their account; but there was no hope of favour unless they would sign the articles and abjure their heresy. In the meantime, the bishop issued certain articles in her majesty's name, one of which was that a Christian magistrate may with propriety punish obstinate heretics with the sword; and commanded all strangers to sign it, or otherwise give sufficient security to appear, at the pleasure of the bishop, before him and the queen, to undergo a circumstantial examination, and be punished according to their deserts. So almost all the foreigners, induced by fear more than any other consideration, signed it, with the exception of some, who chose rather to incur the danger, than, by their signing, to approve of the putting to death of poor people; the issue, however, is yet unknown. Soon after, orders were issued from the court to the sheriff or bailiff of London, to execute the two oldest, according to their sentence: one of them, Jan Pieters, was a poor man, upwards of fifty years old, and had nine children. His first wife was previously burnt at Ghent, in Flanders, on account of her religion; and he married a second wife, whose first husband had likewise been burnt at Ghent for his religious principles. But these two had fled into England on account of persecution, on supposition that they could live there and enjoy liberty of conscience without being exposed to any danger, which circumstance he represented to the bishop, and desired the favour of removing from the country with his wife and children; but he could not obtain it. The other, called Henry Terwoort, was a handsome and respectable man, about twenty-six years old; a goldsmith by trade, and had been married eight or ten weeks before he was apprehended.

"The German and French preachers not succeeding, in much disputation, to induce these men to sign the articles, but having much rather confirmed them in their opinion, by the cruel and unchristian conduct of those who boast of the Gospel and Christian faith, although many English and Germans petitioned in their favour; yet on the 22nd of July, at six o'clock, A.M., they were miserably burnt to ashes, at the same stake, without having been strangled, and without powder, according to the custom at Smithfield, where they used to burn the people who professed our religion.

"This was done the Friday succeeding the Tuesday on which the stake had been erected. I have no doubt but the queen assented to this measure with reluctance; but she was persuaded to it by certain Papists, or other perverse men and enemies of the truth, of whom there are many here, who asserted that the Anabaptists, with whose religion this people are unacquainted, did not only deny God and Christ, and overthrow the salvation of the soul, but also that they rejected all worldly policy, laws, and government, and incited the people to mutiny and sedition, because they taught that the magistracy is ungodly and unchristian; for which reason, no doubt, she was chiefly exasperated at them, so that she would not accept their petition.

"The Lord forgive those who were authors and abettors in this matter, and so misrepresented these poor people to her majesty, as you may judge from their confession, which they signed near me, with their own hand; for, though I do not assent to the whole, and am assured that they are under a mistake in regard to the article concerning the original conception of Christ and the origin of his flesh, yet as they made a Christian confession in express terms, and often confessed orally, in my presence, that Christ is very God and very man, like unto us in flesh and blood, and in all other respects, sin excepted, so be it far from me to acknowledge that they were guilty of death; nay, I would much rather acknowledge them as brethren, and have not the least doubt of their salvation, if they only feared the Lord, and walked before him with a good conscience.

"Touching the two young men who still remain, they continue firm and steadfast, and are in daily expectation of the same punishment. Luke and I endeavoured, if possible, to get them out of prison four days after the execution of the others; we even prevailed on them, through much conversation, to sign the confession (a copy of which I send you), in the hope that the bishop would be satisfied with it. Having read it, he found it good throughout; but he will not receive them into favour unless they sign the first four articles without contradiction, and join the Dutch Church, which they are determined not to do, even if they perfectly agree with us in doctrine; since thereby they would condemn the two that had been executed, and all the rest of their comrades who died or still live in the same faith, and would confess that they had been seduced by the devil, the spirit of lies and error, to this damnable heresy, of which they declare that they are by no means convinced in their own consciences, but that they are much more assured of their salvation in Christ, the very God and very man; they would, therefore, as they say, provoke God in the highest if they would speak contrary to the testimony of their own conscience. Hence we know of nothing else than they will have to suffer the same punishment that was endured by their partners, the more especially as they attempted to break out of prison, having filed off an iron bar of the window, for which cause they are kept more closely in bonds than at any former time, and may consider themselves fortunate if an early and preferable death should release them from the great distress and misery of the prison, for they lie separate from each other, so that they cannot afford each other any consolation, and no one dare to converse with them, on the pain of immediate imprisonment.

"Here, dear mother, you have a distressing history from first to last, of these imprisoned, converted, proscribed, and executed Anabaptists, concerning which, I am likewise aware, that it appears to you very strange and incredible, and that you are very much distressed that those who formerly suffered persecution should now persecute other people on account of their religion, constraining the consciences of others with fire and sword, whereas they formerly taught, and which is the plain truth, that it is the province of no man to lord it over the consciences of others; and that faith is a special gift of God, and is not implanted in men by any human power, but by the Word of God and the illumination of the Holy Spirit. So I say, that I am well aware that the affair has been the cause of extreme distress to you and all the compassionate, as I also hope that it will not be a cause of offence to you, and occasion you to doubt the true faith; and remember, as it is the truth, that some of the pious and learned, as well English as foreigners, who are here, did not approve nor assent to it. I would write more diffusely upon this subject if time would permit. But I will now conclude, and I pray the Lord to strengthen you, together with all who fear God and love the truth, confirming you in all virtue and godliness, to the salvation of your souls.—Amen.

"Your obedient son,
"JACQUES DE SOMERS."*

We give two examples of the manner in which these facts are presented by our historians :—

Strype says: "I find two Anabaptists were burnt in

---

* We are indebted to Benedict for most of the particulars in this narrative. He has borrowed them from "The Martyr's Mirror," a work we have in vain tried to procure. --History of the Baptists. New York, 1848.

Smithfield not long after (July 22nd), namely, John Wiel Macker, and Hendrick Terwoort (who it seems had recanted before, if it were the same), after that they had been sixteen weeks in prison. The Privy Council would not spare them, notwithstanding the earnest intercessions of the Dutch congregations, for divers mighty reasons laid before them. But the chief causes of their execution were, because they would not own them for Christian magistrates, and had been banished a year before."*

Miss Aikin says: "Two of these unhappy men, however, repented of the disingenuous acts into which human frailty had betrayed them, and returning to the open profession of their opinions, were burnt at Smithfield." Obviously a mistake.†

It is difficult to say which feeling most predominates in the mind of an intelligent Christian,—pity, contempt, or indignation, at the perusal of such comment as the following, by one of our church writers: "But though Queen Elizabeth constantly called him Father Fox; yet herein was she no *dutiful daughter*, giving him a flat denial. Indeed, damnable were their impieties, and she was necessitated to this severity, who having punished some *traitors*, if not spurning these blasphemers, the world would condemn her as being more earnest in asserting her own safety than God's honour. Hereupon the writ *De hæretico comburendo* (which for seventeen years had hung only up *in terrorem*), was now taken down and put in execution, and the two Anabaptists, burnt in Smithfield, died in great horror, with crying and roaring."‡ What a specimen of the power of prejudice to blind the mind, and to blunt the sympathies of our nature! Only think of the character of that religion which hails the roasting of men alive, for harmless speculation in the faith, as an acceptable vindication of the honour of the God of love!

---

* Annals, vol. ii., part i., p. 564. He professes to have the latter from Dutch MSS.   † Elizabeth, vol. ii. p. 43.

‡ Fuller's Church History, cent. xvi., p. 104. Crosby, vol. i., p. 74.

The errors were not extirpated. Three years later another hunt for the heretics was ordered. Alva's persecution in the Netherlands had forced many unto this island. The primate and his suffragan were ordered to undertake this work. The character and religion of every foreigner in the kingdom were to be investigated. Into every parish a visitor was to enter, whose special work it was to write the name of every stranger in a register, together with their country, quality, and circumstances. Beyond this they were to extend their inquisitions. Inquiry was to be made into the probable motives of their coming over, the manner of their behaviour, and what church they frequented. Suspected ones were to be reported to the justices of the peace, that they might be brought for trial and punishment. This was necessary, says the writer, "for the Dutch Anabaptists held private conventicles in London, and perverted a great many."*

In 1589 the same fact is admitted by Dr. Some in his reply to Barrow, &c. He affirms that "there were several Anabaptistical conventicles in London and other places." They were not Dutchmen, certainly not exclusively so, for he says that "some persons of these sentiments have been bred at our universities."†

The hostility of Elizabeth to the dissidents was undiminished. "Of toleration, of the rights of conscience, she had as little feeling or understanding as any prince or polemic of her age. Her establishment was formed throughout in the spirit of compromise and political expediency. She took no pains to ascertain, either by assembling of a national synod, or by the submission of the articles to free discussion in Parliament, whether or not they were likely to be agree-

---

* Collier, vol. ii., p. 517.
† Ivimey's History of the Baptists, vol. i., p. 109. We cannot find a copy of Dr. Some's work either in the British Museum or the Red Cross Street Library. Some of the statements of this writer (as given in Ivimey) will appear in another section of this work.

able to the opinions of the majority : it sufficed that she had decreed their reception; and she prepared, by means of penal statutes, strictly executed, to prevent the propagation of any doctrine, or the observance of any rite, capable of interfering with the exact uniformity in religion then re-garded as essential to the peace and stability of any well constituted state."* Age and growing infirmities shed no softening influence on her proud spirit. The primate, by every art in his power, fed this flame. With the queen's hostility to the Puritans of every class, Whitgift had the fullest sympathy.† To the Anabaptists his hatred was intense. At all times it breaks out. ‡ Some says, that "with a view of obviating objections to the principles of ministers, a brief declaration of belief in some leading articles was drawn up in Latin, for their subscription. This contains an assent to the fundamentals of the Christian religion, and a disclaimer of Romish and Anabaptistical errors."§

---

* Miss Aikin's Elizabeth, vol. i., pp. 319, 320.

† "Whitgift, at his first coming to the See, had instructions from the queen to hold a strait rein, to press the discipline of his church, and recover his province to uniformity. This method agreed with the archbishop's sentiments, and was probably suggested by himself."—Collier.

"This man (Whitgift) was thorough in all he did, especially if souls were to be snared, or persons of real piety to be punished. He seemed to take a malicious delight in bending the laws over to the side of perse-cution; and when no law existed which could be thus used, he either made or sought to procure one. He was probably more feared and detested than any man of his day."—Fletcher's History of Independency, vol. ii., p. 145.

‡ The archbishop's views on baptism are thus expressed :—"If I had a child dying without baptism, I should be doubtful of its salvation."— Brooke, vol. i., p. 268.

"Though I do not affirm," he also says, "that children dying without baptism will certainly be lost, yet, because I should fear and doubt the safety of their state, I would have them baptized by a woman rather than not at all."—Examination of Travers. Brooke, vol. ii., p. 319.

§ Reformation, vol. iv., p. 717. A Romish writer charges Elizabeth, in an infamous work published in 1538, with making the country a place of refuge for Atheists, Anabaptists, heretics, and rebels of all nations. The substance of this tract is in Lingard, vol. xiii., p. 535. Note B B.

It is difficult to ascertain with accuracy the extent to which these opinions prevailed. That they were widely diffused admits of no doubt. It has been affirmed by some, and those, too, not of Puritanic principles, that "the Church of England party,—that is, the party adverse to any species of ecclesiastical change,—was the least numerous of the three (parties) during this reign." Hallam, in a note, says, "The following observation will confirm (which may startle some readers) that the Puritans, or at least those who rather favoured them, had a majority among the Protestant gentry in the queen's days. It is agreed on all hands, and is quite manifest, that they predominate in the House of Commons. But that House was composed, as it has ever been, of the principal landed proprietors, and as much represented the general wish of the community when it demanded a further reform in religious matters, as on any other subject. One would imagine, by the manner in which some express themselves, that the discontented were a small faction, who, by some unaccountable means, in despite of the government and the nation, formed a majority of the Parliament under Elizabeth and her two successors."*

Of the prosperity of the kingdom under Elizabeth's government, there can be no doubt. To better hands than those of her ministers, the destinies of a great nation could not be entrusted. Many and grievous as were the civil disabilities under which society groaned; despotic and violent as she ever was; thoroughly politic, *i.e.*, knowing no other rule of action but self-interest in all her dealings with others; trampling on all right in her dealings with some of the most learned and moral of her subjects; yet in all the material elements of prosperity, and the humanizing influence of literature, science, and commerce, her reign had never been surpassed. To her country's well-being, according to her view of what would contribute to it, she was unquestionably

---

* Constitutional History, vol. i., p. 189 (Note).

devoted. On all these grounds she merits the glowing and unbroken eulogy which succeeding ages have awarded her. Beyond this truth cannot go. On other grounds the present generation can give her no praise. The imposing splendour of the sensual blinded her contemporaries to the violation of truth and high moral principles, on which too many of her public measures were based. The haziness is past, and we of the present can look at her conduct in a clearer light, and analyze it with more calmness.

No one, with right conceptions of the nature of true religion, can become familiar with the personal character of this princess without great pain. The head of the church, the great reformer of the religion of the state, claiming the right to dictate to her subjects what they should believe and how they should express their homage to and dependence on God, and inflicting the severest punishment upon them for disobedience; yet, the more we know of the hidden springs of her actions, and the character of her doings, the more the conviction is forced on the mind, that her ignorance of its pure and vitalizing power was profound. Bishops praised her "as the good and godly queen," and the holy incense of Episcopal worship was never wanting to sustain her vanity, and blind her to her real state; but she could "swear like a trooper," and, to say the least,—perhaps stern truth would demand a more decided verdict,—could violate all those decencies which invest female nature with its sweetest charm. The hypocrisy of Leicester, one of her chief favourites, was as deep as his conduct was loathsome. Quoting the sacred volume like a divine, mingling with the Puritan leaders, and ever and anon throwing around them the shield of his high protection, in private life he was luxuriating in every sensual gratification.* The court of Mary

---

* "The queen," said Cecil, "was rushing on to destruction. She had made Lord R. Dudley master of her government and of her own person. Only the fear of France and Mary Stuart prevented the dethronement of Elizabeth."—*Vide* Fraser's Magazine. The article is startling from its revelations. The date, unfortunately, has been mislaid.

would compare with that of her virgin sister with great advantage.* Make all possible allowance for the social condition of society in those days, and enough will remain to justify the decision. Her court was by no means of a higher order. Vice was not very sharply rebuked, and many of her favourites were men of the most profligate habits.†
"Elizabeth, we have no doubt whatever, ran herself into great danger; she indulged in most unbecoming and almost degrading familiarities; she went to the very verge of virtue, but there is no positive evidence that she ever actually overstepped the line." Referring to her connexion with Hatton, the same writer says: "It proves that Elizabeth's passion for Hatton had carried her to lengths quite unbecoming her position: it does not positively prove that it had carried her to the extremest length of all. Our own notion of the relation between them is, she did certainly 'descend very much in her sex as a woman;' and perhaps 'frailties,' not used in the technical sense, might not be too strong an expression. Still this testimony is quite explicit enough to hinder us from pronouncing a positive judgment in her favour, though individually we certainly incline to that side of the balance, and they are almost damaging enough to convert our verdict of 'not guilty,' into one of 'not proven.'" ‡

"Elizabeth was coarse and savage in her personal tastes, we should almost think beyond the standard of her time, though from her capacity she might be fairly expected to

---

* "It was a place in which, according to Faust, 'all enormities reigned in the highest degree.' 'The only discontent I have is to live where there is so little godliness and exercise of religion, so dissolute manners and corrupt conversation generally.'"—Birch, vol. i., pp. 25, 39. *Apud* Lingard, vol. viii., p. 501. (Note.)

† "No married man could hope to retain her favour if he lived on terms of affection with his wife."—Strickland's Queens of England.

‡ Quarterly Review, June 1854, pp. 240-1, 3. Letters given by Sir N. H. Nicholas, in his Life of the Chancellor, express the feelings of the most impassioned lover, if not something more. Dr. H. Campbell, in his "Case of Mary Queen of Scots, and Elizabeth," has raked up, with a malicious pleasure, all the scandal about the latter. —*Vide* Camden, Lingard, Froude, Strickland, &c., &c.

have risen above it." Of her swearing we have spoken. The degrading vice was habitual. It frequently accompanied her infliction of personal chastisement on her maids of honour.* From her royal lips the oath would come, before the Tudor spirit prompted her to spit upon her courtiers, or to box the ears of the gallant Essex. In bull-baiting and bear-baiting she delighted. The latter was one of her favourite pastimes. On one occasion, going to hear a sermon at St. Mary's, Spital, she was followed by two white bears in a cart, that at the close of her devotions they might be ready to contribute to her more congenial gratification.†

"Many good people who are scandalized at the Latin plays at Westminster, will be surprised that in the pious days of England, in the glorious morning of the Reformation, in 'great Elizabeth's golden time,' under kings and queens that were the nursing fathers and mothers, the public acting of plays should be, not the permitted recreation, but the compulsory employment of children devoted to sing the praises of God,—of plays too, the best of which children may now only read in a 'family' edition, some of whose titles a modern father would scruple to pronounce before a woman or a child."‡

Of the religious state of the kingdom, one of the most candid writers on this period of our religious history says: "Towards the conclusion of her reign, the example of the court of Elizabeth was decidedly irreligious, and the contagion spread rapidly among the common people."§ On the

---

* "The queen hath of late used the fair Mrs. Bridge with words and blows of anger."—Sidney Papers. *Apud* Strickland, vol. vii., p. 197.

† She delighted in those brutal sports which marked her era. Bear-baiting formed a prominent feature in many of the festivities which greeted her in those visits to the nobility which her penuriousness or her policy induced her to pay. She had her own master of the bears and dogs, and H. Coleridge tells us that a farthing a day was the salary attached to this office. Men of distinction and wealth frequently held it.—Note on Introduction to the Plays of Massinger, p. 32. Guizot's Shakspeare.

‡ Coleridge's Massinger, p. 36. *Vide* Guizot's Shakspeare, p. 53.

§ Marsden, p. 239. "How cometh it to pass that the common people

other hand, of those whom she and her surpliced flatterers had sought, by every form of oppression, to extirpate, he says, "But after all, the preponderance of real piety lay, we suspect, at the close of the reign of Elizabeth, amongst those who were roughly classed as Puritans. So much constancy in suffering, a zeal as fervent, domestic habits, by the confession of their bitterest enemies, so pure and blameless, religious duties properly discharged in the face of scorn and the instant dread of punishment, can in justice be regarded only as the marks of a piety sincere and deeply seated."* This witness is true. They were the best, the most laborious, and conscientious of her clergy.†

The closing scenes which marked the last days of this mighty queen are most affecting. We can scarcely realize them without the profoundest sorrow. The graphic pen of Sir J. Harrington thus describes her in October, 1601:—"Her taste for dress was gone; she had not changed her clothes for many days. Nothing could please her; she was the torment of the ladies who waited on her person. She stamped with her feet, and swore violently at the objects of her anger. For her protection she had ordered a sword to be placed by her table, which she often took in her hand, and thrust with violence into the tapestry of her chamber."

Another writer says, "The queen kept her bed for fifteen days, besides the three she sat upon a stool; and one day, being pulled up by force, she obstinately stood upon her feet for fifteen hours. When she was near her end, the Council sent to her the Archbishop of Canterbury and other

---

in the country universally come so seldom to common prayer and divine service; and when they do come, be many times so vainly occupied there, or at least do not there as they should do, but for want of this discipline?" —The Lord Keeper's Speech, 1572. Parl. History, vol. i., p. 774.

* Marsden, pp. 244–5.

† "Then it came to pass, and very much, it must be admitted, from their own extravagance, that the Puritans were regarded in the court of Elizabeth, not as men of scrupulous minds, but as a party ill affected to the state."—Marsden, p. 59.

prelates, at the sight of whom she was much offended, cholericly rating them, 'bidding them be packing, saying she was no atheist, but she knew full well they were but hedge-priests.'"* Her kinsman, Sir R. Carey, informs us "that about six at night she made signs for the Archbishop of Canterbury and her chaplain to come near." After she had been examined by his grace as to the grounds of her faith, "he began to pray, and all that were by did answer him. After he had continued long in prayer, the old man's knees were weary: he blessed her, and meant to rise and leave her. The queen made a sign with her hand. My sister Scroope, knowing her meaning, told the bishop the queen desired he would pray still. He did so for a long half hour after, and then thought to leave her. She made, a second time, a sign for the archbishop to continue in prayer. He did so for half an hour more, with earnest cries to God for her soul's health, which he uttered with that fervency of spirit that the queen, to all our sight, much rejoiced thereat."† Exhausted by these efforts, she sank into a deep sleep, from which she never awoke. Thus died "Elizabeth, by the grace of God, Queen of England, France, and Ireland; defender of the true, ancient Catholic faith; most worthy Empress from the Arcade isles to the mountains of the Pyrenees." ‡

---

* Strickland, vol. vii., pp. 294–296.

† Morris, who had been imprisoned wrongfully for proposing a Bill to remedy some ecclesiastical evils, thus indignantly, in a letter to Burghley, writes: "I had thought that the judge ecclesiastical, being charged in the great Council of the realm, to the dishonour of God and of her majesty, of violation and pervertion of law and public justice, and wrong done unto the liberties and freedom of all her majesty's subjects, by their extorted oaths, wrongful imprisonment, lawless subscriptions, and unjust absolutions, would rather have sought means to be cleared of this mighty accusation, than to shroud themselves under the suppressing of the complaint, and shadow of my imprisonment."—Lodge's Illustrations of History, vol. ii., p. 444. Morris had forgot *who* had said, "Men love darkness rather than light, because their deeds are evil."

‡ Quarterly Review, January, 1854, p. 249.

THE FAMILY OF LOVE.

Since the note on page 79 was printed, we have obtained additional information about the founder of this sect. We are indebted to Professor Müller, of Amsterdam, for these details. "In the month of August, 1536, the great assembly of Anabaptists was held at Bockholt, in Westphalia, wherein the different directions (tendencies) among the defenders of Teleio baptism, were manifested and came to light, and were revealed to the conference. It was the grand crisis. Some of the most violent who had escaped from the fall of Munster, but had learnt nothing by that fall, ran as bands of pilgrims through the country, with Jan Willemsz at their head; they were the Anabaptist veri-nominis; others, more calm and sedate, wanting a chief, wandered or rambled as sheep who had no pastor, till they persuaded Menno, in December, 1536, or January, 1537, to place himself at their head. This is the origin of Doopsgezinden, or Teleio-baptists, in the Netherlands. A third party consisted of them who were less violent than the first in practice, but in theory as much fanatic, whom David George (Jovis) proceeded to win for himself, when he had (in November, 1536) his first vision, or pretended to have, from which time dates a total change in his life."

"Hendrik Niclas (or Niclaasson), in accordance with the numerous testimonies of history, began his preaching not before 1540, *i.e.*, four years *after* the severing of the Anabaptists and the Doop; and I may therefore state, with an able historian of our denomination, that *he was not* a Doopsgezinden, nor an adherent of Menno. He was, in many respects, a follower of David Jovis,—not as this man was in the first period of his life (1536), but in the latter. After the removal of David Jovis to Basle, H. Niclas became the leader of his followers in the Netherlands, who had *separated themselves angrily from Menno;* and it may be that some few Doopsgezinden joined him perhaps at Embden.

Then these must have been banished persons, who were attracted and seduced by his boasting of the Love. Besides, H. Niclas did not disapprove of the taking of an oath, from the beginning down to our age considered and practised among us as interdicted by the word of Christ, a tenet which was always, and is now-a-days, respected even by the constitution and the law of the Netherlands. We agree herein with your church to admit of nothing as an article of faith, or of duty in the worship of God, which is not practised by apostolic precept or approved example."

His views on baptism, we may add, are invested in all but impenetrable mystery. The following is from a work called, "*The Upright Christian Faith of the Communion of Saints of the Family of Love, wherein also the upright Christian's Baptism is testified and confessed.*" In the eighth article of this tract will be found the following words:—

"The upright believers, who follow Christ in death and life, are baptized in the living waters of the Holy Ghost by Christ, and superfused superabundantly with full clearness of God."

"We confess that all who are not founded in this upright faith of Christ, and are not baptized in the name of the Father, in the name of the Son, and in the name of the Holy Ghost, are not true Christians; and that, likewise, all who, without that upright faith and baptism, boast to be Christians, are false Christians. Therefore, nobody may boast to be a Christian, who, in the upright faith, has not received the true token of Christianity, viz., the true baptism in the name of the Father, and of the Son, and of the Holy Ghost, or who carries not, essentially, their names in himself. Otherwise he will be found false and lying in the day of love of the righteous judgment before all the saints of God, who are comprised in the communion."*

---

* Letter of Professor Müller. There is a life of David George, by Mr. Cramer, minister of the Mennonite church at Middleburg. Additional information on this sect will be found in the volume of tracts on Liberty of Conscience; Appendix, B. K. Society.

CHAPTER VI.

THE STUART DYNASTY.—JAMES THE FIRST.

WITH a new race of princes, a new, and in many important respects, very different era opened on this England of ours. The Tudor spirit had expended itself. The imperial majesty of the last, and incomparably the greatest, of the race, found no resemblance in the feeble and pedantic character of her successor. Events of the most disastrous kind, and others unfolding the loftiest and purest principles, marked this reign. National honour was never so debased; civil and spiritual tyranny ruled with an iron sceptre; law, both human and divine, was sacrificed to profligate ambition and the lust of power; yet, in the very depths of our national degradation, men were found with the love of liberty so quenchless that they vindicated the rights of humanity, and threw before the world such views of political and moral science as have commanded the homage of the wise and good till the present day.

The seeds of these great changes had been sown during the latter periods of the former dynasty. The great religious movement,—the awakened mind,—the spread of religious truth,—the wide diffusion of the Sacred Scriptures,—the influence of commerce, and other causes, demanded, and of necessity produced them. Elizabeth's strong arm was too feeble to roll back the deepening and swelling torrent of national progress. She frowned, stormed, and threatened, either in person or by the lips of her lord keepers, but her faithful Commons spoke, tremblingly at first, but louder and more firmly the voice of the rising genius of British liberty was heard in the utterances of the Wentworths, the Morrises, the Stricklands, and others. The seeds of constitutional and religious freedom were sown; the harvest, during the reign of the Stuarts, was abundant.*

No careful and candid reader of our history at this period can be ignorant of the fact, or insensible to the influence it exerted, that popular liberty carried on a long and triumphant struggle with despotic and arbitrary power. James's kingcraft was his boast. His son was animated by the same delusion. The divine right of monarchs to do wrong,—to oppress their people,—was a doctrine ardently cherished by them.

No despots of the past ever put forth more blasphemous pretensions. The Senate was doomed, at Whitehall, where they had been summoned, to listen to these words:— "Kings are justly called gods, for that they exercise a manner or resemblance of divine power upon the earth; for if you will consider the attributes of God, you shall see how they agree in the person of a king. God hath power to create or destroy, to make or unmake at his pleasure; to give life or send death; to judge all, and be judged nor accountable to none; to raise low things, and to make high things low at his pleasure; and to God both soul and body are due. And the like power have kings. They make and unmake their subjects; they have power of raising and casting down; of life and death; judges over all their subjects and in all causes; and yet accountable to none but God only. They have power to exalt low things and abase high things, and make of their subjects like men at chess, a pawn to take a bishop or a knight, and to cry up or down any of their subjects as they do their money. And to the king is due both the affections of the soul and the services

---

* Referring to a vindication of its privileges by the House of Commons, in 1571, Lingard says, "This victory was owing to that tone of mind which religious enthusiasm always imparts. It formed a new era in the history of the House of Commons. The members learned to cherish their privileges, to think more highly of their own importance, to resist with greater confidence the arbitrary pretensions of the crown."—History of England, vol. v., p. 318. 4to.

of the body of his subjects."* To such lofty claims were the true manhood of England, at this time, doomed to listen!

To his kingcraft the monarch still clung. Age, and repeated defeats, brought no wisdom to his councils; and in 1621 he thus insulted the patriotism of England in a letter to the Commons:—"These are, therefore, to command you to make known," he said in a letter to the Speaker, to be read to the assembled Commons of England, "in our name, unto the House, that none therein shall presume henceforth to meddle with anything concerning our government, or deep matters of state; and, namely, not to deal with our dearest son's match with the daughter of Spain, nor to touch the honour of that king, or any other our friends and confederates; and, also, not to meddle with any man's particulars which have their due motives in our ordinary courts of justice. . . . You shall resolve, then, in our name, that we think ourselves very free and able to punish and warn misdemeanants in parliament, as well during their sitting as after; which we mean not to spare hereafter, upon any occasion of any man's insolent behaviour there, that shall be ministered unto us.—From Newmarket, December 3rd, 1621."†

His successors clung to the pleasing delusion. But constitutional liberty advanced. Long and fierce was the contest. Step by step the Eliots, the Hampdens, the Pyms, and others of the noble band of patriots who have shed lustre on the British name, advanced in spite of bribes,

---

* Works, pp. 529, 531. He issued a proclamation forbidding his subjects, from the highest to the lowest, from speaking of state affairs, or discussing the conduct of any of the princes in alliance with him.—Aikin's Life of James, vol. ii., p. 195.

† *Ibid*, vol. ii., pp. 281-2. "I heard that the Lord Coke, amongst other offensive speeches, should say to his majesty that his highness was defended by the laws. At which saying, with other speeches then used by the Lord Coke, his majesty was very much offended, and told him he spake foolishly, and said that he was not by his laws, but by God."—Letter to the Earl of Shrewsbury, 1608. Lodge, vol. iii., p. 250.

intimidation, and royal frowns, till the death of Charles proclaimed the overthrow of despotic, of irresponsible power. Later on, the expulsion of James from a throne which he had degraded, and a nation whose liberties he had betrayed, proclaimed the fact that nations were not made for kings, but kings for the people.

Parallel with this was the great and glorious struggle for religious freedom. The progress of the one may always be measured by the advancement of the other. On the side of civil despotism a State Church is generally found. In this case it was so. The flattery of the hierarchy was fulsome in the extreme. Beyond all other men, it encouraged these unhappy princes in their headlong career. The past shows us that a dominant, wealthy, and insolent church is a fearful national curse. That it is a violation of all right, and of necessity has the will, if not the power, to oppress any dissident from its dogmas, or the form of its worship. True statesmanship will always regard and treat it as such. Many of Elizabeth's most sage counsellors felt this. Burghley, Knollis, Walsingham, Leicester, and others, protected many of the persecuted from the crushing fury of the bishops. The successive defeats of the dissidents augmented the insolence of the spiritual princes of the church. The divine right of Episcopacy, broached by Bancroft, was hailed by his brethren. Parker and his brethren had flogged with whips; now the hierarchy used scorpions. With these lofty pretensions, the corruption of Christian doctrine proceeded.

Laud's influence was disastrous in the extreme. He centered the suspicion of the nation on his proceedings, and awakened the fear of the wise and good. The freedom of thought would have been repressed.* A striking instance of this is seen in James's dealing with the great

---

* "The clergy had begun by advancing that the king's authority was sufficient to reform what was amiss in any of his own courts; all jurisdictions, spiritual and temporal, being annexed to his crown."—Hallam, vol. i., p. 324.

Seldon. Referring to a confutation of his History of Tythes, he said, "If you, or any of your friends, shall write against this confutation, I will throw you into prison."* Difference of opinion would have entailed the loss of all that is dear to man in his social and civil relations. Upon the ruins of the nation's dignity he would have based the authority of the church. The senate became a theological school. The most important doctrines,—the Calvinist and Arminian theories,—the tendencies of the high-church principle,—are ever mingled up with "the great remonstrance," and "petitions for the redress of grievances." The Commons felt that the triumph of Laud would be the destruction of those liberties for which they had so long and so earnestly striven. The prostration of the church was the necessary effect. By its degrading flattery to civil despotism,—by the unholy dependence it placed on the will of kings,—by the readiness with which it lent all its power to rivet the chains of slavery on the neck of the people,—it was identified by the popular will as the supporter, if not the originator, of all that was oppressive in kingly government, and the fall of the monarchy was the overthrow of the power of the church. These elements, and others which the historian of this era notices, essentially distinguished the Stuart dynasty. No period of the modern history of this nation is so fraught with national debasement and disaster, as well as with that which gives us brighter proofs of the nation's power, and the unsullied dignity of true Englishmen. With a race of princes the most worthless, we have a race of patriots whose names will excite the veneration of the wise and good in all ages: with a race of statesmen ever ready to sacrifice right to the will of a monarch, we have, in the speeches, the writings, and acts of others, the soundest principles of political science: with a race of bishops, captivated only with the sensual and the formal, who delighted more in compelling the observance of senseless trifles than in the proclamation of Christian virtue or the

---

* Aikin's James I., vol. i., p. 131.

moral improvement of the people, we have divines whose writings will be a ceaseless spring at which the faithful, throughout all time, will quench their thirst for the knowledge of the Lord. Beyond all doubt, the dynasty of this unhappy family was one of extremes, during which the conflict of great principles wrought that change which ultimately placed the Dutchman on the throne, and laid a solid basis for our constitutional freedom.

The accession of James to the English throne was undisputed.* There were no competitors to excite alarm in his pathway. The claims of all who had disturbed the minds of his predecessors now centered in him. His proclamation, by Cecil and the Council, was immediate. The information reached the Scottish king in his capital. He was transported at the tidings. No possessor of the English throne had greater power or wider dominion than the founder of the House of Stuart. The three kingdoms bowed to his authority, and he felt that he had within his reach the means he had long coveted, of gratifying his ambition, and indulging those visions of royal magnificence which had long been floating before him.† His journey to the metropolis of his new dominion was by easy stages, and it was quite an ovation. He was marching to "the land of promise," and everywhere the greetings of his people were hearty and loud. Addressing

---

* James was born in the Castle of Edinburgh, 1566. Of the mode of his baptism there can be no doubt. "At convenient time you are to present her the font of gold, which we send with you. You may pleasantly say that it was made as soon as we heard of the prince's birth, and then it was big enough for him; but now he, being grown, is too big for it. Therefore it may be better used for the next child, provided that it be christened before it outgrow the font."—Keith, p. 357. Turner, vol. iv., p. 86 (Note).

James also refers to "the font wherein I was christened."—Works. London, 1616. Of Prince Henry's baptism the reader will find a lengthy account in a volume of Tracts illustrative of Traditional History of Scotland. Edinburgh, 1836.

† Lingard, vol. vi., p. 3. 4to.

his first parliament, he thus alludes to it:—"Shall I ever, nay, can I ever be able, or rather so unable in memory as to forget your unexpected readiness and alacrity, your ever memorable resolution, and your most wonderful conjunction and harmony of your hearts, in declaring and embracing me as your undoubted and lawful king and governor? Or shall it ever be blotted out of my mind how, at my first entry into this kingdom, the people of all sorts rid and ran, nay, rather flew to meet me;—their eyes flaming nothing but sparkles of affection, their mouths and tongues uttering nothing but sounds of joy; their hands, feet, and all the rest of their members, in their gestures, discovering a passionate longing and earnestness to meet and embrace their new sovereign?"*

The hopes and fears of the great religious parties gathered around the new chief of the nation. There were grounds on which all were warranted to expect the favour of the monarch. Romanists recalled the devotedness and suffering of his mother for the old faith, and the sympathy which the Scottish king had, not unfrequently, manifested with it;† and though, probably, despairing of the restoration of their church to its former supremacy and glory, yet they very naturally expected a modification of the sharp laws under which they had suffered during the former reign.

The Nonconformists, and even the Separatists, on the other hand, were sanguine that not only would their claims be heard by a sympathizing judge, but that large and important concessions would be made to their just and Scriptural demands. The ground on which these hopes were based was broad and solid. The discipline of Geneva had been enthroned in the northern kingdom, by the successful efforts of Knox and his brethren. James had been nurtured in it. All his

---

* Parl. History, vol. i., p. 977. James's speech to his Parliament.

† He even solicited the Pope to confer a cardinal's hat on Drummond, Bishop of Vaison.—Aikin's James I., vol. i., p. 33. Lingard, vol. ix., p. 439. (Note.)

public acts were associated with it. The English Episcopate, and the constitution of the church, had been condemned by him in the severest language, and on his own kirk he had lavished the warmest expressions of affection. They had not forgotten, that "with head uncovered and hands uplifted to heaven, he had protested that their Presbyterian Church was the purest in the world; that the English service was but an evil said mass in English; and that except the adoration of the host, it wanted nothing of the mass itself."* The church had more reason for alarm. Hope and fear would mingle in the minds of the prelates at the prospect of the change which the growing infirmities of Elizabeth assured them could not be distant. The succession of a Presbyterian monarch to a queen devoted to the most splendid Episcopacy in the world, was an event which might be disastrous. But wise men swayed the destinies of the church at this crisis, though not invested with spiritual power. Another religious revolution would be fearful. The contending elements were more varied and powerful now than before, and there was no master mind to grasp and control them. The sympathies of the leading statesmen at this time, from many causes, would be in favour of the hierarchy. Whitgift, too, was alert. His emissaries had visited the monarch. Of the devotedness of the prelates to his interest he was fully assured; and if the royal word was of any worth, their fears were allayed by the assurance of James, that without their counsel and consent he would make no alteration in the ecclesiastical condition of the kingdom. The bishops had promised him an obsequiousness to which he had been little accustomed, and a zeal to enhance his prerogative which they afterwards too well displayed.†

Old Thomas Fuller, in his quaint, but racy style, thus describes the conflict:—"And now it is strange with what

---

* In 1590, before his Parliament.—Marsden, p. 249.
† Hallam's History, p. 297.

assiduity and diligence the two potent parties, the defenders of Episcopacy and Presbytery, with equal hopes of success, made (besides particular and private addresses) public and visible application to King James I.; the first to continue, the latter to restore, or rather to set up their government. So that whilst each side was jealous his rival should get the start by early stirring, and rise first in the king's favour, such was their vigilance that neither may seem to go to bed; incessantly diligent, both before and since the queen's death, in despatching posts and messages into Scotland, to advance their several designs," &c.*

Such was the condition of religious parties when the first of the Stuarts came to take possession of his long-coveted crown. The character of James presents us with a singular mixture of contrarieties. A glance at it is requisite to our design. The present has reversed the decisions of the past. "The Solomon of his age" is now regarded as only, in the language of a contemporary, "the wisest fool in Christendom."† Extremes seem to have centered in him. With the loftiest pretensions to political wisdom, his simplicity was extreme.‡ Boasting of his unbounded authority, he was governed by a succession of the most unprincipled and worthless men. With a style of the most imposing regality there were associated vices of the lowest and most degrading kind. Grave at times, yet volatile; impetuous, yet patient; studious, yet frivolous;—in a word, so varied and changing as to justify the conflicting opinions which the pen of history has recorded both of the man and the king. His duplicity was unbounded. "Early trained to dissimulation, by the time he was sixteen his mastery in this despicable art was entire. No motive had power to influence him which did

---

* Church History, book ix., p. 5. *Vide* Bishop Goodman's Court of James I., vol. i., p. 28. (Note.)

† Sir P. Warwick's Memoirs, p. 3. (Note.)

‡ "Sagacity that often wore the appearance of consummate wisdom, of folly scarcely distinguishable from that of an idiot."—Marsden, p. 247.

not touch his personal gratification or selfish interest. Lost to all filial affection, the sufferings of his misguided and unfortunate mother were lost upon him."* Of the extent to which this despicable vice was cultivated by James, we can have no more striking instance than his treatment of his all-powerful favourite, upon whose worthless head he had showered the highest honours:—" The Earl of Somerset never parted from him (James) with more seeming affection than at this time, when he knew Somerset should never see him more. . . The Earl, when he kissed his hand, the king hung about his neck, slubbering his cheeks, saying, 'For God's sake, when shall I see thee again? On my soul, I shall neither eat nor sleep until you come again.' The Earl told him on Monday (this being on Friday). 'For God's sake let me,' said the king; 'shall I—shall I?' then lolled about his neck. 'Then, for God's sake, give thy lady this kiss for me.' The Earl had scarcely entered his coach before the monarch said, 'I shall never see his face more.'"† His extravagance was boundless. "Already," says Cecil, " our sovereign spends £100,000 yearly in his house, which was wont to be but £50,000."‡ Coming from a country where money was scarce, he had no conception of its value, and he squandered away the treasure of the kingdom with the most lavish hands on many of his needy countrymen

---

* Lingard, vol. viii., p. 214. "But his opinion is, that it cannot stand with his honour that he be a consenter to take his mother's life; but he is content how strictly she be kept, and all her old knavish servants hanged, chiefly they who be in hand."—The Master of Grey (James's Ambassador, 1586), Goodman, vol. i., p. 129.

† Court and Character of James I. Secret History of James I., vol. i., pp. 411–12.

Tytler says, "He was influenced by favourites through life." He was "an early adept in diplomatic hypocrisy." "The king was known to be so great a dissembler that few trusted his professions."—History of Scotland, vol. viii., pp. 133, 203, 245, 333. "James, however, was all his life rather a bold liar than a good dissembler."—Hallam, vol. i., p. 297.

‡ Cecil to Lord Shrewsbury, September, 1603. Lodge's Illustrations, vol. iii., p. 34.

who followed him,* and the worthless favourites who ruled him according to their will.† "Such were the crowds that followed his majesty of the former, that the Privy Council issued orders to prevent the emigration of his northern subjects to the newly-acquired English Goshen."‡ His wants were always great, and his recklessness often brought him into collision with his Commons, and led him to the adoption of means for raising of money which laid the foundation of the ruin of his son, and the disasters which more or less marked his family. Bribery was shameless, and the sale of all offices was notorious.§

This rough outline of the character of the king is requisite to our design. Ignorant of it, the facts which our subsequent narrative will embody would lose much of their interest.

At an early period the Puritans laid their claims before the Presbyterian monarch. Their grievances were embodied in a petition. It was called the Millionary one, from the number of subscribers to it.|| Their demands were moderate. At no time could they have been conceded with a better

---

* "This vast treasure was bestowed on the needy Scots, who, like horse-leeches, sucked the exchequer dry; so that honour and offices were set to sale to fill the Scots' purses and empty the kingdom's treasure."—Sir E. Payton's Catastrophe of the House of Stuart. Secret History of James I., vol. ii., p. 343.

† "His favourite Scot, who from a lowly position was raised to the highest honour. His tyranny for a season was complete. Offices about the court were sold to the highest bidder: no plunder of the public was obtained without purchase; and the king's titles were bought and sold, whilst no seclusion could resist the intrusion of his potent influence."—Thomson's Life of Villiers, Duke of Buckingham, vol. i., p. 91.

‡ Osborne's Traditional Memorials of James I. Secret History of the Court of James I., vol. i., p. 143.

§ "Every inferior department which was not filled by their relations or dependents, was sold without scruple to the highest bidder."—Lingard, vol. ix., p. 151. *Vide* note also. Proof of this abounds in Lodge's Illustrations, vol. iii.

|| "It was subscribed by 825 ministers, from twenty-five counties."—Hallam, vol. i., p. 296.

grace. "Many of these have since been wrung, by a necessity they could not resist, from churchmen of succeeding days; some, in a far better spirit, have been cheerfully conceded in our own time, by churchmen as well-affected, as learned, and as pious as the most unyielding of their forefathers."* We need not recapitulate their claims. We have mentioned them before. They asked for nothing which was inconsistent with the existence of the established hierarchy.

Policy demanded that some regard should be paid to their modest request. A conference was proposed. Some of the most eminent of the nonconforming clergy should meet with the bishops, and in a Christian and fraternal spirit confer, under the presidency of the king, on the various points in dispute. Hampton Court was selected as the place for this celebrated ecclesiastical gathering. The project was suited to the tastes of the king. It would give the royal theologian, who had been trained in all the dialectics of the schools in his northern states, an opportunity of exhibiting his skill in the discussion; whilst his fairness, in trying to hold the balance between the contending parties, and to bring them into a more fraternal union, would be manifest to his people. But it was one of the first pieces of kingcraft with which he sought to betray and impose on his people. A more glaring and shameful piece of hypocrisy was never practised in the worst days of Romish tyranny. Four Puritans and eighteen churchmen, with the king at their head, met on the 14th of January, 1603. The archbishops of both provinces, eight bishops, seven deans, and two others, formed the clerical party. On the other side were Dr. Reynolds, Dr. Sparkes, Mr. Knewstubs, and Mr. Chaderton. Everything, after the first day's proceedings, was a mere sham. Practically, the monarch and his ecclesiastical staff had settled the matter before the representatives of the dissenting brethren had uttered a word in conference. "During the

---

* Marsden, p. 251.

first day," says a candid writer, "the Puritans were not present, being expressly excluded by his majesty's commands. Yet in their absence the questions were discussed, *and, in fact, decided, on which they were most anxious to obtain a hearing.* The king opened the proceedings with a speech, in which he expressed his satisfaction that he was in the presence of grave, learned, and reverend men; not as before, elsewhere, a king without state, without honour; where beardless boys braved him to his face. He said he was averse to any innovations; at the same time, should anything be found to need redress, he wished it to be done, though as quietly as possible, and without any visible alteration; a remark which he several times repeated; and on this account he had called in the bishops by themselves."*
Over three days this farce was extended. The arguments of the Puritans were heard only with contempt and insolence. Truth was with them, but the union of royal and episcopal interest triumphed over them for a season. We cannot narrate the proceedings of this synod. Our readers will find ample details of them in the authors indicated below.† We can only give one sample of the way in which the royal theologian dealt with questions which were shaking the church to its centre. Dr. Reynolds had been pleading for the restoration of the prophesyings, as Grindal and other dignitaries of the church had recommended. For the benefit of the church, and the more efficient discharge of clerical duty, he also advocated provincial synods, under the presidency of the bishops. "The king," says Bishop Barlow, "was stirred at this; yet, which was admirable in him, without passion or show, thinking that they aimed at a Scotch Presbytery, which he said agreed with monarchy as God and the devil. 'Then Jack and Tom, and Will and Dick shall meet, and, at their pleasure, censure me and my Council, and all our proceedings: then Will shall stand up

---

* Marsden, p. 257. † Marsden, Price, Neal, Brooks, Fletcher, &c.

and say, "It must be thus;" then Dick shall reply, and say "Nay, marry, but we will have it thus;" and here I must once reiterate my former speech, *Le roy s' avisera,*'" &c.* Looking at Dr. Reynolds, the royal hypocrite said, "Well, doctor, have you anything else to say?" *Dr. Reynolds.* "No more, if it please your majesty."—*The King.* "If this be all your party hath to say, I will make them conform themselves, or else I will harry them out of the land, or else do worse." "The jeers and pleasantries of Jeffries, on the judgment seat, were scarcely more unfeeling."† From the character of the monarch, as already delineated, our readers will feel no surprise at his treatment of these Christian men. But what shall we say of the bishops? They were the anointed of the Lord; the successors of apostolic men; yet the profound learning of Reynolds, the holy character of his colleagues, the moral worth and transparent sincerity of their and the doctor's motives, ought to have called forth manifestations of the most exalted tenderness and sympathy. But littleness, under the mask of lofty pretensions, in the flush of triumph, never feels thus. His Grace of Canterbury, in the fulness of his joy, exclaimed, "that, undoubtedly, his Majesty spake by the especial assistance of God's Spirit." The Bishop of London, on his knees, protested "that his heart melted within him, as, he doubted not, did the hearts of the whole company, with joy, and made haste to acknowledge to Almighty God, his singular mercy in giving us such a king, as since Christ's time the like had not been seen." So writes the episcopal historian of this celebrated conference. Well might a subsequent member of the same church, compelled by the force of truth, say, in reference to this, "that the scene that followed was one of the most humiliating upon the page of English history." "The Puritans had been unfairly treated, browbeaten, jeered at, silenced."‡

---

* Collier, vol. ii., p. 681. † Marsden, p. 262.
‡ *Ibid*, pp. 266–7. Welwood's Memoirs, p. 21. Mosheim's Ecclesiastical History, vol. v., p. 386.

We will only add a sentence or two from one of the most able of modern historians, but by no means one partial to the character of the Puritans. "His measures towards the Nonconformist party had evidently been resolved upon before he summoned a few of their divines to the famous conference at Hampton Court. In the account that we read of this meeting, we are alternately struck with wonder at the indecent and partial behaviour of the king, and at the abject baseness of the bishops, mixed, according to the custom of servile natures, with insolence towards their opponents."*

The spirit of the monarch manifested itself, in relation to religion, in the proclamation for his first parliament. After various directions, he says:—"Next, and above all things, considering that one of the main pillars of this estate is the preservation of unity in the profession of sincere religion of Almighty God, we do also admonish that there be great care taken to avoid the choice of any persons, either noted for their superstitious blindness one way, or for their turbulent humour other ways, because their disorderly and unquiet spirits will disturb all the discreet and modest proceedings in that greatest and gravest Council."†

His hatred to the Puritans was intense. In a letter, supposed to be addressed to the Earl of Dunbar, his treasurer in Scotland, he says: "And so farewell from my wilderness, which I had rather live in (as God shall judge me), like an hermit in his forest, than be a king over such a people as the pack of Puritans are that overrule the Lower House."‡

James held "no bishop, no king," for as real an article in the mystery of monarchy, as they did "no ceremony, no bishop," in that of the hierarchy.§

---

* Hallam's Constitutional History, vol. i., p. 297.
† Parliamentary History, vol. i., p. 968.
‡ Hallam's Constitutional History, vol. i., p. 308.
§ Court of James I. Secret History, vol. i., p. 175.

It is not very difficult to account for this. The pliancy of the Episcopate, and the imposing splendour of its ceremonies, were in perfect harmony with James's notion of his regal state, and deepened his dislike to the naked platform of Geneva and the republican notions of its advocates, to a great extent, no doubt. He believed the bishops "were useful instruments to turn a limited monarchy into absolute dominion, and subjects into slaves, the design in the world he minded most." Upon men like James this would operate with invincible power. We have a glance at it in his address to Dr. Reynolds. The Jack and Tom, the Will and Dick, the beardless boys censuring him and his Council, were not fancies, but stern realities. The experience of the past suggested this. The Presbyterian power had checked him in his northern states. The struggle between his despotic authority and the liberal tendencies of the reformed clergy had been long and fierce. No monarch in Christendom had been more roughly handled by his spiritual teachers. Humbled by stern advocates of freedom, preached at in public assemblies, the worst terms of reproach applied to his majesty, deprived of liberty for months, his experience of the Presbyterian government was destitute of every element of pleasure. "Admit that our king be a Christian king," said John Ross, in a sermon, in 1594, "yit, but amen de ment, he is a reprobate king. Of all the men in this nation, the king himself is the maist fynest, and maist dissembling hypocrite." "All kings," said David Black, two years later, "were children of the devil; but that in Scotland the head of the court was Satan himself." James's vocabulary of abuse was not scanty. "Loanes, smaikes, snivelling knaves," were terms often applied by the royal lips to these holy men. He "frequently declared that he never looked upon himself to be more than King of Scotland in name, till he came to be King of England; but now, he said, one kingdom would help him to govern the other, or he had studied kingcraft to very little purpose from his cradle to that time."* These facts will throw much light on the ecclesiastical proceedings during his reign, both in relation to doctrine and the constitution of the church, to which we must now ask the attention of our readers.

Whitgift,† who had died soon after the Hampton Court conference, was succeeded in the primacy by the Bishop of London. Bancroft was a man after the king's own heart. A not unfriendly pen thus truthfully describes him:—
"Bancroft was a man of vehement zeal, but of the most grasping avarice, as appears by an epigrammatic epitaph on his death, in Arthur Wilson:—

> 'Here lies His Grace, in cold earth clad,
> Who died with want of what he had.'"

We find a characteristic trait of this Bishop of London, in this conference (Hampton Court). Ellesmere, Lord Chancellor, observed, that livings rather want learned men, than learned men livings, many in the universities pining for want of places: "I wish, therefore, that some may have single coats (one living) before others have doublets (pluralities); and this method I have observed in bestowing the king's benefices." Bancroft replied, "I commend your memorable care that way; but a doublet is necessary in cold

---

* We are indebted for these extracts to Buckle's History of Civilization, &c., vol. ii., chap. iii., p. 253; chap. iv., pp. 261-2. His pages are crowded with similar examples.

† Wigginton says, "The archbishop hath treated me more like a *Turk* or a *dog* than a man or a minister of Jesus Christ." Another Puritan of that day says, as quoted by Bancroft, "Of all the bishops that ever were in the see of the Archbishop of Canterbury, there was never any did so much hurt to the church of God as he hath done. No bishop that ever had such an aspiring and ambitious mind as he; no, not Cardinal Wolsey. None so proud as he; no, not Stephen Gardiner of Winchester. None so tyrannical as he; no, not Bonner. . . . He sits upon his cogging-stool, which may truly be called the chair of pestilence. His mouth is full of cursing against God and his saints. His feet are swift to shed blood. There is none of God's children but had as lieve see a serpent as meet him."—Hanbury's Mem., vol. i., p. 38.

weather." Thus an avaricious bishop could turn off, by a miserable jest, the open avowal of his love of pluralities.*

With the knowledge of the king's feeling towards the Puritans, the hierarchy entered on their work. The royal head of the church had agreed to interpose the shield of his protection against any attack on the Episcopate, while the spiritual lords had bound themselves to support the prerogative of the king. This understanding was early arrived at, and the ends aimed at were steadily pursued by both. Hallam has correctly said: "The real aim of the clergy in thus enormously enhancing the pretensions of the crown, was to gain its sanction and support for their own. Schemes of ecclesiastical jurisdiction, hardly less extensive than had warmed the imagination of Becket, now floated before the eyes of his successor, Bancroft. He had fallen, indeed, upon evil days, and perfect independence of the temporal magistrate could no longer be attempted; but he acted upon the refined policy of making the royal supremacy over the church, which he was obliged to acknowledge and professed to exaggerate, the very instrument of its dependence upon the law. The favourite object of the bishops in this age was to render these ecclesiastical jurisdictions, no part of which had been curtailed in our hasty reformation, as unrestrained as possible by the courts of law."†

In 1604, the first convocation after the accession of James was held. It has become memorable for its work. Bancroft presided, though only then Bishop of London, and the spirit of the dominant sect revealed itself. We cannot narrate all its proceedings. Suffice it to say, that the doctrine which had been propounded by Bancroft, so gratifying to Episcopal pride, that the bishops governed the church and the inferior clergy, *jure divino*, by a right derived from God alone, was affirmed. To deny the Church of England to be a true

---

* D'Israeli's Miscellaneous Literature, p. 331.
† Constitutional History, vol. i., p. 323.

church; to say that its worship was erroneous, or any part repugnant to Holy Scriptures, or that any of its ceremonies were superstitious; to deny the authority of archbishops, bishops, deacons, or to separate from the communion of the church, and form separate assemblies, was to expose the parties to excommunication. Bancroft and his brethren carried out these decisions with no gentle hand. The best of the clergy, finding no prospect of relief, were compelled to quit the church; some wasted their lives in prison, others escaped to foreign lands. Everything was done which the monarch and his spiritual advisers could do to crush out the spirit of Puritanism from the city and parochial churches, and their success must have exerted an all-powerful influence on the morals of society. It could not be otherwise. The policy of James and his minions could only be realized by exposing to scorn the teaching and saintly character of the Puritan ministers. The truthful pen of Lucy Hutchinson gives us some glimpses of the social and moral life of England at this time, while it presents us with the outline of the true Puritan character during the same trying period. "At court these were hated (the godly ministers), disgraced, and reviled, and in scorn had the name of Puritans fixed upon them. And now the ready way to preferment there was to declare an opposition to the power of godliness under that name: so that these pulpits might justly be called the scorner's chair; those sermons only pleasing that flattered them in their vices, and told the poor king that he was Solomon, that his sloth and cowardice, by which he betrayed the cause of God and the honour of the nation, was gospel meekness and peaceableness, for which they raised him above heaven, while he lay wallowing like a swine in the mire of his lust." In lower circles, "if any, out of mere morality and civil honesty, discountenanced the abominations of those days, he was a *Puritan*, however he conformed to the superstitious worship: if any showed favour to any godly, honest person, kept their company, relieved them in want, or protected them against violent or unjust oppressors, he was a *Puritan:* if any gentleman in his county maintained the good laws of the land, or stood up for any public interest, for good order or government, he was a *Puritan:* in short, all that crossed the views of the needy courtiers, the proud, encroaching priests, the thievish projectors, the lewd nobility and gentry; whoever was zealous for God's glory or worship, could not endure blasphemous oaths, ribald conversation, profane scoffs, Sabbath breach, derision of the Word of God, and the like; whoever could endure a sermon, modest habit, or conversation, or anything good, all these were *Puritans:* and if Puritans, then enemies to the king and his government, seditious, factious hypocrites, ambitious disturbers of the public peace, and finally, the pest of the kingdom: such false logic did the children of darkness use to argue with against the hated children of light, whom they branded besides as illiterate, morose, melancholy, discontented, crazed sort of men, not fit for human conversation: as such they made them not only the sport of the pulpit, which was become but a solemn sort of stage, but every stage, every table, and every puppet play, belched forth profane scoffs upon them; drunkards made them their songs; all fiddlers and mimics learned to abuse them, as finding it the most gainful way of fooling."* We will only add from another source the following:—"The vicious multitudes called all Puritans that were strict and serious in a holy life, though ever so conformable; so that the same name in a bishop's mouth signified a Nonconformist, and in an ignorant

---

* Memoirs of Colonel Hutchinson, pp. 27, 28. "The generality of the gentry of the land soon learned the court fashion, and every great house in the country became a sty of uncleanness."

Macaulay, referring to the habits of the Puritans, with the hand of a master sketches some of their leading traits. There is an element of truth in his description, but only a moiety. "It was a sin to hang garlands on a Maypole, to drink a friend's health, to fly a hawk, to hunt a stag, to play at chess, to wear lovelocks, to put starch into a ruff, to touch the virginals, to read the 'Fairy Queen.'"—History, vol. i., p. 81.

drunkard's mouth, a godly obedient Christian. Now the ignorant rabble hearing that the bishops were against the Puritans, were the more embolden against all those which they gave the name to, and their rage against the godly was the more increased; and they cried up the bishops, partly because they were against the Puritans, and partly because they were earnest for that way of worship which they found most suitable to their ignorance, carelessness, and formality; and thus the interest of the diocesans, and of the profane and ignorant sort of people, was unhappily twisted together."*

The glory of the hierarchy was the curse of the spiritual life of the church. The Calvinian element, which had still marked its teaching so late as Whitgift, and which, in an eminent degree, distinguished the Puritans, gradually, indeed rapidly, gave way to the Arminian, long before the close of James's reign.† Macaulay has truly said: "Opinions which, at the accession of James, no clergyman could have avowed without imminent risk of being stript of his gown, were now the best title to preferment. A divine of that age, who was asked by a simple country gentleman what the Arminians held, answered, with as much truth as wit, that they held all the best bishoprics and deaneries in England."‡ James had denounced Arminius. To the Synod of Dort he had sent some English divines to aid the Dutch in their opposition to his teaching; yet, under the same monarch, the views of the Dutch heretic were patronized, and shed a withering influence upon the religion of the nation.

---

* Baxter's Life, &c., by Calamy, p. 48.
† "Arminianism crept in, to the corruption of sound doctrines, till at length they had the impudence to forbid the preaching of those great and necessary truths concerning the decrees of God."—Mrs. Hutchinson's Life of her Husband, p. 27. Bohn's Standard Library.
‡ History of England, vol. i., pp. 79, 188.
"We know King James's round answer when some asked him wherefore he preferred not good men to bishoprics? 'The devil an honest man,' says he, 'will accept them.'"—Hanbury, vol. ii., p. 252.

Montague, Mainwaring, Sibthorpe, and Laud, names which will pass under review again, were the chief instruments in effecting this doctrinal change. The country was alarmed. The senate was alarmed. Arminianism and Popery were twins. The one always followed the other; and neither were compatible with the liberties of the nation. Again and again the House remonstrated with the thoughtless monarch on the progress of the error. Again and again the Senate House rung with the thunders of some zealous Puritan, as in glowing language he condemned the foe of British freedom. The records of parliament are full of them :—" I desire that we may consider the increase of Arminianism an error that maketh the Grace of God lackey it after the will of man : that maketh the sheep to keep the shepherd : and makes mortal seed of an immortal God. I desire that we may look into the very belly and bowels of this Trojan horse, to see if there be not in it men ready to open the gates of Romish tyranny and Spanish monarchy: for an Arminian is the spawn of a Papist; and if there come the warmth of court favour upon him, you shall see him turned into one of those frogs of the bottomless pit: and if you mark it well you will see an Arminian reaching out his hand to a Papist; a Papist to a Jesuit; a Jesuit gives one hand to the Pope and the other to the King of Spain," &c.* Mainwaring had been compelled to appear before the Commons and ask pardon for his doctrine. The House felt that the purity of Christian truth as well as the protection of liberty were in their keeping. The senate was the conservator of both. In the spirit of indignant remonstrance the following was added about Mainwaring :—"Yet was this man also immediately after our rising (when he was censured and obliged to ask pardon) released from his imprisonment, reported to have the honour to kiss the king's hand ; obtained his pardon in folio; was preferred to a rich living ;

---

* Speech of Mr. Rouse, 1628. Parliamentary History, vol. ii., pp. 444-5.

and, if some say true, cherished assured hopes of dignity in the church. If these be steps to church preferment, God be merciful to those churches which shall fall under the government and feeding of such a clergy," &c.* The fact is true, from whatever cause it may arise, that the pulpit was prostrated to the very worst of purposes. The contrast between this period and the era of the Reformation was very striking. The rugged boldness of Latimer and his brethren is wanting. "From the pulpit," says one, "came all our future missions, God not being served there as he ought. The court sermons informing his majesty he might, as Christ's vicegerent, command all, and that the people, if they denied him supplement, or inquired after the disposal of it, were presumptuous people unto the ark of the state; not to be done under the severest curse," &c.† The doctrines of passive obedience and non-resistance were more frequently heard than those of Paul. Bishop Goodman tells us that "these flatterers proceeded further, that if princes should intend to destroy their subjects, yet their subjects were bound to obey them : yea, further, if they should destroy all religion, and labour as much as possible to bring in atheism, yet their subjects had no other way to resist them but with their prayers and tears to God," &c.‡ "Yesterday Dr. Buckeridge preached before the king, and proved by Scripture and history, with many excellent examples, the supremacy of the king, and that in all ages the authority of the kings governed and ruled all presbyters and clergy. At this sermon were all the Puritans of Scotland that were here."§

The connexion between correct Christian doctrine and a holy life is closer than some suppose. The one will ever

---

* Speech of Sir R. Grosvenor, 1628. *Ibid*, pp. 470-1.

† Secret History of James I., vol. i., p. 193.

‡ Annals of James I., vol., i., p. 268. *Vide* Robinson's Claude, vol. ii., notes, for various examples.

§ Lodge, vol. iii., p. 186. Letter to the Earl of Shrewsbury, September 24th, 1606.

produce the other. Many of the clergy, both of the higher and lower order, were examples of this. It is said that the notorious Bishop of Lincoln, "when any one preached (before the king) who was remarkable for his piety, desirous of withdrawing the king's attention from truths he did not wish to have his majesty reminded of, would, in the sermon-time, entertain the king with a merry tale, which the king would laugh at, and tell those near him that he could not hear the preacher for the old bishop, prefixing an epithet expletive of the character of these merry tales."* The character of Williams, first Bishop of Lincoln, and afterwards raised to the Archiepiscopal See of York, is thus delineated:—"In Bacon's place comes Williams, a man on purpose brought in, at first to serve turns, but in this place to do that which none of the laity could be found bad enough to undertake; whereupon this observation was made, that first no layman could be found so dishonest as a clergyman."†

---

* Kennet's History of England, vol. ii., p. 729. D'Israeli's Modern Literature, p. 331. Of the same bishop the following is recorded:— "Andrews, Bishop of Winchester, and Neil of Ely, were present with James, soon after the Commons had refused him supplies in 1621, when the monarch asked them aloud 'if he might not levy money upon his subjects when he wanted it, without applying to parliaments?' 'God forbid,' said Ely, 'you might not! for you are the breath of our nostrils.' 'Well, my lord,' said James to Andrews, 'and what say you?' 'Sir,' said Winchester, 'I am not skilled in parliamentary cases.' 'No put-offs,' said the king, 'answer me presently.' 'I think, then,' said Andrews, 'that it is lawful for you to take my brother Neil's money, for he offers it.'"— Aikin's James I., vol. ii., p. 271.

† Court of James I. Secret History, vol. i., p. 449. Hackett, in his Life of Williams, mentions an instance of baseness and treachery which must always stamp his character with infamy. He says that in an interview with Buckingham, "his grace had the bishop's consent, with a letter asking that he would be his grace's faithful servant in the next session of parliament, and was allowed to hold up a seeming enmity, and his own popular estimation, that he might sooner do the work."— Life of Williams, pp. 77—80. He was not alone in this revolting work. Many episcopal dignitaries forgot the Christian in the base proceedings of the politician.

Lodge gives us the following illustration of the social life of many of the clergy of this period. It is the Vicar of Hope to whom he is referring:—"In the latter day, when all the justices but himself and one other were risen, he would have had the said vicar licensed to sell ale in his vicarage, although the whole bench had commanded the contrary; whereupon Sir J. Poole being advertised, returned to the bench (contradicting his speech), who, with Mr. Bainbridge, made this warrant to bring before them, him, or any other person that shall for him, or in his vicarage, brew or sell ale, &c. He is not to be punished by the justices for the multitude of his women, until the bastards whereof he is the reputed father be brought in."*

The alarm of the Commons at the Popish tendencies of James and his favourite advisers was not without foundation. Lingard admits that he was willing to connive at the silent introduction of the Catholic missionaries into the country, and even to receive one at court, as his tutor in the Italian language.† On another occasion James said:—"And for myself, if that were yet the question, I would with all my heart give my consent that the Bishop of Rome should have the first seat. I, being a western king, would go with the Patriarch of the West. And for his temporal principalities over the signories of Rome, I do not *quenell* it, neither let him in God's name be *primus* Episcopus inter omnes Episcopus et Princeps Episcoporum, so it be no other ways but as St. Peter was Princeps Apostolorum."‡

"Secret treaties were entertained with the court of Rome. . . . The Papists lost not their credit at court, where they now wrought no longer by open and direct ways, but

---

* Illustrations of English History, vol. iii., p. 280.

† History of England, vol. viii., pp. 190, 244; vol. ix., p. 154.

‡ Mrs. Thompson's Life of the Duke of Buckingham, vol. i., p. 364. He ordered his son's chaplain, when in Spain, to go "as near the Roman form as lawfully can be done, for it hath ever been my way to go with the church of Rome, usque et aras." *Ibid*, 377. *Vide* Marsden, pp. 343–45.

humouring the king and queen in their lusts and excesses, found the most ready way to destroy the doctrine of the Gospel was to debauch its professors."* No one conversant with his court and his favourite divines can doubt this. The power of Laud was increasing. By his influence everything in the church, which could, was made to resemble Rome as much as possible. He was the founder of the High Church School, which from that time to this has confounded the form with the substance, and ignored every claim to piety which does not bear the name and superscription of the Beast.

It would be difficult to trace, in the space we have allotted to ourselves, the effects of this combination of very powerful influences on the morals of the community at large. That they were of the very worst kind, admits of no doubt:— the luxury and corruptions of the court and the higher classes; the pride, the oppression, and the sycophancy of the bishops and the clergy;† and the ejection of the wisest and best of the Nonconforming ministers, largely contributed to this result.

The course of the narrative now demands advertence to another event, which has exerted an influence on the English Baptists. It transpired in that land from which so many had fled to our own island home, in the hope of protection from the power of the persecutors. Holland had sheltered large

---

* Mrs. Hutchinson, p. 27.

† "Tobey Mathews, Archbishop of York, on receiving some of James's works, threw himself on his knees to receive them from the messenger, kissed them, promised to keep them as the apple of his eye, and to read them over and over again."—Lingard, vol. ix., p. 105.

"Mr. Nichols, in his Plea of the Innocents, expressly affirms, p. 218, that conferring with the particular persons in his parish, after he had preached some good space amongst them, about the means of salvation, of four hundred communicants he scarce found one but that thought and professed a man might be saved by his own well-doing, and that he trusted he did so live by serving God and good prayers."—Robinson, vol. ii., p. 288.

numbers of Protestant refugees during the Marian persecutions. It now welcomed another class, glad to escape to its reclaimed swamps from the crushing tyranny of the Protestant hierarchy of England. It was about the year 1606. A company of Brownists or Separatists left for Amsterdam. An English church already existed there, but rather Puritan than Separatist. The exiles were headed by their pastor, J. Smith. He had ministered in the English church, but was compelled to leave it, and for some time he officiated probably as the pastor of a Separatist church, at Gainsbro', in Lincolnshire. Others followed, and in 1608, Robinson and most of the remaining members of his flock, arrived in the same city.* To trace the history of these pilgrims, the conflicts, the separations which marked them, is not our province. Only on one case we detain the attention of the reader,—the separation of John Smith and the formation of the English Baptist church in that city. We stop not to investigate the causes which led to this. Ivimey and Adam Taylor will supply this information to those who are curious enough to inquire into them. We do not dismiss the subject from want of interest. Whatever contributes to the formation of character, or is productive of results which affect communities, especially in their highest relations, can never be matter of indifference to the thoughtful.

Upon two points differences had grown up in the church. Smith, Helwys, and certain others had renounced the Calvinistic doctrine, and had embraced Arminianism. Holland, at this time, was shaken by the teaching of the man who gave his name to this system. The religious war was carried on with the fiercest spirit. Not only the English Separatists, but the Dutch churches, were divided by the strife. To calm it, and uproot the error, the Synod of Dort was convened.† England sent some of her best theologians to aid in the

---

* Life of Robinson. Works, vol. i., p. 25.
† *Vide* History of the Council of Dort, by Thomas Scott.

work. The power and prevalence of Arminian sentiments is a sufficient comment on the efficiency of national Synods or Œcumenical Councils. But these exiles imbibed another error, probably graver at that time in the eyes of their brethren, for "they advocated the practice of believers' and adult baptism, to the exclusion of infants from that ordinance."* The adoption of these views not only involved separation from the communion of the church with which Johnson and Ainsworth were connected, but the formation of a new one. Smith and Helwys were not alone in this. A considerable number, we cannot say a majority, simply because we do not know the extent of the membership of the community of the Amsterdam church, sympathised with them. Upon the very threshold of their enterprise a formidable difficulty presented itself. Who should baptize them? There were Baptists in Holland, those who administered the ordinance by immersion, as well as those who adopted the mode at present practised by our brethren

---

* Robinson's Works, vol. iii., p. 461. The editor says: "It is rather a singular fact that zealous as were Mr. Smith and his friends for believers' baptism, and earnest as were their opponents on behalf of infant baptism, the question of the mode of baptism was never mooted by either party. Immersion baptism does not appear to have been practised or pleaded for by either Smith or Helwys, the alleged founder of the General Baptist denomination in England. Nothing appears in these controversial writings to warrant the supposition that they regarded immersion as the proper and only mode of administering that ordinance. Incidental allusions there are, in their own works and in the replies of Robinson, that the baptism which Mr. Smith performed on himself, must have been rather by effusion or pouring. Nor is this supposition improbable, from the fact that the Dutch Baptists, by whom they were surrounded, uniformly administered baptism by immersion." Robinson's Works, vol. iii., p. 461. The remark of the editor is equally true of a considerable period of the controversy in this country. The all but universal practice of immersion in the English Church, rendered the discussion of the mode unnecessary In Tombes's replies to his many opponents, the claims of infants are the points in dispute. Upon the mode of Smith's baptism, we shall have more to say presently; and we only add that there were a portion of the Dutch Baptists who uniformly administered baptism by immersion.

in the Netherlands. From some cause or other, application was not made to any of them, and the story goes that after much prayer Smith baptized himself, then Helwys, and then the remainder of the company. He has since been called a Sebaptist. The story has been used with uncommon, but to us amusing gravity, by the opponents of Baptist principles, and repelled with no small amount of indignant feeling as a calumny on the men.* Crosby, Ivimey, Taylor, and others in the past, and of living authors Messrs. Underhill and Cutting, have displayed considerable ingenuity in shielding their brethren from reproach in this matter. To us it is of no moment whether it be true or false, beyond the interest which we have in it as an historical fact. Writers who can find in it materials for accusation, will never have their fancied complacency disturbed by us. They are perfectly welcome to all their ingenuity can extract from it. We lay the whole case before our readers. Adam Taylor has assumed that Robinson was the first reporter of this charge, and that it did not appear till some years after the event. Robinson's work was printed in 1614, and the separation took place certainly not later than early in 1609, more probably in the very year Robinson left for Leyden. Robinson certainly was not the originator of the story. The following was published four years earlier than his work :—

"By what rule baptized you yourself? What word or example had you for that in all the Scriptures? Do you affirm the baptism of children to be the mark of the Beast, because, you say, there is no word nor example in all the Scripture to prove that they may be baptized : and yet durst you presume without either word or example to baptize yourself ? If you go about to prove that lawful which you have done, by any word or example in the Scripture, I say you cannot set one step forward to that purpose, but you must allow thereby the baptism of children. I marvel you did not prevent this objection, which will be as hard a bone for you to gnaw upon as you think the baptism of children is to us. It was a wonder you would not

---

* Hanbury, vol. i.

receive your baptism first, from some one of the elders of the Dutch Anabaptists; but you will be holier than all, and see how you have marred all!"*

The following is Robinson's statement :—"If the church be gathered by baptism, then will Mr. Helwys's church appear to all men to be built upon the sand, considering the baptism it has and had; which was, as I have heard from themselves, on this manner:—Mr. Smith, Mr. Helwys, and the rest, having utterly dissolved and disclaimed their former church, state, and ministry, came together to erect a new church by baptism; unto which they also ascribed so great virtues, as that they would not so much as pray together before they had it. And after some straining of courtesy who should begin, and that John Baptist (Matt. iii. 14) misalleged, Mr. Smith baptized first himself, and next Mr. Helwys, and so the rest, making their particular confession. Now to let pass his not sanctifying a public action by public prayer (1 Tim. iv. 4, 5); his taking unto himself that honour which was not given him, either immediately from Christ or by the church (Heb. v. 4), his baptizing himself, which was more than Christ did (Matt. iii. 14); I demand unto what church he entered by baptism; or entering by baptism into no church, how his baptism could be true by their own doctrine? Or, Mr. Smith's baptism not being true, nor he by it entering into any church, how Mr. Helwys's baptism could be true, or into what church he entered by it? These things then being, all wise men will think that he had small cause either to be so much enamoured of his own baptism, or so highly to despise other men for the unorderly or otherwise unlawful administration of it."†

The substance of Mr. Taylor's arguments are very fairly condensed by Benedict, under the following particulars :—

---

* A Description of the Church of Christ, as against certain Anabaptists, &c. By J. H. London, 1610, p. 23.

† Works, vol. i., p. 168. London, 1851.

"1. It is not easy to trace the story to an earlier date than the middle of the seventeenth century, that is, nearly half a century after he became a Baptist.

"2. Bishop Hall, who wrote at this time, and appears to have had an intimate acquaintance with the persons and circumstances, would have seized with avidity a fact like this; yet he never alludes to it; a strong presumption that no such report was then in circulation. The righteous soul of this good prelate seems to have been sore vexed at the conduct of the whole company of the Separatists in leaving the church; and in conformity to the spirit of the times, he was assiduous to detect all their imperfections, and exceedingly severe in his castigations.

"3. F. Johnson, in his Christian Plea, and H. Ainsworth, in his Reply to it, though they frequently mention Mr. Smith and his sentiments, make no allusion to this circumstance. When we reflect that they were, at first, Mr. Smith's associates, and afterwards his avowed opponents, it is probable that either had never heard the report, or knew it to be false.

"4. This is rendered still more probable by consulting Mr. Smith's Character of the Beast. There was the fairest occasion, in that work, to mention such a circumstance; and yet it does not appear to be alluded to by either party. This work was in the form of a dialogue, and all the objections of his opponents are put down before Mr. Smith proceeds to answer them; and as the fact of his Se, or self-baptism, was an event of but yesterday, if it had really taken place, it is indeed singular that nothing was said about it in this severe scrutiny of errors and mistakes, from Mr. Clifton and others concerned in the discussion.

"From some expressions in the writings of this man, and from what appears in a book published by his followers in less than five years after his death, Mr. Taylor draws the conclusion that Smith and one of his companions baptized each other, as was the case with Roger Williams and some others."*

Our readers will see how part of Mr. Taylor's argu-

---

* "As the whole company, in their estimation, were unbaptized, and they knew of no administration in any of the settlements to whom they could apply, they with much propriety hit on the following expedient:— Ezekiel Holliman, a man of gifts and piety, by the suffrages of the little company was appointed to baptize Mr. Williams, who, in return, baptized Mr. Holliman and the other ten."—Benedict's History of the Baptists, p. 450. Many examples of a like kind might be adduced from Ecclesiastical History.

ment is weakened by the paragraph we have inserted from an earlier work than Robinson's, which he had not seen.*

Mr. Underhill has offered a new and very different argument. He questions the fact altogether. He states it in a letter to the venerable Dr. Benedict, of the United States, the Baptist historian. He says :—

"In a visit I lately paid to Amsterdam, I found some more interesting manuscripts relative to the church of which John Smith was pastor, with the original Confessions of Faith published by him and his company. I was also able to discover and elucidate the name of Sebaptist, given to Smith, and so often used as a name of reproach. As these documents are now being copied for me, I am not able to send you the particulars, but the general facts are as follows :—

"On Smith and his people becoming Baptists, the question arose how they were to commence the practice of the rite, and by whom it should be administered. The Dutch Baptists or Mennonites held at that time the opinion that baptism should be administered only by a minister or elder in office. As Smith did not agree in several matters with the Dutch, they were unwilling to resort to them for baptism, and became of opinion that it might be originated among themselves; they were therefore called "Se-baptists,"—persons baptizing themselves;—not that each one dipped, or baptized *himself*, but among them they commenced the practice. After this, Smith and several more came to be of the same opinion on this and other points with the Dutch, and applied to be admitted to communion with them. The Dutch received them, but at the same time required a recantation of their error. A *fac-simile* of this document I possess. The heading is in Latin, purporting that the persons whose names are subscribed, renounce the sentiment that they may 'se ipsos baptizare,'—baptize themselves,—as contrary to the order of Christ. It thus appears that the equivocal phrase, 'se ipsos baptizare,' became the foundation of the charge that Smith baptised himself. But from the controversy which arose it is evident that the meaning of the words is as I have stated it.

---

* The following work we have not seen, but it is contradictory to Mr. Taylor's theory :—"Plain Evidences : the Church of England is Apostolical : the Separation Schismatical. Directed against Mr. Ainsworth, and Mr. Smith the Sebaptist, &c. By Richard Bernard, preacher of the Word of God at Worksop. Set out by authority, 1610."—*Vide* Robinson's Works, vol. ii., p. 2, Preface.

"Among the names which follow is the autograph of John Smith and his wife Mary. A few remained of the first opinion, among whom was Thomas Helwys. I have seen a MS. letter of his, in which this subject is taken up and argued with the two Dutch pastors to whom this letter is addressed, and he also treats of the succession of the ministry in reference to the same subject, in a printed work still extant. A copy of this letter I hope soon to possess. I may, therefore, confidently affirm that the charge of baptizing himself is, with repect to Smith, a calumny, but arose from the circumstances referred to. In no other way can we account for the silence with respect to it, observed by himself in his writings and in those of his friends."*

In this conclusion, the last writer on this subject whom we have seen, fully concurs.† How far this is justified by the facts, we shall leave our readers to decide, after we have laid the documents before them. Mr. Underhill had only, we apprehend, seen one. The whole, for the first time, we now submit to our readers. It is only right to add that Mr. Underhill himself now gives up this theory.

It is admitted, on all hands, that from some cause or other, the church over which Smith and Helwys presided was divided, but the cause of division is not so manifest. Smith, with some twenty-four persons, was excluded from the church, and these sought communion with one of the Mennonite churches in the city. It is more than probable that it was one of the Waterland, one of the most liberal of the Mennonite churches, and their mode of baptism was by sprinkling, or affusion. "The said English were questioned about their doctrine of salvation, and the ground and the form (mode) of their baptism." "No difference was found between them and us." This statement is singular, as the members of this community were not immersionists.

---

* The Watchman (U. S.), July 14th, 1853.

† Historical Vindications, &c., by S. S. Cutting, Professor of Rhetoric and History in the University of Rochester. Boston, 1859. Page 60, note (a).

To satisfy their brethren, Smith and his friends made the following acknowledgment, on which Mr. Underhill has founded his defence :—

"The names of the English who confess this their error, and repent of it, viz., that they undertook to baptize themselves contrary to the order appointed by Christ, and who now desire, on this account, to be brought back to the true church of Christ as quickly as may be suffered.

"[Names of men.] [Of women.]

"We unanimously desire that this our wish should be signified to the church."*

The date of this is uncertain. It called forth, we think, the following letter :—

"BELOVED IN THE LORD,—Your approved care, diligence and faithfulness in the advancement of God's holy truth, being the good experience (to God be given the glory) well known unto us, makes us that we can do no less than, with our best hopes, hope that, through the grace of God (his word and Spirit directing you), we shall find you so still. And therefore we are with much gladness and willingness stirred up to write to you, praying you, as you love the Lord and his truth, that you will take wise counsel, and that from God's Word, how you deal in this cause betwixt us and those who are justly, for their sins, cast out from us. And the whole cause in question being Succession (for so it is in deed and in truth), consider, we beseech you, how it is Antichrist's chief hold, and that it is Jewish and ceremonial, an ordinance of the Old Testament, but not of the New. Furthermore, let it be well considered that the Succession which is founded upon neither the times, person, nor place, can be proved to any man's conscience, and so herein we should ground our faith, we cannot tell upon whom, nor when, nor where. We beseech you consider, how can we, if faith forsake the evident light of God's truth to walk in such darkness? And this is our warrant by the Word of truth. First, from Baptism. John Baptist, being unbaptized, preached the baptism of repentance, and they that believed and confessed their sins he baptized. And whosoever shall now be stirred up by the same Spirit to preach the same Word, and men thereby being converted, may, according to John his example, wash them with water, and who can forbid? And we pray that we may speake freely herein, how dare any man or men challenge unto

---

* The original, with the names, will be found in the Appendix, Note D.

themselves a pre-eminence herein, as though the Spirit of God was only in their hearts, and the Word of God now only to be fetched at their mouthes, and the ordinance of God only to be had from their hands, except they were apostles? Hath the Lord thus restrained his Spirit, his Word, and Ordinances, as to make particular men lordly over them, or the keepers of them? God forbid. This is contrary to the liberty of the Gospel, which is free for all men, at all times, and in all places: yea, so our Saviour Christ doth testify, wheresoever, whosoever, and whensoever, two or three are gathered together in his name, there is he in the midst of them. And thus much in all Christian love we do advertise you, that this ground of truth is and will be maintained against all the world, and that by the great adversaries of our faith in divers other main points, who will be glad to have such an advantage against you if you shall publish or practice any things against this ground in the xviii. of Matthew, and the professors of Christ shall sustain much reproach by it; and therefore we earnestly entreat you, even by the love of Christ that is in you, that you will be well advised what you do in these things.

"And now for the other question, that elders must ordain elders; or if this be a true perpetual rule, then from whom is your eldership come? And if one church might once ordain, then why not all churches always? Oh, that we might be thought worthy to be answered in these things, or that the poor advice of so few, so simple, and so weake, might prevail with you to cause you to look circumspectly to your ways in these things! The Lord that knoweth all hearts, knoweth ours towards you herein, that we do desire that there may be found no way of error in you; but that you and we might walk uprightly in the ways of God, casting utterly away all the traditions of men, and this, we are persuaded, is your unfeigned desire also; now fulfil our persuasion herein, and try your standing in these points, and respect not how many hold these things with you, but respect from what grounds of truth you hold them.

"Thus bechewing *(sic)* the Lord to persuade your hearts that your hands may not be against his truth, and against us, the Lord's unworthy witnesses, we take leave, commending you to the gracious protection of the Almighty, and to the blessed direction of his Word and Spirit, beseeching the Lord to do by you according to the great love and kindness that you have shown unto us. Grace and peace be with you. Amen.—Your brethren in Christ,

"Thos. Helwys,
"William Piggott,
"Thos. Seamer,
"John Morton.

"*Amsterdam,*
this 12th of March, 1610.

"P. S.—We have written to you in our own tongue because we are not able to express our minds in any other, and seeing you have an interpreter. And we have been much grieved, since our last conference with you, because we dishonoured the truth of God much for want of speech, in that we were not able to utter that poor measure of knowledge which God of his grace hath given us."

There is also a confession of faith, consisting of thirty-eight articles, and signed by thirty-nine individuals, which it is probable was presented by Smith and his friends to the church at the same time.* A short confession, also signed by Smith, is preserved, but on what occasion it was prepared, or to whom presented, the MS. affords no clue.†

The following will throw some additional light on this subject. It will be seen, from this and a subsequent page, with what caution our Dutch brethren acted in the new and delicate affair. This letter has no date. The writer was Lubbert Gerrits.‡ It was addressed to the church at Leeuwarden, the chief town of the province of Tariso, asking the advice of the brethren about "the English persons, of whom formerly they got intelligence, who long ago entreated, by iterations, to unite with our church:"—

"Jesus, the eternal Wisdom of the Father, be with you, heartily-regarded brothers and fellow-servants in the Lord.

"Our purpose is, dearly beloved in Christ, to inform you by this about the state of the affairs here with us and the English persons (about whom some informations have been given you already), who have, a long time since and continually, requested the union with our churches. In the first place, know that, as well by the ardent requests of the persons already mentioned as by the insisting desires of some of our brethren by whom their doings and godly walks are perfectly known, we have been brought thus far that we, by no

---

* Appendix, Note E.   † Note F.

‡ Gerrits was one of the principal Waterland ministers in Amsterdam. He, and the not less celebrated Hans de Ries, drew up, in behalf of the English Baptists, the Confession of Faith, generally known under their names. It has been translated into Latin, English, German, &c., and is generally quoted as the authentic exposition of the religious views of the Dutch Baptists (Confessio fidei Johannis Risfii et Lubberti Gerardi). This creed has no authority now in the Mennonite Church.—Dr. Müller.

means, could shut our ears any longer before them with a good conscience, but have represented their affair to our whole brotherhood, in order to see, with our congregation, what will be the results which the merciful God will allow us, as the affair here principally concerned us most. Therefore, first of all, we ministers have, according to the desire of our brethren, summoned these English before us, and again most perfectly examined them as regards the doctrine of salvation and the government of the church, and also inquired for the foundation and form of their baptism, and we have not found that there was any difference at all, neither in the one nor the other thing, between them and us; while we have also, concerning their baptism, received as an answer, that they, in baptizing, have taken notice of 1° Act ii. 38: 'Repent and be baptized, every one of you, in the name of Jesus Christ,' &c., in order to demonstrate repentance and to explain fundamentally the death from sins (which is also symbolized by baptism) according to the manner of Peter here,—2° of Act viii. 37: 'If thou believest with all thine heart, thou mayest,' &c., in order to add to all this the belief in Jesus Christ, that he is the Son of God, and to demand this from him who is to be baptized; and after this they have baptized him, receiving the promise from the christened one that he will bend himself under the whole Gospel, with the doctrine of it; it might be that they did understand it or did not yet understand it; so then we remark, that they have not taught persons with an impure understanding, nor instructed them who were to be baptized to found their baptism on any misunderstanding whatsoever, as has sometimes happened with other Baptists, but that they have only followed therein the Scriptural foundation, and have, therefore, acted unanimously with us.

"All this is afterwards and at a due time explained before the brethren, and we have represented to them our judgment upon their baptism, according to the desire of the brethren, and because we were considered the maintainers of the congregation; and then we have advised them to take this into consideration (as they desired also), and admonished them to bring the affair before God in their prayers. And, after some weeks, again having met, we have demanded to relate to us, every one of them in particular, what was given in their hearts by God, and so we found that most of the brethren, only a few excepted, had the same opinion as we represented them, and, therefore, agreed with us. Now then, the state of the affair is, that, though we have obtained here a reasonable result in the affair among our brethren, we, however, have resolved (as we thought this much better) not to go on before we had informed our neighbouring fellow-ministers about this matter, in order to instruct ourselves and our congregation by them out of the Word of the Lord, if it were that we were erring.

"Our opinion and our best idea about this affair is, then, that these English, without being baptized again, must be accepted; and we ourselves, also, are too scrupulous, and should not venture to baptize them again, as this is said also by every one of us, and by far the greatest part of the congregation, as we have told already; and this being the reason, viz., that we know, and have seen and observed, we ourselves, that formerly those persons that belonged to the Munster party, the Amsterdam naked-walkers, the Harerswonde* sect, and that of the Old Cloister, who were already baptized, not are re-baptized, as they did not dare to do it in that time, but have accepted them without re-baptizing them; while, at the same time, even in our days, their baptism is considered as valuable. Moreover, the manner in which, and the foundation on which baptizing these persons [the English] is performed, are, according to our opinion which we have of these affairs, when we mutually consider them, much better and more Christian-like than the former which were suffered among us, and still are suffered.

"Now then, if it be the case, dearly beloved brethren, that you think that we err in this affair, you will act well to come hither, and to teach us and the congregation with the Word of God, as this is the kind and fraternal prayer and desire of us and the whole congregation. We are most willing to be taught by any one whosoever, if we are erring and lack the truth in this affair. Be so kind and teach the English also with the Word of God, if it were necessary that they ought to be baptized again; for they declare that they have no objection to be baptized again, if you can prove with the Word of God and with reason, that their baptism is a less valuable one than that of the Flemings, Frisians, and other Baptists (to take into consideration, and distinguish the baptism of those that are baptized by their minister himself, for we ourselves do distinguish the act of baptizing by which he has baptized himself; this is an affair quite different; at present the other baptism is the question—do notice this). We have no courage to do this, because they are very intelligent people, who will not at all be blinded with discourses without good reason. We pray you once more, pay attention to that which we desire; notice our proposition, and consider all things well. If it be your opinion that we are erring, come to us and deliver us from error, and bring us into the right way; if this were not your opinion, you can satisfy us by being silent, and leaving the affair to God and our conscience."

---

* Harerswonde, a village in the neighbourhood of Leyden, the seat of certain notorious Anabaptists in the first times.

To this request the brethren at Leeuwarden forwarded the following reply :—

"Mercy and peace from God our Father and your Lord Jesus Christ, be, very dear and beloved brethren, with us all who love our Lord Jesus Christ, without end.

"Very dear, and in God, beloved brother and fellow-servant in the Lord, Lubbert Gerritsen, and you, beloved fellow-servants, we wish you altogether, with all our hearts, all good things from the Lord, with our Christian greetings. We have received your letter sent to us, and understood the contents of it for the greatest part; this in particular, that you, dear brother, request us, and are desiring very humbly to come to you at Amsterdam, on May 23, *stilo novo;* the cause of which, being, as we understand, to make peace with the English who are with you there. In consequence of this, we write, our dear brother, as an answer, on this moment, that our visit would be very inconvenient to us at this time. Misfortune also teaches us to pay particular attention to your request; for several times we have been in Holland, according to the desire and letters of others, and in order to settle several affairs; and, indeed, we have then given our best advice that we could give, it has availed very little for the promotion of peace, and even ingratitude and cooling of love were the consequences, which we most sadly have taken to heart, as the Lord knows. Therefore, dear brethren, if it had been convenient to us to come to you, which you most seriously desired, we are yet very scrupulous about this matter of uniting yourselves with the English, as long as we have no more knowledge of their affairs. It is, indeed, a very critical thing, and ought seriously to be taken into consideration, what might be the consequences on our side that are still in peace; for experience teaches us very well, &c.

"Therefore, dear brethren, our opinion would be in these affairs, that we should desire to deal with our congregations, which we acknowledge to serve unworthily, with open doors and not secretly, for it concerns them as well as us. And if it were that we were all with you, and saw and heard all things, we should not be inclined to consent for our own persons, in any affair whatsoever, unless it were that we, in the first place, received from you a short account of the chief articles of your doctrine and the customs of the congregations, which you have pointed out for them, in writing, and on which these persons would be inclined to unite themselves with you, in order to afford us the opportunity to examine these with our congregations everywhere; for, as the affair would be spoken of everywhere among us, as you yourselves write us, dear brethren, if they were not informed of it, it requires much responsibility. Therefore, we should be inclined to take care, that our congregation also knew everything that we should do and advise in this affair, that we, afterwards, will not be involved in any trouble or unquietness. For as neither we ourselves, without the congregation, nor they without us, are one body, so we think it necessary (though we are unworthy servants) not to do anything without their knowledge, as we know, dear brethren, the condition of our congregation here perfectly well. This is, as nearly as possible, our humble opinion of these affairs. Do not take it amiss. If you were anything else but happy, it would grieve our hearts very much. For this time no more, but that we recommend you altogether to the Lord and his mercy, and offer you our kind greetings in the Lord of peace. Pray God for us. We remain most willingly your debtors.—*May 5, old style, a° 1610.*

"Undersigned by us, in Leeuwarden:—

"HANS MATHYSZOON, "JAN JANSZOON SCHELLINCKWOUN,
"ANA ANESZ, "YEME DE RYNCK."
"DYRCK DOEDESZ,

Dissatisfied with this reply, the Amsterdam brethren again addressed the following epistle to their friends in Prussia:—

"Loving, and in God beloved, brethren and fellow-servants in the Lord, Jan Schellinckwoun or Hans Mathÿs, with your fellow-helpers in the service of the Lord, we wish you the peace of the Lord and a merciful illumination in Christ, in all your ways.—Amen.

"May it please you, that we inform you that we are very much desiring for some answer on that which, a long time ago, we have asked and desired concerning the affair with the English, with which affair we have acquainted you. We are very surprised that this affair seems to have been taken at heart by you so very little, for which we are ashamed before these persons, and scarcely know what to answer that this affair is put off such a long time. Therefore, our request and serious desire is, that you do not defer this affair any longer, but shortly, and within a fortnight after the date of this, send us some answer, either by coming yourselves, if it be possible that we may be valued by you so much, or by writing us something concerning the two following questions:—

"Firstly, What there may be in the confession which, according to your desire is sent to you, as you wished to examine it with your congregations in comparing it with the Word of God,—that deserves to be rejected and to be improved?* Secondly, What, according to your opinion, and according to the Word of God, must be thought of their being baptized? Concerning the last question, on this especially we should like very much to receive an answer and good instruction as soon as it is possible. And if you do not send us this within the time above-mentioned, we shall take it, therefore, that you leave it to us and put it wholly in our hands to do, or to leave this, what we, with our congregation, think best of all, after the wisdom which we possess, and that you will be contented and quite at ease in this afterwards. Therefore, act with diligence, beloved brethren, if you think it necessary, in virtue of God's Word, to warn us in one thing or another, and to teach us to our welfare; and forward it to us most speedily, as we asked already, that we the sooner the better may be able to do what our duty is.

"Besides this we have nothing else to mention, but the hearty greetings to you, our dear brethren and fellow-servants in the Gospel of the Lord, yonder in Friesland. Jesus remain everlastingly with you with his Spirit.—Amen.

"*At Amsterdam, July* 16 *a*°, 1610, *stilo novo.*"

The correspondence was closed with the following decided refusal to have anything to do with the affair of the English :—

"Our loving greeting, and great affection of our hearts to you, very dear and beloved brethren and fellow-servants in the kingdom of God, Lubbert Gerrits and your fellow-servants. We, undersigned, may not conceal from you our astonishment at your ardent and impetuous writing to us, in which you demand our answer within a fortnight, or that we afterwards shall be quiet about the alliance or union with the English, in your town, having taken place or intended, &c. We are, dear men, after very much thinking about the affair, about which you demand and request most ardently and impetuously the advice from us in Friesland; though it is an affair quite new and never heard of. Therefore, it were very necessary that all churches in Prussia and the whole of Germany, and wherever established, were acquainted with it, as you yourselves, dear brethren, know very well what words and promises have been given by us in formerly transacted affairs, viz.: not to do anything without asking the advice of every one in particular. What astonishment will be occasioned in several congregations, as well as with private persons everywhere, at this alliance or union of this people with their absurd labour and service, you, yourselves,

---

* Probably the Confession, Appendix, Note E.

dear men, may easily understand, and therefore, it is not necessary widely to explain this. In short, we thought it very advisable (save correction) still to tarry a little time in this affair, not to be so zealous and ardent, but to apply much more all diligence, trouble, and labour that is possible, in order to prevent ruin, harm, hurt, and perdition of the churches concerning the Westerland peace-making or union: if this first was brought to an end, that fire extinguished, and everything was brought again to peace, quietness, and silence, it would be a hearty joy and gladness of soul to us. Do not leave so easily the old friends, by choosing new ones, who, perhaps, will not be so good. We take very much at heart the augmentation of the kingdom and the improvement of the Church of Christ (God, our Lord, knows it); but if the scattering of our friends is connected with it, it is not to be desired. This harm is woe to our hearts; your intemperate zeal is partly the cause of it as well. We will finish this affair here, though we had to say much more concerning it.

"As regards the request for our advice and examination which you desire about the thirty-eight articles of creed presented to us,—this is all in vain; as they are all revealed in printed books before the eyes of every man, we may now expect with you a general judgment of it from all men. Therefore, we think it rather impertinent to demand this from us in particular. Time will teach us that commodity has yet been nothing else with many, *obiter*, seen once and read over once, expect what time will reveal; in this affair, also, we have to do something else.

"Finally, that you demand principally, and before all things, our advice and opinion about their baptism, this makes us astonished very much, because you yourselves have not shown your opinion nor thoughts about this piece, and this you ought to have done. If we, then, had seen this, we ourselves might have examined it, and ours put together with it, in order to choose the best with each other. But to give a short answer and correction, we say, that we do not know such use, custom, or ordinance from the Holy Scriptures, and, therefore, we are scrupulous and have no courage to say much of this. It is an affair never heard of, therefore we will leave it as it is; and we shall behave ourselves according to the instruction given us in the Word of God, and not according to the work and actions of men. We think, for this instance, to have sufficiently answered your writing and your request; you, certainly, will perform your service and the duty of your office in this and all other affairs, if our answer cannot satisfy you,—with the observation only to inform every one, and in all places already-mentioned, about the condition of the affairs. Deliberate together most seriously, and keep watch over the flock of the Lord. Let us try to restore, first of all, the present harm, before some new affair is intended; to this we exhort you, this we pray from you. Be recommended, all together, to the eternal and Almighty God and his merciful Word, and to his eternal and merciful protection. We, altogether, your unworthy brethren and fellow-servants, offer you our hearty greetings. Farewell!

"Dyrck Doedes, 1610 7/18
"Mr. Doume Lybrants,
 "by me, Hans Mathysz.

"*July* 18*th*, 1610. (I am nearly tired of this. by anxiety.)"

Upon the minds of the brethren this letter had little effect. The English were finally admitted into the fellowship of the church, and a subsequent page will disclose to us the manner of their admission.

The effect of this change of sentiment on the community was not powerless. It awakened the most virulent hostility from the wise and the good in Holland. Not only the "charity which thinketh no evil" was violated, but truth itself was sacrificed, to the injury of a dissenting friend.* It had other results. Judging from the statements of an opponent, it gave an extension to Baptist statements of no ordinary magnitude. Of this truthfulness we have collateral proof.

Mr. Pagit, in his Arrow against Separation, says "that out of a few members in the Brownist's churches, more fell to Anabaptism than out of many thousand members of the Presbyterian churches amongst the Dutch, or out of all the English Reformed churches there."

"Brown's church, at Middleborow, abundance turned Anabaptists, which discontented him. Smith himself, the great leader in this new way, turned Anabaptist. So also did

---

* As a sample, and that a rather mild one, take the following:—"As I acknowledge the unblamable conversations of many amongst you, so do many Papists, Anabaptists, and other vile heretics and schismatics, walk as unblamably this way as you: and yet are they not true shepherds of Christ's sheep."—Robinson's Reply to Bernard, vol. ii., pp. 409-10.

Cann, at last, as I have heard. Johnson and Ainsworth's church, at Amsterdam, abundance of them turned Anabaptists, and were, therefore, excommunicated. So also hath it fallen out in England : the church that came from Holland, many of the members fell to Anabaptism, both of Shadrack Sympson's and Thomas Goodwin's, and some separated upon it into distinct congregations."* He attributes this to the logical tendency of Independency.

"The tendency of Independency doth, as it were of course, breed Anabaptism ; so that, if they judge Anabaptism a pestilent error, as others do, they should renounce their Independency, which is so natural an occasion of it. St. Austin said of Anabaptism, that it shaketh the very foundations of the church. And holy Philpot, the martyr, said it was undoubtedly set on foot by the devil to destroy the Gospel."†

"The reason is plain, because no man can be true to the principles of Independents and Brownists, but they must turn Anabaptists." How far this reasoning of the accuser of our brethren be true, we stop not to say. Certainly, others besides Jessey, Simson, Lawrance, Blackwood, and Allen, mentioned by this author, have felt its force, and we greatly mistake if multitudes more will not yet acknowledge its power.

Before dismissing this matter of the English in Holland, a word or two on the subsequent condition of the church may not be uninteresting to the reader. Little, indeed nothing, is known in this country about it. From the date of this correspondence up to 1614, the period when Helwys left Holland, its history is unknown. Nor could we fully fill up this gap in our annals till now. Supposing that materials might exist in some of the archives of our Dutch brethren, we sought information in Holland, and

---

* Lamb's Fresh Suite against Independency, p. 37.
† *Vide* his Letter to an Anabaptist, in Fox. *Ibid*, p. 33.

the result we now lay before our readers. "Assisted by one of the two professors of our seminary," says Professor Müller, "I have made further researches, and I have the pleasure to impart to you the following results. We have ascertained by various dispersed notes, that the above-said English Baptists at Amsterdam, held their usual meeting in the building known as 'the Cake-House of John Munter,'* where some of them dwelt, and where old and necessitous people belonging to the Waterland church found a refuge. John Munter was one of the most considerable and rich members of that church. The records of the consistory contain nothing about the English in question, nor about their desire to unite with the Waterlanders, before November 6th, 1614.†

"On that day the consistory resolved to bring the proposal of the English to join the community on the next Sunday, before the brethren, granting them a fortnight or three weeks for taking it into consideration. This was done accordingly on the 9th of November, and ample details of their affairs were given at the same time.

"On the 18th of January, 1615, when some young people, desiring to be baptized, were presented to the community, the consistory declared that on the next Wednesday the English would be taken up in the community, according to their demand, provided none of the members objected to it, as no one had done until that time. On the following Tuesday, the 20th of January, the English (worshipping) in the 'Cake-House,' numbering about thirty individuals, male and

---

* "Some of our churches had formerly peculiar bakehouses for the baking of bread, &c., for the necessitous people amongst them. Perhaps the building alluded to here was such a house, and at the same time afforded accommodation as a dwelling for indigent members."—Professor Müller.

† These are evidently to be distinguished from Smith's party, and no doubt are the remains of the early church over which Helwys presided.

female, were called before the consistory, in the 'Spyker' (an old granary, adapted for a meeting-house of the Waterlanders, of which transmutation there are many instances), and asked :—' 1st. If they persisted in their demand to join the community ? 2nd. If they stood firm in their agreeing to our interpretation of the dogmas and professions of faith, which they had signed with their own hands? when they fully declared such to be the case, except a few, about four, who stood not firm in some points, having a different opinion, principally in what regards magistracy, and from taking an oath; but who promised to behave themselves quietly and to make no opposition.

"The consistory, however, objected to take up these few who differed in opinions, but all the English declared forthwith, that if some were struck out, all of them would stick to their seclusion, as they were too much attached to each other to separate. To this demand the consistory would not accede, unless the community granted leave to take up also those few whose opinions differed from those of the Waterlanders, and refused once more to the signing of the professions of faith, from which not one of these had refrained himself. On that night this matter remained undecided, to the regret of all.

"But already, on the early morning of Wednesday, the 20th of January, the English returned to the consistory and declared that they had amply discussed the matter during the last night, and were happy to state, that to their great relief and joy, eventually the four dissenting, advised to, and approved of, the joining of the others to the community, even if they were to be rejected. Accordingly they were admitted in the community, after those being baptized who were to be baptized (administered by Hans de Ries), in the open congregation, *without baptism*. Room has been left in the memorial for filling in their names, but it has been omitted to set them down. It appears, however, clearly, that on the same day were baptized, amongst many others, four English: Swithin Grindall, a young man; Thomas Odell, a spur maker; Anthony Thomassen, an old man, husband of Lysbeth, an English woman; and Thomas Huysbertsen, glover, a bachelor, in the 'Cake-House.'

"After their joining us, the English, however, continued their separate worship in the 'Cake-House,' where they preached in English. Even on the 8th of June, in 1620, their preacher, Thomas ―――, was confirmed to full service (*i.e.*, to administer baptism and the Lord's Supper, &c.) by the old minister, Reinier Wybrands, and his colleague, Peter Andriessen, and until 1637 baptism was frequently administered in their place of worship, although it does not appear by whom." A list of names and dates of persons baptized follows, which we omit, as adding nothing of interest to the narrative; but the close of the list presents us with the name of Jane Morton, the wife, we have little doubt, of the John Morton whose name occurs in the letter of Helwys. We give this record: "September 26th, 1630, Janneker (Jane) Morton, and 12th December, 1638, Michael Wallis: the five first, because they were baptized formerly by Mr. Smith; the latter, because he was baptized an adult in England."

"It is consequently evident," the Professor adds, "that although the English congregation had in some respects a separate existence, it was nevertheless closely united to the Waterlanders. Those who were baptized and admitted were instantly considered as members of the Waterland church, and while those who wanted relief were assisted, likewise those who misbehaved were censured by the consistory. The marriages of the English were concluded by the Waterlanders, of which five instances can be quoted." We omit them, as of no comparative interest to our readers.

"Several of the English, probably those who understood Dutch better, were baptized in the church of the Waterlanders, and not in their own place of worship. The instances noted in the memorial are the following. 'The list extends from 1615 to 1645, and in it are the names of Piggott, Overton, Drew, Armfield, &c., children, no doubt, of some of those whose names are attached to the confession. Some in this list were admitted as members, without baptism, being already baptized adults in England.'

"Later on, the difference between the English and the Waterlanders cannot be traced any further. No mention is made any more, as formerly, of an 'Englishman' or 'Englishwoman,' and the names are wholly Dutchified; nay, already in 1615, behind the name of Swithin Grindall, we read, in Dutch, called Swithin Janssoon, and behind the name Margaret Morris, Grietje Thomas.

"The union of the two parties had become so close, that on the 8th of July, 1640, an Englishman, Joseph Drew, was proposed by the Waterland consistory as minister, which offer he accepted on the 8th December, 'although he was rather afraid that his language might be an objection, he being used to the English.' It does not appear that he actually officiated as minister. He and his two brethren, Alexander and John, belonged to the most respectable number of the English congregations."

To these statements Dr. Müller says: "I, for myself, add the following remark: It appears to me that the persons mentioned in the memorial, who were not yet baptized, were admitted to the Waterlanders by the baptism not of immersion, but of sprinkling. This mode of baptizing was, from the days of Menno, the only usual mode amongst them, and it is still amongst us. The Waterlanders, nor any other of the various parties of the Netherland Doopsgezinden, practised at any time baptism by immersion. Had they made an exception, in that use, on behalf of the English, who in their country had not yet received baptism, it is more than probable that the memorial would have mentioned that alteration. But they cared only for the *very nature* of the baptism,* and were therefore willing to admit even those who were baptized by a mode differing from theirs, just as we are wonted to do now-a-days."

This narrative supplies us with very valuable material, and enables us to correct some mistakes into which previous writers on our history have fallen. The course of the English refugees in Amsterdam may be thus traced. Smith's first negotiation to unite with the Waterlanders, in 1610, was, after some application, successful; later on, Helwys, in 1611 or 1612, returned to England, which evidently led the people, who were left behind, to seek a union with the Dutch Church, and which was consummated in 1615.

We have now arrived at a period in our annals when our information becomes more abundant, and the movements of our brethren much more distinct and traceable. In the past, the persecuting edicts of monarchs, and the ruthless proceedings of the professed ministers of Christ, have been our guides; the existence of the Anabaptists has been indicated by the sufferings of the Gatehouse and the Fleet, or the fires of Smithfield. Though suffering will still mark their course, intense and very cruel, for another generation or two, still we can listen to their own statements, and are less dependent, consequently, on the prejudiced accounts of their bittered foes for our knowledge of their principles and our estimate of their characters. As we hear their own voice, and become more familiar with their proceedings and their great principles, the mists which ignorance and malice have gathered around them disappear, and they stand before us invested with a moral grandeur which few, if any, of their contemporaries could surpass.

We have seen that Mr. Helwys, and probably some of his brethren, returned to England about 1611 or 1612. The unhappy condition of the Amsterdam church may have had

---

* "As founded on full ages." The meaning is, that they baptized only **adults**, and that by sprinkling.

some weight in his decision.* The motives which he avows are of the very highest kind, though his judgment in the matter may not meet with unmixed approval. He thought it wrong to flee from persecution. It had "been the overthrow of religion in this island; the best, ablest, and greater part being gone, and leaving behind them some few who, by the others' departure, have had their affliction and their contempt increased, hath been the cause of many falling back, and of their adversaries rejoicing." London was fixed on as the place of their future residence. Many causes would contribute to this decision. Here "they continued their church state and assemblies for worship as publicly as the evils of the time would admit." Mr. Taylor regards this as the first General Baptist church formed in England. The claim, we think, cannot well be questioned, though Crosby appears to be of a different opinion.† There is no evidence to sustain his views. We refer not only to the fact in the former part of this chapter, but the General Baptist historian has supplied an amount of evidence that must silence every doubt. Still Helwys held some opinions which the intelligent members of that section of our body would repudiate. The doctrine "that the New Creation, which is begotten of God, needeth not the outward Scripture, or ordinances of the church, to support him, but is above them (1 Cor. xiii. 10, 1 John ii. 27), seeing he hath in himself three witnesses,

---

* "Neither is it likely, if he, and the people with him at Amsterdam, could have gone on comfortably as they desired, that the unlawfulness of flight would ever have troubled him," &c.—Robinson's Works, vol. iii., p. 159.

† Crosby, vol. i., p. 270. His own witnesses fail him. "Mr. Helwys, elsewhere and rightly, disclaims all free will, or power in a man's self to work out his salvation, but teacheth that 'this grace, which is his mercy in Christ, God hath given to all, though all receive it not.'" "That original sin is an idle term, and that there is no such thing as men intended by the word (Ezek. xviii. 20); because God threatened death only to Adam (Gen. ii. 17), not to his posterity; and because God created the soul."—Robinson, vol. iii., pp. 232–3, 246. Other instances will be found pp. 251, 253, 258.

the Father, the Word, and the Holy Ghost, which are better than all Scripture; or creation, though such as have not attained the new creation need them for instruction, comfort, and to stir them up," &c. (2 Peter i. 19; 1 Cor. xi. 26; Eph. iv. 12, 13,*) would find no welcome from them.

Crosby supposes that the Baptists were mixed up more or less with other Christian organizations. The facts of their prevalence, and, yet, of the absence of all records of their separate organization, he would thus reconcile. No one, we apprehend, acquainted with the estimate in which these religious outcasts were held by all classes of the community, as indicated by the facts laid before our readers, can doubt this. The success of Helwys and his friends was considerable. Of his death we know nothing.†

---

* Quoted by Robinson, vol. iii., p. 268.

† On the fly-leaf of a book of 212 pages, entitled, "A Short Declaration of the Mistery of Iniquity," printed "anno 1612," without any indication of the place where it was printed, there is the following passage written by the author:—

"Heare, O king, and dispise not yᵉ counsell of yᵉ poore, and let their complaints come before thee.

"The king is a mortall man, and not God, therefore hath no power over yᵉ jmmortall soules of his subiects, to make lawes and ordinances for them, and to set spirituall lords over them.

"If the king have authority to make spirituall lords and lawes, then he is an jmmortall God, and not a mortall man.

"O king, be not seduced by deceivers to sin so against God, whome thou oughtest to obey, nor against thy poore subiects, who ought and will obey thee in all thinges, with body, life, and goods, or els let their lives be taken from yᵉ earth.

"God save yᵉ king.   "THOMAS HELWYS.
Spittlefield, neare London."

Our friend, Mr. Wenger, who kindly copied this for us, says:—"I am inclined to think the volume from which this passage is copied was what we should call a presentation copy, and that the fly-leaf contained what was intended to occupy the place of a dedication. The reasons which suggest this are certainly not conclusive, yet deserving of attention. 1. The handwriting is beautiful, and betrays special care. 2. The closing line, 'God save the king,' would hardly have been added in an ordinary copy. 3. The signature, 'Thomas Helwys,' is placed as low down, and as

Under the date of 1616, Sir S. D'Ewes says: "In the Low Countries the heretical faction of the Anabaptists, under the new and false name of Arminians, began openly to defend the errors of their Pelagian blasphemies, which to this day, like all weeds, have grown to such a rankness as they have almost outgrown the truth. Notwithstanding, our learned King James did now labour earnestly, by Sir D. Carlton, his ambassador, with the States, to have these heretics suppressed, as he had at first after the death of Arminius,* the enemy of God." In 1629 he commends the zeal of the

---

completely in the corner, as you would expect in a piece intended for the king's eye: but it is most beautifully written, though in plain unadorned characters."

In the same library there are two other works by this writer. The following is the Title of a Tract of 144 leaves, 8vo., printed in 1611. "A Short and Plaine Proofe, by the Word and Workes of God, that God's Decree is not the Cause of anye Man's Sinne or Condemnation:

AND

That all Men are Redeemed by Christ;

AS ALSO

That no Infants are Condemned."

The following is one of 94 pages, and was printed in the same year:—

"An advertisement or admonition unto the congregations which men call the New Fryesters, in the Lowe Countries, written in Dutche, and published in Englis.

"Wherein is handled four principall pointes of religion:—

"1. That Christ took his flesh of Marie, having a true earthlie, naturall bodie.

"2. That a Sabbath, or day of rest, is to be kept holy everie first day of the weeke.

"3. That there is no succession nor privilege to persons in the holie thinges.

"4. That magistracie, being an holy ordinance of God, debarreth not anie from being of the church of Christ.

"After these followes certen demandes concerning God's decree of salvation and condemnation."

[These scarce works are in the Bodleian Library at Oxford.]

* "King James, after the death of James Arminius, Professor at Leyden, in Holland, an arch Anabaptist, &c. . . . He called him a blasphemer, an atheist, &c., terming the deceased Anabaptist, Arminius, the enemy of God."—Life of Sir S. D'Ewes, vol. i., p. 82.

Commons "that the true religion might not be intermixed with Popish ceremonies or idolatrous actions, nor the pure doctrine of the Church of England be corrupted with the blasphemous tenets of the Anabaptists, in derogation of God's grace and providence; which tenets had been freely broached by Sebastian Castellio, in Latin, and by other Anabaptists in England, about seventy years past; and now, some twenty years past, in the Low Countries, by James Arminius and his fellow Anabaptists, in Latin and Dutch." From other sources the same conclusions would be reached. Though we have no distinct proof of the separate organization of our churches at this time, yet the evidence is abundant as to the wide prevalence of our opinions.* Johnson, referring to the denial of infant baptism, says: "How greatly it spreadeth, both in these parts (Holland, 1617) and of late in our own country, that is, England."†

Important as this movement of Helwys and his friends was, it was not alone. The pen was wielded, and from the press various works issued in defence of Baptist principles. Against the ignorance, the intolerance, the cruelty of the ruling faction, they appealed. Sentiments were uttered then which have exerted the most benignant influence on society. Sentiments which surpliced hypocrites, wanton courtiers, and a sensual monarch, could not appreciate, but which Williams, Taylor, Milton, and Locke, in after years, heard

---

* D'Ewes' Life, vol. i., pp. 97, 400. The Knight is very angry with the Anabaptists, and in every instance identifies them with the followers of Arminius.—*Vide* pp. 102, 120, 201, 388, 405–6.

† Crosby, vol. i., p. 94.

"There was also another sect amongst the Anabaptists, that were called the Puritans; from whence the Precisians of our kingdom, who, out of self-will and fancy, refuse to conform themselves to the order of our Church, have borrowed this name."—King James's Works, p. 371.

"Pagit also mentions a kind of Anabaptists, so called (*i. e.*, Separatists) because they pretended to be separated from the world."—Heresiog, p. 35. Hanbury, vol. i., p. 35.

with rapture and propagated with success. Scarcely were they heard at first. The rigid Presbyterians, as well as the Right Divine Episcopalians, repudiated them. But they were not powerless. In the senate and in the church they worked, and on them rests the mighty structure of England's liberties.

In 1614 there resided in London a humble citizen, who obtained his daily bread with difficulty. Persecution was in part the cause of this. He had been an exile, and probably had mingled with his brethren in Holland. His scholarly attainments were considerable. With the Greek of the New Testament he was familiar. Of the exact period of his return to London we know nothing. The rage against the Puritans was not abating. Episcopacy and arbitrary power were in the ascendant. To the wilds of the New World multitudes of the holiest of the nation were repairing, to find in the wilderness a home, and to lay the foundation of a purer civil and ecclesiastical commonwealth. Leonard Busher*—a name that will never perish—issued his work: "*Religious Peace; or, A Plea for Liberty of Conscience. Long since presented to King James, and the High Court of Parliament then sitting, by Leonard Busher, Citizen of London; and printed in the Year* 1614." We cannot analyze this book, or present an outline of the noble sentiments it advocates. The exterior may be rough, but there is a massive grandeur about it which is well worthy the mighty theme it embodies. It will pass before us again. Still there are two or three sentences the production of which justice demands:—

"*I read that Jews, Christians, and Turks, are tolerated in Constantinople, and yet are peaceable, though so contrary the one to the other. If this be so, how much more ought Christians not to force one another to religion? And how much more ought Christians to tolerate*

---

* He was probably a descendant of one of the Walloon refugees. We find a Domynic Busher amongst them, as a subscriber of £100 to a loan to Elizabeth in 1588.—Burns's History of the French and Walloon Church, &c., pp. 6, 7.

Christians when the Turks do tolerate them? SHALL WE BE LESS MERCIFUL THAN THE TURKS? OR SHALL WE LEAVE THE TURKS TO PERSECUTE CHRISTIANS? IT IS NOT ONLY UNMERCIFUL, BUT UNNATURAL AND ABOMINABLE: YEA, MONSTROUS, FOR ONE CHRISTIAN TO VEX AND DESTROY ANOTHER FOR DIFFERENCES AND QUESTIONS OF RELIGION."

"And the king and parliament may please to permit all sorts of Christians; yea, Jews, Turks, and Pagans, so long as they are peaceable, and no malefactors, as is above mentioned, which if they be found to be, under two or three witnesses, let them be punished according to God's Word. Also, if any be found to be willing liars, false accusers, false allegers and quoters of Scripture, or other men's writings,—as some men willingly do,—let them be punished according to right and justice; it is due desert, not persecution. *But let God's Word have its full and free passage among them all; even to the end of their lives, in all bountifulness, longsuffering, and patience: knowing that it is ordained by God's rich mercy to lead infidels and such as err into repentance and amendment, out of the snare of the devil, by whom they are taken and deceived.*"

The whole work breathes this loftiness of spirit; the same enlarged view and nobleness of purpose pervade it. We can only give another example:—

"*That for the more peace and quietness, and for the satisfying of the weak and simple, among so many persons differing in religion, it be lawful for any person or persons, yea, Jews and Papists, to unite, dispute, confer and reason, print and publish any matter touching religion, either for or against whomsoever; always provided they allege no Fathers for proof of any point of religion, but only the Holy Scriptures.*"*

Not only is the broadest liberty for thought and utterances on religious matters pleaded, but the doctrine of "unlicensed printing" was within the wide circle of his advocacy. Another and yet another of these compositions

---

* Tracts on Liberty of Conscience, pp. 24, 33, 51. Cecil, in reply to a letter from the Archbishop of York, who pleaded with him for the use of gentler means with the Puritans, says: "I love not to procure or yield to any toleration; a matter which I well know no creature living dare propound to our religious sovereign."—Lodge, vol. iii., p. 128. The spirit of the great Burghley had not rested on his son.

followed,* pleading the cause of the oppressed with a power and earnestness which at that time had no parallel. Presbyterians and Separatists asked for toleration, but it was for the liberty of a sect. The Anabaptists only, though despised and persecuted, pleaded the claims of all, and maintained that no power, civil or ecclesiastical, had authority over conscience.

Other events, which have exerted an unmistakable and not less powerful and benignant influence on the church, transpired about this time. They form an epoch in the world's history. They have given an impulse to commerce, to liberty and religion, which arrested the downward tendency of this nation, and have contributed more than anything else to its present greatness. Whilst in many places, in England especially, the power and life of the Church were dying out, from the pressure of the multiplied ceremonies and superstitious forms which clothed it,† the Redeemer was, from other causes, giving it a new and more Scriptural development, and preparing a wider circle in which its triumphs should be won. We have seen already, that many devout men, despairing of liberty in England, and anxious for freedom from the intolerable oppression of the hierarchy, had fled, some to Holland, and others to the wilds and wastes of the new world. To the latter, the church over which Robinson, the antagonist of Smith and Helwys, presided, resolved to go. As a religious community they

---

* "Persecution for Religion Judged and Condemned. 1615." "A most Humble Supplication of many of the King's Majesty's Subjects. 1620." Both these works will claim attention again.

† The decay of piety towards the close of the reign of James, *i. e.*, when his pernicious example and worthless character had wrought their full effect upon the nation, is an afflicting topic. The lewdness of his court was such, that those who drew the sword against his son and brought him to the scaffold, do not hesitate to contrast the many virtues of King Charles, and the discourse of his courtiers, with the low and infamous bebaucheries of the court of James."—*Vide* Mrs. Hutchinson's Memoirs. Marsden, p. 337.

would emigrate. The history of the enterprise is one of thrilling interest. Genius has adorned it with some of her noblest efforts. In the pages of the historian and of the poet it forms a commanding and glowing episode, and the pencil of the painter has pourtrayed it in a lasting form. To the pages of Bancroft and others we must refer our readers for the full details.* Only a sentence or two will our limits allow. The Puritan character, with all its excellencies and defects, marked the civil and ecclesiastical constitution of the colony, which after almost unparalleled suffering this noble band of Christian heroes succeeded in founding. Suffering for conscience sake had not taught them forbearance. Dissent from the opinions of the ruling power was not tolerated. Hence the annals of the State are marked with blots of the deepest hue. Roger Williams was persecuted, and had to flee for his life. He subsequently established another colony, founded on the broadest principles of civil and religious freedom, and gave rise to the Baptist body in that distant land.†

From the struggles and mistakes of the Pilgrim Fathers we must turn to another scene. It is the last of the long series of sacrifices which pampered bigotry and ignorance offered in this kingdom. Other victims followed, as we shall presently see, but their tortures were more refined and protracted. This was the last *auto-da-fé* which the church offered to attest the purity of its faith, and the accordance of its spirit with the tender and loving mind of the Prince of Peace. The episcopal city of Lichfield was the spot selected for this act of devotion. The victim was the very embodiment of all the heresies of the past. In him were embodied "the wicked heresies of the Ebionites, Cerienthians, Valentinians, Arians, Macedonians, of Simon Magus, of Manes, Manichees,

---

* Bancroft's History of the United States.

† *Vide* Life of Roger Williams, by Professor Knowles. Dr. R. Elton's smaller, but interesting, volume may be consulted.

of Photinus," and, to crown all, "of the Anabaptists, and of other heretical, execrable, and unheard-of opinions, by the instinct of Satan, by him excogitated and holden." He held "that the baptizing of infants is an abominable custom. That there ought not to be in the church the use of the Lord's Supper to be celebrated in the elements of bread and wine; and the use of baptism to be celebrated in the element of water, as they are now practised in the Church of England. But that the use of baptism is to be administered in water only to converts of sufficient age and understanding, converted from infidelity to the faith." Edward Wightman was of Burton-on-Trent. Few, excepting episcopal judges, would doubt his insanity. An asylum, where he might have indulged his wild fancies, would have been a more appropriate place than the martyr's stake.* Before the bishop the heretic was called, but reasoning and threats were powerless. The warrant for his execution informs us that his lordship was aided by "other divines and learned in the law;" the aforesaid wicked crimes, heresies, and other detestable blasphemies and errors "were stubbornly and pertinaciously, knowingly, maliciously, and with an hardened heart, published, defended, and dispersed," &c. Only one alternative remained. The Church could do no more. Her tender mercies were exhausted. "As a blasphemous and condemned heretic" he was "left to the secular power to be punished with condign punishment." The bidding of the church was heard. "We, therefore," says the royal executioner, "as a zealot of justice and a defender of the Catholic faith, and willing that the holy church, and the rights and liberties of the same, and the Catholic faith to maintain and defend, and such like heresies and errors everywhere, so much as in us lies, to root out and extirpate, and heretics

---

* "Wightman was a visionary who should have been placed in the hands of a keeper rather than in the hands of the executioner."--Vaughan's History of England, vol. v., p. 121.

so convict to punish with condign punishment, holding that such an heretic, in the aforesaid form convict and condemn, according to the laws and customs of this our kingdom of England, in this part accustomed, ought to be burnt with fire. We command thee (the sheriff) that thou cause the said Edward Wightman, being in thy custody, to be committed to the fire in some public and open place below the city aforesaid, for the cause aforesaid, before the people; and the same Edward Wightman cause really to be burnt, in the detestation of the said crime, and for manifest example of other Christians, that they may not fall into the same crime." Evidently there was a burning sense in which royal theologians and episcopal divines understood Paul, "*By the terrors of the Lord we persuade men.*"

The closing period of this reign was marked by the stronger development of those principles which were disastrous to the highest interests of the nation, and finally led the first Charles to the scaffold. The graphic pen of Macaulay thus describes the opposing elements:—

"Theories tending to Turkish despotism were in fashion at Whitehall. Theories tending to republicanism were in favour with a large portion of the House of Commons. The violent prelatists, who were to a man zealous of their prerogatives, and the violent Puritans, who were to a man zealous for the privileges of parliament, regarded each other with animosity more intense than that which, in the preceding generation, had existed between Catholics and Protestants."*

Every year augmented this. The folly, the debasement of this despicable creature, increased till, after an illness of some fourteen days, he closed his ignoble reign the 27th of March, 1625. We shall be forgiven if, in addition to the remarks on a previous page, we offer one or two on the character of James.

---

* History, vol. i., p. 82.

His personal appearance is thus described by a contemporary:—"His eye large, ever rolling after any stranger that came in his presence, insomuch as many for shame have left the room, as being out of countenance. His beard was very thin; his tongue too large for his mouth, and made him drink very unseemly, as if eating his drink, which came out into the cup of each side of his mouth. His skin was as soft as taffate sarsnet; which felt so because he never washed his hands, only rubbed his finger ends slightly with the wet end of a napkin. His legs were very weak, having had, as some thought, some foul play in his youth, or rather before he was born, that he was not able to stand at seven years of age; that weakness made him ever leaning on other men's shoulders."*

The social habits of the monarch were as filthy as his person. His drunkenness was excessive. The presence of the most illustrious of his guests had no influence on him. From under the table the royal drunkard was not unfrequently taken by his attendants from the company of his visitors.† The disgusting vices of the monarch were reflected with the fullest accuracy by his courtiers. "The court of the king was a nursery of vice and licentiousness; he had brought in with him a company of poor Scots, who, coming into this plentiful kingdom, surfeited with riot and debaucheries, and got all the riches of the land only to cast away. The honour, wealth, and glory of the nation, when Queen Elizabeth left it, were soon prodigally wasted by this thriftless heir; the nobility of the land utterly debased, by setting honours to public sale, and conferring them on persons that had neither

---

* Weldon's Court and Character of James I., p. 177–179.

"It was no light thing that, on the eve of the decisive struggle between our kings and parliaments, royalty should be exhibited to the world stammering, slabbering, shedding unmanly tears, trembling at a drawn sword, and talking in the style alternately of a buffoon and a pedagogue. —Macaulay's History, vol. i., p. 74.

† History of England, vol. i., p. 166.

blood nor merit to wear, nor estates to bear up their titles, but were fain to invent projects to pill (plunder) the people and pick their purses for the maintenance of vice and lewdness."* "Ebriety was not confined to the male sex, and on some occasions females of the highest rank, who had spent weeks in the study of their respective parts, presented themselves to the spectators in a state of the most disgusting intoxication."† "Those whom I never could get to taste good liquor, now follow the fashion, and wallow in beastly delight. The ladies abandon sobriety, and are seen to roll about in intoxication."‡

The Earl of Worcester, in a letter to Lord Shrewsbury, thus speaks of the maids of honour: "But the plotting and malice amongst them is such, that I think envy hath tied an invisible snake about most of their necks to sting one another to death."§ The details so supplied by contemporaries, are, at least, many of them, totally unfit for our pages, and more than justify the statement of a modern writer, that "to remain incorrupt in the reign of James, would have argued almost superhuman strength of character."‖

Four days before James's death, great religious preparations were made for the solemn event. The drunken sensualist went through the form of confession, devoutly making his professions of faith to the Lord-Keeper Williams. The sacrament was then administered with great solemnity, and the bishop says "that the dying monarch received it with that zeal and devotion as if he had not been a frail man, but a cherubim clothed with flesh and blood." "Our only

---

* Life of Colonel Hutchinson, p. 27.

† Lingard, vol. ix., p. 109.   ‡ *Ibid.* vol. ix.

§ Lodge's Illustrations, vol. iii., p. 68.   *Vide* Sir A. Weldon's Secret History of James I., vol. i., p. 399; ii. p. 387 (note).

‖ *Vide* Hallam, vol. i., p. 331 (note).   Life of Villiars, vol. i., p. 133. Bishop Williams was charged with an improper intimacy with the mother of Buckingham. *Ibid*, vol. i., pp. 208, 308. Bishop Goodman doubts the truth of the charge, vol. i., p. 286.

comfort," says the courtly prelate, " is this, that as he lived like a king, so he died like a saint. Never have you read of any king that left this world more resolved, more prepared, as though he had embraced himself for bed rather than for his grave."* We cannot forget a sentence from another pen: "The wicked have no bands in their death." Thus "the monarch who broke the heart of Arabella Stuart by long imprisonment and blighted hopes, and who beheaded Raleigh, and denied restitution to his son Carew, died well! So self-deceived is the rich man; so easy is it to substitute profession for practical Christianity."†

The funeral of the monarch lasted from ten in the morning to seven in the evening. Charles was present as chief mourner. Williams pronounced the warmest eulogy on the king. Though an habitual swearer, drunkard, and a notorious liar, yet he was equal to Solomon in every view, and his superior in many things. The bishop told them that the abandoned prince "was now reigning gloriously with God in heaven." The strain of Bishop Hall was equally disgraceful.‡

---

* Williams's Sermon; Somers' Tracts, vol. ii., p. 51. "He breathed forth his blessed soul most religiously, and with great consistency of faith and courage."—Laud's Diary. London, 1695, p. 15.

† Life of Villiars, vol. ii., pp. 146-7.

‡ *Vide* D'Ewes' Journal, vol. i., p. 267; Rushworth, vol. i., p. 171; Marsden, p. 367.

APPENDICES.

A.—Page 66.

(From a Book of Ceremonies. *Vide* Strype's Ecc. Memorials, vol. vi., pp. 170-74.)

THE RITES AND CEREMONIES OBSERVED ABOUT THE SACRAMENT OF BAPTISM.

FIRST, the catechism which goeth before the baptism; and it is as much as to say, a *teaching* and *instruction*. For in the primitive church, where many came to the Christian faith, at the year of age and discretion, it was used that such, before they were admitted to baptism, should be taught the articles of the faith, and the sum of Christian religion, and should promptly and readily render the same to their pastors or curates; which were yet to be used, if any such would desire to receive baptism. But in baptism of infants, which for lack of age cannot be instructed, the priest shortly expresseth then such instruction, and then chargeth the godfather and godmother further to teach the child or children when they come to lawful age; and then beginneth to make a cross upon the forehead of the child that is offered to be baptized; entokening that he is coming to be professed and totally to be dedicated to Christ crucified; whom he will never be ashamed openly before men to confess and acknowledge.

Then he maketh another cross upon the breast, from whence cometh the belief; signifying that it is not enough to confess Christ with mouth openly, unless he doth steadfastly believe in heart inwardly. And, therefore, the minister calleth Almighty God to take away the blindness of his heart, and to make him apt to receive grace in baptism.

And then he putteth hallowed salt into his mouth, to signify the spiritual salt, which is the Word of God, wherewith he should be seasoned and powdered; that thereby the filthy savour of stinking sin should be taken away; preserving him from corruption, and making him a more apt vessel to continue in the moisture of wholesome and godly wisdom. And, therefore, the minister prayeth that he may be replenished with heavenly food, and that he, receiving his grace of baptism, may obtain his everlasting reward. Then the minister maketh the sign of the cross on the child's forehead; adjuring the devil to depart, and no more to approach to him, but to acknowledge his sentence of damnation, and to give glory unto God and to Christ, which triumphed on the cross over him in his own person; praying that this child, now purged from the wicked spirit, may be the sanctified temple of the Holy Ghost.

After this is read the Gospel, taken out of Matt., chap. xix., beginning, *Ablati, sweet Jesus, pueri et;* wherein is showed, that the oblation of young children is acceptable to Christ, of whose church, without baptism, they cannot be made members. Wherefore the people, according to this example, offereth their children to the minister to be baptized.

Then the minister wetteth with spittle the nose, thurles, and ears of him that shall be baptized; putting us in remembrance of the miracle of the deaf and dumb made by Christ, who looking up into heaven, putteth his spittle with his finger to his ear, and touching his tongue, saith, *Ephatha*, *i.e.* to say, *Be opened.* And so he healed him; signifying thereby the grace and godly influence descending from heaven, which, by the operation of the Holy Ghost, openeth our nose to take the sweet savour of the knowledge of Christ; and our ears to hear his Word and commandment.

Then the minister exhorteth the godfather and godmother, with all others that are present, to pray to God that the child may worthily receive the blessed sacrament of baptism, to the honour of God, and to the salvation of his soul, and confusion of his ghostly enemy the devil; and so the minister and all they together say, *Pater Noster.*

Then immediately the minister maketh the sign of the cross in the right hand of the infant, which cross should, in all our lifetime, admonish us valiantly to defend Christ, and withstand the crafty assaults of our enemy the devil, and all our corrupt and perverse affections and designs. And so blessing the child in the name of the Father, the Son, and the Holy Ghost, taketh it by the right hand, and biddeth it enter into the church, then to be admitted as one of Christ's flock and congregation, and so proceedeth to the font.

And then entering towards the baptism, the first inquisition is made of the name of him that should be baptized, to the intent that by giving in his name, he may now profess himself to a new master, Christ. For of a certain, such professions were made by such in Scripture, and giving in their name.

Then there followeth a stipulation under prescript words: the minister demanding certain questions, and he that is baptized, or his sureties, making answer to any questions and demands particularly. [Which demands, questions, and answers (to the intent the godfather, with others then present, may know what is a Christian man's profession at his baptism), we think it very convenient and meet to be uttered hereafter in English], and first to this interrogation by the minister.*

The minister saith, "Forsakest thou the devil?" He, or his sureties for him, answereth, "I forsake him." The minister saith, "And all his

---

* The words within brackets [ ] were added in the margin by Bishop Gardiner's own hand.

works?" It is answered, "I forsake them." The minister saith, "And all his pomps and vanities?" The answer is, "I forsake them."

After this the minister, with holy oil, anointeth the child before, upon his breast, and behind, between his shoulders. Which unction signifieth that our hearts and affections should be wholly dedicated to Christ, and established in a perfect faith in his mercy; which the oil doth commonly signify in Scriptures. And the anointing between the shoulders with the sign of the cross, signifieth that we should be bold and strong to bear the yoke of our Lord; and particularly to sustain such cross of persecutions, trouble, and afflictions, as our most merciful Lord shall lay upon us.

That further, the minister maketh inquisition of his belief that is to be christened, saying, "Believest thou in God, the Almighty Father, Maker of heaven and earth?" It is answered, "I believe." The minister saith, "Believest thou in Christ, his only Son, our Lord?" and the answer is made, "I believe." The minister saith, "Believest thou in the Holy Ghost, the holy Catholic Church, the communion of saints, the remission of sins, the resurrection of the body, and after death, to have everlasting life?" It is answered, "I believe." All which promises and professions of renouncing the old errors, and believing and embracing the truth, made in baptism, every Christian man ought to have in his after remembrance.

And after this the minister saith unto him that is to be baptized, these words, "What asketh thou?" It is answered, "Baptism." The minister demandeth further, "Wilt thou be baptized?" It is answered, "I will." For there is no man saved against his will, but willingly. For as man by his own free will, obeying the serpent, did perish; so when God calleth by grace, by the conversion of his own mind, every man truly believing and intending to work accordingly, is saved.

Then the minister calleth the child by the name, and baptizeth it in the name of the Father, and the Son, and of the Holy Ghost; putting it into the water of the font, and taking it out again; or else pouring water upon the infant, whereby the person christened hath not only the remission of all his sins, by the operation of the Holy Ghost, but also by the same is signified the death and resurrection of Christ, the only cause of our health and salvation. And, moreover, that we should clearly mortify our evil desires and corrupt affections; and so washed from sin, walk in a new, pure, and godly life and conversation.

Then after this baptism, he is anointed with holy chrism on the head, as the supreme and principal part of man. Signifying thereby, that he is made a Christian man by the head of the congregation, and that he is anointed with the spiritual unction of the Holy Ghost, that by his assistance and grace he may obtain everlasting life.

Then he that is baptized is clothed with a white vestment, in token of his manumission and freedom from his former captivity of the devil. And it signifieth also a Christian purity and innocence, which, after the washing away of the spots of his old sins, he ought studiously to conserve and keep, and so to come to the presence of Christ at the day of judgment, and remain with him in glory everlasting.

Finally, the minister putteth a candle-light in the right hand of him that is baptized, in token that he should, through all his lifetime, show before all men a light of good example and godly works; that he may be always in readiness with the saints, to meet our Lord, and receive the fruitions of everlasting joy.

B.—Page 75.

THE SENTENCE AGAINST JOAN OF KENT, WITH THE CERTIFICATE MADE UPON IT.

In Dei Nomine, Amen. Nos Thomas, permissione divina Cantuarien. Archiepiscopus, totius Angliæ primas et Metrapolitanus, Thomas Smith Miles, Willielmus Cooke Decanus de Arcubus, Hugo Latimer Sacræ Theologiæ Professor, et Richardus Lyell Legum Doctor, illustrissimi, invictissimi in Christo Principis et Domini nostri Domini Edwardi sexti, Dei Gratia Angliæ, &c., per Literas suas Regias Patentes, dat. duodecimo die mensis Aprilis, Anno Regni sui tertio, contra te Joannam Bocher, alias nuncupatam Joannam de Kente, coram nobis super hæretica pravitate, juxta et secundum Commissionem dicti Domini nostri Regis detectam et declaratam, ac in ea parte apud bonos et graves Notorie et Publice, diffamatam, rite et legitime procedentes, auditis, visis, intellectis, cognitis, rimatis, et matura deliberatione discussis et ponderatis dicti negotii meritis et circumstantiis, servatisq; in omnibus et per omnia in eodem negotio de jure servandis in quomodolibet requisitis : judicialiter et pro tribunali sedentes, Christi nomine invocato ac ipsum solum Deum præ oculis nostris habentes ; Quia per acta inactitata, deducta, probata, confessata, ac per te sæpius coram nobis in eodem negotio recognita, comperimus et clare invenimus te, tum per confessiones, tum per recognitiones tuas coram nobis judicialiter factas, nefandum et intollerabilem errorem, hæresin damnatam et scandalosam opinionem subscriptam, juri Divino et Fidei Catholicæ obviantem, contrariam et repugnantem : viz.—"That you believe, that the Word was made flesh in the Virgin's belly; but that Christ took flesh of the virgin, you believe not; because the flesh of the virgin, being the outward Man, was sinfully gotten and born in sin; but the Word, by the consent of the inward Man of the virgin, was made flesh." Manutenuisse: quem quidem errorem, hæresin damnatam et scandalosam opinionem, juri divino et Fidei Catholicæ, obviantem, contrariam et repugnantem, &c. Idcirco nos Thomas Archiep. &c., te Joannam Bocher, alias Joannam de Kente prædictam, de meritis, culpis, obstinaciis et contumaciis, &c., de et super horrendo hæreticæ pravitatis reatu confessam, ad Ecclesiæ unitatem redire nolentem, hæreticam opinionem credentem, præmissorum prætextu fuisse et esse, cum animi dolore et cordis amaritudine Judicamus. teq; ex nunc tanquam pertinacem et obstinatam hæreticam, judicio sive curiæ seculari ad omnem juris effectum, qui exinde sequi debeat, aut poterit, relinquendam fore decernimus et declaramus, et sic per præsentes de facto relinquimus: Teq: Joannam Bocher, alias Joannam de Kent, memoratam hæreticam, pertinacem, in majoris Excommunicationis sententiam occasione præmissorum incidisse et incurrisse, nec non excommunicatam fuisse et esse, etiam sententialiter et definitive pronunciamus et declaramus, per hanc nostram sententiam definitivam, quam ferimus et promulgamus in his scriptis. Lecta fuit hæc sententia per prænominatos, Reverendum, &c.

C.—Page 81.
EXAMINATION OF GILES VANBELLER.

In the Name of God, Amen. I, Giles, a Dutchman born, now of the diocese and jurisdiction of York, arrested and detected of heresy, here before you, Master William Clyff, Doctor of Law and Vicar-General to the most Reverend Father in God, Lord Edward, Archbishop of York, Primate of England and Metropolitan in Ordinary, openly confess and acknowledge that I have heretofore spoken, affirmed, declared, divers erroneous opinions and articles against the true faith of holy church, and contrary to the determination of the same. Which articles and erroneous opinions the principal hereafter follow:—

I have divers and sundry times affirmed, said and taught, defended and holden, in the parish of Worksop, of the said diocese, that there is no priest but God only; and that no priest hath power to consecrate the very body of Christ, as he was here reigning on earth; for the apostle had no power to consecrate the body of Christ, and that no priest had power to take away man's sins.

Item: That the sacrament of the altar is but bread, except it be received by faith and in the name of Christ. *Item:* That God doth not dwell in temple or church made by man's hands, but in a faithful * man to God. *Item:* That no man can make any water holier than God made it: therefore the water in the font, nor the holy water in the church, is holier than the water in the river, for the water in the river is as holy as the water in the font, if a man be baptized in it, and the words of baptism be spoken over him. *Item:* That any man may baptize in water as well as a priest.

Item: That no bishop can make one ground holier than another. That no man is bound to fast. That no man ought to keep any holy day but the Sunday. That prayers made to saints be of no value. That no man ought to go on pilgrimage. That a man may be confessed of another man, as well as of a priest. That there is no purgatory. Also, I have kept, holden, taught, and read some books called the New Testament, in the Dutch tongue; a false and corrupt translation, prohibited for me to have, to the infection and evil example of Christian people. For which cause, articles, and erroneous opinions, and many other by me holden and believed

---

* A word we cannot make out. We think it is Christian.

upon, I was brought before you, to them, and every of them, to make answer; by whom I am now sufficiently and truly enforced that these articles, and every of them, be erroneous and heretical, and contrary to the true understanding and interpretation of the Holy Scripture, and the holy doctrine of the good and Catholic doctors opposed by our mother the holy church, and her determination, slanderous and evil sounding to all true and faithful (as before) ears. Whereas, I do now acknowledge and confess, and believe upon the true Catholic faith in all points; and do, above all and every, these erroneous opinions and heresies, personified on all manners of heresies, contravening the determination of the said mother holy church; and in case, hereafter, I be found culpable in this or any other like contraries to the determination aforesaid: I do submit myself to the holy canon and laws of the church, and promise, and do show by these holy evangelists, here by me bodily touched, that, from henceforth, I will no more speak, declare, affirm, teach, pronounce, hold in belief the said erroneous opinions, in any order, nor anything that is or shall be condemned for heresy by holy church's determination. Ne, that I will hereafter use, read, teach, keep, buy or sell, any books, volumes, or quires, any works called Luthen, or any other man's books, or his heretical sects, or of any other, containing heresy in them, or prohibited by the laws of holy church; . . . nor be conversant or familiar, if meeting with any person or persons suspected or defamed of heresy. But, so soon as I shall know any such, I shall forthwith, upon such my knowledge, detect them, and every of them, to his or their ordinary or ordinaries, with all their heresies and errors, submitting myself most humbly to our mother holy church and to your correction. In witness whereof to this my present submission, I have subscribed my name, and set the sign of the cross.

+ GILES VANBELLER.

D.—Page 209.

Nomina Ænglorum qui hunc errorem suum agnoscunt, ejusque pœnitentiæ agunt, viz., quod incœperint se ipsos baptizare, contra ordinem a Christo constitutum, quique jain cupiunt hinc veræ Christi ecclesiæ veniri, ea quâ feri possit expeditione.

Nomina virorum, &c.   Nomina feeminarum, &c.

Cupimus unanimiter votum hoc nostrum ecclesiæ significari.

HUGH BROMHEAD,	ANN BROMHEAD,
JARVASE NEVILL,	JANE SOUTHWORTH,
JOHN SMYTH,	MARY SMYTH,
THOMAS CANADYNE,	JOAN HALTON,
EDWARD HANKIN,	ALIS ARNFIELD,
JOHN HARDY,	ISABELL THOMSON,
THOMAS PYGOTT,	MARGARET STANLY,
FRANCIS PYGOTT,	MARY GRINDALL,
ROBERT STANLY,	MOTHER PYGOTT,

APPENDICES.

ALEXANDER FLEMING,	ALIS PYGOTT,
ALEXANDER HODGKINS,	MARGARET PYGOTT,
JOHN GRINDALL,	BETTERIS DICKINSON,
SOLOMON THOMSON,	MARY DICKINSON,
SAMUEL HALTON,	ELLYN PAYNTER,
THOMAS DOLPHIN.	ALIS PARSONS,
	JOANE BRIGGS,
	JANE ARGAN.

E.—Page 211.

A SHORT CONFESSION OF FAITH.

ARTICLE 1. We believe, through the power and instruction of the Holy Scriptures, that there is one only God, who is a Spirit, eternal, incomprehensible, infinite, almighty, merciful, righteous, perfectly wise, only good, and only fountain of life and all goodness; the Creator of heaven and earth, things visible and invisible.

2. This only God in the Holy Scriptures is manifested and revealed in Father, Son, and Holy Ghost, being three, and nevertheless but one God.

3. The Father is the original and beginning of all things; who hath begotten his Son from everlasting before all creation : that Son is the everlasting word of the Father, and his wisdom. The Holy Ghost is his virtue, power, and might, proceeding from the Father and the Son. These three are not divided, nor separated in essence, nature, property, eternity, power, glory, or excellency.

4. This only God hath created man good, according to his image and likeness, to a good and happy estate, and in him all men to the same blessed end. The first man was* fallen into sin and wrath; and was* again by God, through a sweet comfortable promise, restored and affirmed to everlasting life, with all those that were guilty through him; so that none of his posterity (by reason of this institution) are guilty, sinful, or born in original sin.

5. Man being created good, and continuing in goodness, had the ability, the spirit of wickedness tempting him, freely to obey, assent, or reject the propounded evil: man being fallen and consisting (*sic*) in evil, had the ability, the T— himself moving him freely to obey, assent, or reject the propounded good; for as he through free power to the choice of evil, obeyed and affirmed that evil; so did he through free power to the choice of good, obey and reassent that propounded good. This last power or ability remaineth in all his posterity.

6. God hath before all time foreseen and foreknown all things, both good and evil, whether past, present, or to come. Now as he is the only perfect goodness, and the very fountain of life itself, so is he the only author, original, and maker of such things as are good, holy, pure, and of

---

* Interlined.

nature like unto him; but not of sin, or damnable uncleanness. He forbiddeth the evil, he forewarneth to obey evil, and threateneth the evil doer: he is the permitter and punisher. But evil men, through free choice of all sin and wickedness, together with the spirit of wickedness which ruleth in them, are the authors, originals, and makers of all sin, and so worthy the punishment.

7. The causes and ground, therefore, of man's destruction and damnation are the man's free choice of darkness or sin, and living therein. Destruction, therefore, cometh out of himself, but not from the good Creator. For being perfect goodness and love itself (following the nature of love and perfect goodness), he willeth the health, good, and happiness of his creatures; therefore hath he predestinated that none of them should be condemned, nor ordained, or willed the sinner, or means whereby they should be brought to damnation: yea, much more (seeing he hath no delight in any man's destruction, nor willing that any man perish, but that all men should be saved or blessed) hath he created them all to a happy end in Christ, hath foreseen and ordained in him a medicine of life for all their sins, and hath willed that all people or creatures, through the preaching of the Gospel, should have these tidings published and declared unto them: Now all they that with penitence and faithful hearts receive and embrace the gracious benefits of God, manifested in Christ, for the reconciliation of the world, they are and continue the elect which God hath ordained before the foundation of the world, to make partakers of his kingdom and glory. But they which despise and contemn this proffered grace of God, which love the darkness more than the light, persevere in impenitence and unbelief, they make themselves unworthy of blessedness, and are rejected, excluded from the end whereto they were created and ordained in Christ, and shall not taste for ever of the Supper of the Lord, to which they were invited.

8. The purpose which God, before the foundation of the world, had for the reconciliation of the world (which he saw would fall into wrath and want of grace), he hath in the fulness of time accomplished; and for this purpose hath sent out of heaven his everlasting Word, or Son, for the fulfilling of the promises made unto the fathers, and hath caused him to become flesh . .* in the womb of a holy virgin (called Mary) by his word, and power, and working of the Holy Ghost. Not that the essence of God, the eternal Word, or any part thereof, is changed into a visible mortal flesh or man, ceasing to be Spirit, God, or God's essence; but that he, the everlasting Son of God, continuing that he was before, namely, God or Spirit, became what he was not, that is, flesh or man; and he is in one person true God and man, born of Mary, being visibly and invisibly, inwardly and outwardly, the true Son of the living God.

9. This Person, God and Man, the Son of the living God, is come into the world to save sinners, or to reconcile the sinful world to God the Father: therefore now acknowledge him to be the only Mediator, King,

---

* Word wanting.

Priest and Prophet, Lawgiver and Teacher, which God hath promised to send into the world, whom we must trust, believe, and follow.

10. In him is fulfilled, and by him is taken away, an intolerable burden of the Law of Moses, even all the shadows and figures; as, namely, the priesthood, temple, altar, sacrifice; also the kingly office, kingdom, sword, revenge appointed by the law, battle, and whatsoever was a figure of his person or office, so thereof a shadow or representation.

11. And as the true promised Prophet he hath manifested and revealed unto us whatsoever God asketh or requireth of the people of the New Testament; for as God, by Moses and the other prophets, hath spoken and declared his will to the people of the Old Testament; so hath he in those last days, by his Prophet, spoken unto us, and revealed unto us the mystery (concealed from the beginning of the world), and hath now manifested to us whatsoever yet remained to be manifested. He hath preached the promised glad tidings, appointed and ordained the sacraments, the offices and ministeries, by God thereto destinated; and hath showed by doctrine and life, the law of Christians, a rule of their life, the path and way to everlasting life.

12. Moreover, as a High Priest and Mediator of the New Testament, after that he hath accomplished the will of his Father in the foresaid works, he hath finally given himself obediently (for the reconciliation of the sins of the world) to all outward suffering, and hath offered up himself in death upon the cross unto the Father, for a sweet savour and common oblation.

13. We acknowledge that the obedience of the Son of God, his suffering, dying, bloodshed, bitter passion, death, and only sacrifice upon the cross, is a perfect reconciliation and satisfaction for our sins and the sins of the world; so that men thereby are reconciled to God, are brought into power, and have a sure hope and certainty to the entrance into everlasting life.

14. Christ, our Prophet and Priest, being also the promised, only spiritual, heavenly King of the New Testament, hath erected, or built, a spiritual kingdom, and united a company of faithful, spiritual men; these persons hath he endowed with spiritual, kingly laws, after the nature of the heavenly kingdom, and hath established therein justice, righteousness, and the ministers thereof.

15. Having accomplished and performed here upon the earth, by dying the death, his office of the cross, he was afterwards buried, thereby declaring that he was truly dead; the third day he rose again, and stood up from the dead, abolishing death, and testifying that he was Lord over death, and that he could not possibly be detained by the hands of death, thereby comfortably assuring all the faithful of their resurrection and standing up from death.

16. Afterwards, forty days spent, he conversed amongst his disciples, and ofttimes showed himself unto them, that there might no doubt be had concerning his resurrection; after that, being compassed by a cloud, he was carried up into heaven, and entered unto his glory, leading

captivity captive, and making a show of his enemies, hath gloriously triumphed over them, and is sat at the right hand of the Majesty of God, and is become a Lord, and Christ, glorified in body, advanced, lifted up, and crowned with praise and glory, and remaineth over Mount Sion, a Priest and King for everlasting.

17. The holy office of this glorified Priest, King, Lord, and Christ, in the heavenly glorious being, is to help, govern, and preserve, by his holy Spirit, his holy church and people in the world, through the storm, wind, and troubles of the sea; for, according to his priestly office, as an overseer or steward of the true tabernacle, is he our Intercessor, Advocate, and Mediator by the Father. He teacheth, comforteth, strengtheneth, and baptizeth us with the Holy Ghost, his heavenly gifts and fiery victims, and keepeth his spiritual supper with the faithful soul, making it partaker of the life-giving food and drink of the soul, the fruit, virtue, and worth of his merits obtained upon the cross; the only and necessary good signified in the sacraments.

18. And according to his kingly office, in his heavenly[*] being he governeth the hearts of the faithful by his Holy Spirit and Word; he taketh them into his protection, he covereth them under the shadow of his wings, he armeth them with spiritual weapons for the spiritual warfare against all their enemies, namely, the Spirit of wickedness, under heaven, and whatsoever dependeth on them in this earth. He, their most Glorious, Almighty, Heavenly King, standeth by them, delivereth and freeth them from the hands of their enemies, giveth them victory and the winning of the field, and hath prepared for them a crown of righteousness in heaven. And they being the redeemed of the Lord, who dwell in the house of the Lord, upon the Mount Sion, do change their fleshly weapons, namely, their swords into shares, and their spears into sythes, do lift up no sword, neither hath nor consent to fleshly battle.

19. All these spiritual good things and beneficial, which Christ, by his merits, hath obtained for the saving of sinners, we do graciously enjoy through a true, living, working faith. Which faith is an assured understanding and knowledge of the heart, obtained out of the Word of God, concerning God, Christ, and other heavenly things which are necessary for us to know, and to believe to salvation, together with a hearty confidence in the only God, that he, as a gracious and heavenly Father, will give and bestow upon us, through Christ, and for his merits, whatsoever is helpful and profitable for body and soul for salvation.

20. Through such a faith we obtain true righteousness, forgiveness, absolution from sin through the bloodshed of Christ, and true righteousness, which through the Christ Jesus, by the co-operation of the Holy Ghost, is plentifully shed and poured into us, so that we truly are made, of evil men, good; of fleshly, spiritual; of covetous, liberal; of proud, humble; and through regeneration are made pure in heart, and the children of God.

---

[*] Interlined.

21. Man being thus justified by faith, liveth and worketh by love (which the Holy Ghost sheddeth into the heart) in all good works, in the laws, precepts, ordinances given them by God through Christ; he praiseth and blesseth God, by a holy life, for every benefit, especially of the soul; and so are all such plants of the Lord trees of righteousness, who honour God through good works, and expect a blessed reward.

22. Such faithful, righteous people, scattered in several parts of the world, being the true congregations of God, or the church of Christ, whom he saved, and for whom he gave himself, that he might sanctify them, ye whom he hath cleansed by the washing of water in the word of life: of all such is Jesus the Head, the Shepherd, the Leader, the Lord, the King, and Master. Now although among these there may be mingled a company of seeming holy ones, or hypocrites; yet, nevertheless, they are and remain only the righteous, true members of the body of Christ, according to the spirit and the truth, the heirs of the promises, truly saved from the hypocrites and dissemblers.

23. In this holy church hath God ordained the ministers of the Gospel, the doctrines of the holy Word, the use of the holy sacraments, the oversight of the poor, and the ministers of the same offices; furthermore, the exercise of brotherly admonition and correction, and, finally, the separating of the impenitent; which holy ordinances, contained in the Word of God, are to be administered according to the contents thereof.

24. And like as a body consisteth of divers parts, and every part hath its own proper work, seeing every part is not a hand, eye, or foot; so is it also in the church of God; for although every believer is a member of the body of Christ, yet is not every one therefore a teacher, elder, or deacon, but only such who are orderly appointed to such offices. Therefore, also, the administration of the said offices or duties pertaineth only to those that are ordained thereto, and not to every particular common person.

25. The vocation or election of the said officers is performed by the church, with fasting, and prayer to God; for God knoweth the heart; he is amongst the faithful who are gathered together in his name; and by his Holy Spirit doth so govern the minds and hearts of his people, that he by them bringeth to light and propoundeth whom he knoweth to be profitable to his church.

26. And although the election and vocation to the said offices is performed by the foresaid means, yet, nevertheless, the investing into the said service is accomplished by the elders of the church through the laying on of hands.

27. The doctrine which by the foresaid ministers must be proposed to the people, is even the same which Christ brought out of heaven, which he, by word and work, that is, by doctrine and life, hath taught, which was preached by the apostles of Christ, by the commandment of Christ and the Spirit, which we find written (so much as is needful for us to salvation) in the Scripture of the New Testament, whereto we apply whatsoever we find in the canonical book of the Old Testament, which

hath affinity and verity, which by doctrine of Christ and his apostles, and consent and agreement, with the government of his Spiritual kingdom.

28. There are two sacraments appointed by Christ, in his holy church, the administration whereof he hath assigned to the ministry of teaching, namely, the Holy Baptism and the Holy Supper. These are outward visible handlings and tokens, setting before our eyes, on God's side, the inward spiritual handling which God, through Christ, by the co-operation of the Holy Ghost, setteth forth in the justification in the penitent faithful soul; and which, on our behalf, witnesseth our religion, experience, faith, and obedience, through the obtaining of a good conscience to the service of God.

29. The Holy Baptism is given unto these in the name of the Father, the Son, and the Holy Ghost, which hear, believe, and with penitent heart receive the doctrines of the Holy Gospel. For such hath the Lord Jesus commanded to be baptized, and no unspeaking children.

30. The whole dealing in the outward visible baptism of water, setteth before the eyes, witnesseth and signifyeth, the Lord Jesus doth inwardly baptize the repentant, faithful man, in the laver of regeneration and renewing by the Holy Ghost, washing the soul from all pollution and sin, by the virtue and merit of his bloodshed; and by the power and working of the Holy Ghost, the true, heavenly, spiritual, living Water, cleanseth the inward evil of the soul, and maketh it heavenly, spiritual, and living, in true righteousness or goodness. Therefore, the baptism of water leadeth us to Christ, to his holy office in glory and majesty; and admonisheth us not to hang only upon the outward, but with holy prayer to mount upward, and to beg of Christ the good thing signified.

31. The Holy Supper, according to the institution of Christ, is to be administered to the baptized; as the Lord Jesus hath commanded that whatsoever he hath appointed should be taught to be observed.

32. The whole dealing in the outward visible supper, setteth before the eye, witnesseth and signifyeth, that Christ's body was broken upon the cross, and his holy blood spilt for the remission of our sins. That the being glorified in his heavenly Being, is the alive-making bread, meat, and drink of our souls: it setteth before our eyes Christ's office and ministry in glory and majesty, by holding his spiritual supper, which the believing soul, feeding and *   the soul with spiritual food: it teacheth us by the outward handling to mount upwards with the heart in holy prayer, to beg at Christ's hands the true signified food; and it admonisheth us of thankfulness to God, and of verity and love one with another.

33. The church discipline, ôr external censures, is also an outward handling among the believers, whereby the impenitent sinner, after Christian admonition and reproof, is severed, by reason of his sins, from the communion of the saints for his future good; and the wrath of God is denounced against him until the time of his contrition and reformation; and there is also, by this outward separation of the Church, mani-

---

* Word wanting.

fested what God before had judged and fore-handled, concerning this secret sinner, by reason of his sin. Therefore, first before the Lord, the prejudging and predetermining of the matter must pass * in respect of the sinner * and the after-judging and handling by the church. Therefore the church must carefully regard that none in the church be condemned with it, and be condemned in the Word of God.

34. The person separated from the church may not at all be admitted (so long as he proceedeth in sin) to the use of the holy supper or any other * handling, but he must be avoided therein, as also in all other things betokening the communion of saints or brotherhood. And as the rebellious life, conversation, or daily company of the godless and perverse, or anything with them, is dangerous and hurtful, and ofttimes promoteth scandal and slander to the godly, so must they withdraw themselves from the same rebels, avoiding them in all works and ends whereby their pure souls might be polluted and defiled: yet so that always the Word of God take place, and that nothing take place or be performed that is contrary to love, mercy, Christian discretion, promise, or any other like matter.

35. Worldly authority or magistracy is a necessary ordinance of God, appointed and established for the preservation of the common estate, and of a good, natural, politic life, for the reward of the good and the punishing of the evil: we acknowledge ourselves obnoxious, and bound by the Word of God to fear, honour, and show obedience to the magistrates in all causes not contrary to the Word of the Lord. We are obliged to pray God Almighty for them, and to thank the Lord for good reasonable magistrates, and to yield unto them, without murmuring, beseeming tribute, toll, and tax. This office of the worldly authority the Lord Jesus hath not ordained in his spiritual kingdom, the church of the New Testament, nor adjoined to the offices of his church. Neither hath he called his disciples or followers to be worldly kings, princes, potentates, or magistrates; neither hath he burdened or charged them to assume such offices, or to govern the world in such a worldly manner; much less hath he given a law to the members of his church which is agreeable to such office or government. Yea, rather they are called of him (whom they are commanded to obey by a voice heard from heaven) to the following of his unarmed and unweaponed life, and of his crossbearing footsteps. In whom approved nothing less than a worldly government, power, and sword. This then considered (as also further, that upon the office of the worldly authority many other things depend, as wars * to hurt his enemies in body or goods * with evilly or not at all will fit or consort with the Christ, and the crucified life of the Christians), so hold we that it beseemeth not Christians to administer these offices; therefore we avoid such offices and administrations, notwithstanding by no means thereby willing to despise or condemn reasonable discreet magistrates, nor to place him in less estimation than he is described by the Holy Ghost, of Paul.

---

* Cannot decipher the word.

36. Christ, the King and Lawgiver of the New Testament, hath prohibited Christians the swearing of oaths; therefore it is not permitted that the faithful of the New Testament should swear at all.

37. The married estate, or matrimony, hold we for an ordinance of God, which, according to the first institution, shall be observed. Every man shall have his one only wife, and every woman shall have her one only husband; those may not be separated but for adultery. We permit none of our communion to marry godless, unbelieving, fleshly persons out of the church; but we censure such (as other sinners) according to the disposition and desert of the cause.

38. Lastly, we believe and teach the resurrection of the dead, both of the just and the unjust, as Paul (1 Cor. xv.) soundly teacheth and witnesseth: The soul shall be united to the body, every one shall be presented before the judgment seat of Christ Jesus, to receive in his own body wages according to his works. And the righteous, whosoever hath lived holily, and through faith brought forth the works of love and mercy, shall enter into everlasting life with Christ Jesus, the Bridegroom of the Christian host. But the unsanctified, which have not known God, and have not obeyed the Gospel of Jesus Christ, shall go into everlasting fire. The Almighty, gracious, merciful God, preserve us from the punishment of the ungodly, and grant us grace and gifts helpful to a holy life, saving death, and joyful resurrection with all the righteous. Amen.

We subscribe to the truth of these Articles, desiring further information. [Forty-two names are attached to this document. We cannot decipher the whole, but the following are plain. A line is drawn through some of them. The * mark them. † Uncertain.]

* JOHN SMYTH,	* ———————,
HUGH BROOMHEAD,	* MATTHEW PIGOTT,
* JOHN GRINDALL,	MARY SMYTH,
* SAMUEL HALTON,	JANUS ———,
THOMAS PIGGOTT,	MARGARETT STAVELEY,
JOHN HARDIE,	† ISABELLA THOMSON,
* EDWARD HAWKINS,	* JANE ARGAN,†
THOMAS JESSOPP,	MARY DICKINS,
ROBERT STAVELEY,	BETTRISS DICKENS,
* ALEXANDER FLEMING,	DOROTHE HAMAND,
JOHN ARNFELD,	* ELNH. BUYWATER,
HANNAH PIGGOTT,	ANN BROOMHEAD,
THOMAS SOLPHIN,	ALEXANDER PARSONS,
SOLOMON THOMSON,	* JOAN HAUGHTON,
ALEXANDER HODGKIN,	* JOANE BRIGGE,
URSULA BYWATER,	ALEXANDER PIGOTT,
DOROTHEA OAKLAND,	MARGARET PIGOTT,
JOHN ———,	ALEXANDER ARMFIELD,
FYLIS ———,	ELNH. WHITE,
	DOROTHE THOMSON,
	MARGARET MORRIS.

[We judge the whole of these signatures autograph.]

F.—Page 211.

We believe with the heart and with the mouth confess :—

(1.) That there is one God, the best, the highest, and most glorious Creator and Preserver of all; who is Father, Son, and Holy Spirit.

(2.) That God has created and redeemed the human race to his own image, and has ordained all men (no one being reprobated) to life.

(3.) That God imposes no necessity of sinning on any one; but man freely, by Satanic instigation, departs from God.

(4.) That the law of life was originally placed by God in the keeping of the law; then, by reason of the weakness of the flesh, was, by the good pleasure of God, through the redemption of Christ, changed into justification of faith; on which account, no one ought justly to blame God, but rather, with his inmost heart, to revere, adore, and praise his mercy, that God should have rendered that possible to man, by his grace, which before, since man had fallen, was impossible by nature.

(5.) That there is no original sin (lit., *no sin of origin or descent*), but all sin is actual and voluntary, viz., a word, a deed, or a design against the law of God; and therefore, infants are without sin.

(6.) That Jesus Christ is true God and true man; viz., the Son of God taking to himself, in addition, the true and pure nature of a man, out of a true rational soul, and existing in a true human body.

(7.) That Jesus Christ, as pertaining to the flesh, was conceived by the Holy Spirit in the womb of the Virgin Mary, afterwards was born, circumcised, baptized, tempted; also that he hungered, thirsted, ate, drank, increased both in stature and in knowledge; he was wearied, he slept, at last was crucified, dead, buried, he rose again, ascended into heaven; and that to himself as only King, Priest, and Prophet of the church, all power both in heaven and earth is given.

(8.) That the grace of God, through the finished redemption of Christ, was to be prepared and offered to all without distinction, and that not feignedly but in good faith, partly by things made, which declare the invisible things of God, and partly by the preaching of the Gospel.

(9.) That men, of the grace of God through the redemption of Christ, are able (the Holy Spirit, by grace, being before unto them *grace prevement*) to repent, to believe, to turn to God, and to attain to eternal life; so on the other hand, they are able themselves to resist the Holy Spirit, to depart from God, and to perish for ever.

(10.) That the justification of man before the Divine tribunal (which is both the throne of justice and of mercy), consists partly of the imputation of the righteousness of Christ apprehended by faith, and partly of inherent righteousness, in the holy themselves, by the operation of the Holy Spirit, which is called regeneration or sanctification; since any one is righteous, who doeth righteousness.

(11.) That faith, destitute of good works, is vain; but true and living faith is distinguished by good works.

(12.) That the church of Christ is a company of the faithful; baptized after confession of sin and of faith, endowed with the power of Christ.

(13.) That the church of Christ has power delegated to themselves of announcing the word, administering the sacraments, appointing ministers, disclaiming them, and also excommunicating; but the last appeal is to the brethren or body of the church.

(14.) That baptism is the external sign of the remission of sins, of dying and of being made alive, and therefore does not belong to infants.

(15.) That the Lord's Supper is the external sign of the communion of Christ, and of the faithful amongst themselves by faith and love.

(16.) That the ministers of the church are, not only bishops ("Episcopos"), to whom the power is given of dispensing both the word and the sacraments, but also deacons, men and widows, who attend to the affairs of the poor and sick brethren.

(17.) That brethren who persevere in sins known to themselves, after the third admonition, are to be excluded from the fellowship of the saints by excommunication.

(18.) That those who are excommunicated are not to be avoided in what pertains to worldly business (*civile commercium*).

(19.) That the dead (the living being instantly changed) will rise again with the same bodies; not the substance but the qualities being changed.

(20.) That after the resurrection, all will be borne to the tribunal of Christ, the Judge, to be judged according to their works; the pious, after sentence of absolution, will enjoy eternal life with Christ in heaven; the wicked, condemned, will be punished with eternal torments in hell with the devil and his angels.*

JOHN SMITH.

I believe with the heart and confess with the mouth:—

(1.) That there is only one God, one Christ, one Holy Spirit, one church, one truth, one faith, one true religion.

(2.) In the Godhead are three persons really distinct,—Father, Son, and Holy Spirit, co-eternal, co-equal, co-original; all and singular of them one and the same God, not divided, but really distinct among themselves in their *specialities*, viz., in Creation, Redemption, and Sanctification.

(3.) God the Father is self-existent from himself, not from another; God the Son is also self-existent, not from himself, but from the Father; God the Holy Spirit is also self-existent, but not from himself, but from the Father and the Son: so that the Divine essence of these three is the same, and one in number.

(4.) This Trinity in unity ought to be worshipped both in spirit and in truth, and whosoever shall so worship God shall be happy in eternal life; and the rule of so worshipping God is thoroughly expressed by God him-

---

* This has no date. The MS. is in Latin.

self in the Old and New Testament, by the hands of prophets and apostles. And whoever shall worship God in any other method than that expressed in these two Testaments, shall be cast from the presence and favour of God to eternal death with demons and their angels.

(5.) I believe and confess that our Lord Jesus Christ, preached by the apostles, was Messiah himself, promised from eternity, concerning whom the prophets prophesied and wrote.

(6.) I believe all things written and contained in the Law and the Gospel are true, divine, and are to be affirmed and maintained by all.

(7.) Christ, the only begotten Son of God, was Priest, Prophet, and King, according to the order of Melchisedec, for ever. And his church ought to be governed by no other in heaven, earth, or hell, but by himself.

This prophetic office is (1) to reveal the will of the Father, and (2) to appoint a ministry, and (3) to teach internally, or to be effectual through the ministry.

His priestly office is, First, To teach us, and otherwise than any other priest, that is, not only to the ears by words, but in our hearts by the Holy Spirit; Second, To offer himself a propitiatory sacrifice for all and singular the sins of the whole world; Third, To pray and intercede for us continually with the Father. So that his sacrifice is enough and sufficient for the people of all and every nation in the whole universe, for their redemption and salvation, if it be by them received in true faith, and held fast to the end.

His kingly office consists in his resurrection from the dead, and his ascension into heaven to the right hand of the Father, living, and casting beneath his feet, hell, death, sin, and final condemnation; governing with all power in heaven and earth, spiritually, his church; adorning her with spiritual gifts, and at length freeing her from all the evil; and openly thrusting down the conquered into eternal punishment.

His true and visible church is a certain number of people, separated from the world by the Word of God, and by the baptism of faith and repentance, gathered together and constituted.

Christ allowed full power and authority to his church, assembled together, *cordially* and *unanimously*, to choose persons to bear offices in this church. And these and no other are to be included, viz. (the offices), of pastors, of teachers, of elders, of deacons, of sub-ministers, who, by the Word of God, from every part are qualified and approved.

All antichristian offices of whatever kind they may have been, are not to be admitted into this church, but utterly extirpated.

All human traditions and opinions are to be pursued with cordial hatred (lit., the hate of the heart), and avoided; and if ever they should be adopted by any, they are not to be encouraged, but immediately put down.

But before I proceed, or come to an end, that it may not (I pray) be a hindrance to you to have known me as an Englishman, lately of the English church, but convinced by the Word and Holy Spirit of God, I give up all its errors, and renounce its maternity, and with the whole soul and mind, desire to enter by baptism into the true church.

I believe that there are but two sacraments to be administered and embraced in the church of Christ, viz., Baptism and the Lord's Supper, and these sacraments are to be administered to, and participated by, those who are penitent and manifest faith; so that both of them are to be denied to all infants and all unbelievers, because they do not belong to such.

Lastly, I grieve most of all for sin; and with sadness and great grief I do confess myself to be the greatest sinner, and heretofore to have lived in great and daily sins; but I expect and seek their remission through Jesus Christ, the eternal Son of God, and after death to enter into eternal life. In his name, therefore, with all the powers of body and mind, I wish and seek to enter, by baptism, into the true church, and to persevere.

What doth hinder, therefore, that I should not be baptized?

RICHARD OVERTON.

[The above has no date. Neither can we ascertain to which community in Holland it was addressed. The writer is probably the author of a book entitled :—

"MAN'S MORTALITIE: or, a Treatise wherein 'tis proved, both Theologically and Philosophically, that whole Man (as a *rationall Creature*) is a Compound wholly mortall, contrary to that common distinction of *Soule* and *Body*: And that the present going of the *Soule* into *Heaven* or *Hell* is a meer *Fiction*: And that at the *Resurrection* is the beginning of our *immortality*, and then Actual *Condemnation*, and *Salvation*, and not before.

"With all doubts and Objections Answered, and resolved, both by Scripture and Reason; discovering the multitude of *Blasphemies*, and Absurdities that arise from the fancie of the *Soule*.

"Also, divers other Mysteries, as, of Heaven, Hell, Christ's humane residence, the extent of the Resurrection, the New Creation, &c., opened, and presented to the tryall of better Judgments.

"By R. O.

"'*That which befalleth the sons of men, befalleth beasts; even one thing befalleth them all: as the one dyeth, so dyeth the other; yea, they have all one breath, so that man hath no preheminence above a beast; for all is vanity.*'—ECCLESIASTES iii. 19.

"AMSTERDAM: Printed by *John Caune*. *Anno Dom.* 1644."]

G.

SMITH'S CONFESSION.

THE following is now, for the first time, given to the English public. It was issued by the remainder of John Smith's company. The only knowledge we have of it is from Robinson's remarks on it (Robinson's work was published in 1614).* From the latter work, Crosby has extracted a few fragments. It is a translation from the Dutch, executed for the author by his friend Professor Müller, from the copy preserved in the archives of the Church at Amsterdam. This Creed must not be confounded with another, articles from which have been given by Crosby, and subsequently by Mr. Underhill, in a fragmentary form.† The title of the one differs somewhat from the other. Mr. Underhill regards the latter as the joint production of Smith and Helwys, and wonders that his name is not attached to it. The mystery, we think, can be solved. It is clear, that the one which we have given in a former note, with the forty-two names attached, was the Confession of Faith presented to the Waterland church on the application of Smith and his companions for fellowship with that community, and is altogether different from the one which he has given. He says, "A *fac-simile* of the subscriptions before the editor begins thus: 'We subscribe to the truth of these articles, desiring further instruction. Forty-two names follow, and among them those of John Smyth, and of Mary Smyth, his wife.'"‡ I need not say that this is altogether a mistake. A moment's comparison will settle the question. The one now given covers a wider circle, and embraces a larger variety of subjects. Its teaching will pass under review in the second volume of this work. As the first Baptist Creed, at least of modern times, it will be perused with great interest by most of our readers:—

I.

We confess, that there is a God (Job xi. 6), against all Epicureans and Atheists, who say with the heart, or pronounce with the mouth, that there is no God. (Pslm. xiv. 1.; Job xxii. 13.)

II.

That there is only one God in number (1 Cor. viii. 6), against the heathens, and some others, who introduce many gods.

III.

That God is incomprehensible and inexpressible, *i.e.*, that the essence or substance of God cannot be comprehended by the understanding, nor expressed by words of men and angels.

---

* "A Survey of the Confessions of Faith, published in Certain Conclusions, by the remainder of Mr. Smith's company, after his death."—Robinson's Works, vol. iii., p. 237.

† Hansard Knollys Society. Confessions of Faith, Introd., p. vii. Crosby, vol. ii., Ap. No. 1. ‡ *Ibid*, p. vii.

IV.

That God has not designed the creatures and holy writings to teach us, how God is in his essence or substance, but how he is in his working (operating) and attributes. (Rom. i. 19-21.)

V.

That the words Father, Son, and Holy Ghost, do not declare God's essence or substance, but only his back or nearest parts that can be known of God. (Rom. i.)

VI.

That God is to be known by his names, attributes, and works expressed in the creatures and revealed in the Scriptures. (John xvii. 3.)

VII.

That to understand and conceive God in the mind, or in the understanding, is not the saving knowledge of God; but to be like to God in his effects and properties,—to be made conformable to his divine and heavenly attributes: this is the true saving knowledge of God, whereunto we ought to give all diligence. (2 Cor. iii. 18; Matt. v. 49; 2 Peter i. 4.)

VIII.

That this God is revealed as Father, Son, and Holy Ghost (Matt. iii. 16), and is infinite in mercy, in all omnipotence, holiness, righteousness, truth, glory, and eternity. (Pslm. xc. 2; cii. 27.)

IX.

That God, before the foundation of the world, did foresee and determine the issue and event of all his works (Acts xv. 18); and that he accomplishes at the just time, instantly, all things by his disposition, according to the pleasure of his will (Ephes. i. 11); and that we consider, therefore, as an abomination, the understanding (sentiment) of those who teach that all things happen by luck and fortune. (Acts iv. 27, 28; Matt. x. 29, 30.)

X.

That God is not the author and worker of sin or wickedness (Pslm. v. 4; Jas. i. 13); but that He only has foreseen and determined what evil the free-will of angels and men would do: yet he gave no influence, instinct, motion, or inclination to the least sin.

XI.

That God has created, in the beginning, the world, namely, the heavens, the earth, and all things which are therein (Gen. i.; Acts xvii. 24); so that things which are seen, were not made of things which do appear. (Heb. xi. 3.)

XII.

That God has created man for salvation (bliss, happiness) in his own image, in a state of innocence, without a spot of sin (Gen. i. 27; ii. 25). He created them male and female, namely, an only male and an only female (Gen. i. 27). He formed man of the dust of the ground, and breathed into his nostrils the breath of life; and man became a living soul (Gen. ii. 21, 22); and God has blessed them, and said unto them, Be fruitful, and multiply, and replenish the earth, and subdue it, and have dominion over all that is therein. (Gen. i. 28.)

XIII.

That, therefore, marriage be honourable amongst all, and the bed undefiled, namely, between a man and his wife (Heb. xiii. 4; 1 Cor. vii. 2); but God shall judge adulterers and fornicators.

XIV.

That God created man with a free will, having the faculty to choose what is good, and to avoid what is evil; or, to choose what is evil, and to avoid what is good: and that this liberty of will was a natural power and property, created by God in the soul of man. (Gen. ii. 16; xvii. 3; xvii. 10; Gen. i. 17; vii. 31.)

XV.

That Adam, when falling, was not moved or caused by God, or by any instigation of God: that he has fallen out of his innocence, and has died the death, only from the temptation of Satan, while his free-will yielded freely therewith (or consented). (Gen. iii. 6.)

XVI.

That Adam died the same day that he sinned (Gen. ii. 17): for the reward of sin is death (Rom. vi. 23); and it is that the apostle calls (Ephes. ii.) dead in sins and transgressions; that is, a loss of innocence, of peace of conscience, and of the comfortable presence of God. (Gen. iii. 7.)

XVII.

That Adam being fallen, did not lose any natural power or faculty which God created in his soul; because the work of Satan, who is sin, cannot abolish God's works and creatures; and therefore, being fallen, he still retained freedom of will. (Gen. iii. 23, 24.)

XVIII.

That original sin is not a Scriptural term, and that there is no such thing as men intended by the word (Jerem. xviii. 20); because as God threatened death only to Adam (Gen. ii. 17), not to his posterity, for their sins, and because God over-rates the soul. (Heb. xii. 9.)

XIX.

That if original sin might have passed from Adam to his posterity, yet is the issue thereof stayed by Christ's death, which was effectual before Cain and Abel's birth, as Christ is the Lamb slain from the beginning of the world. (Rev. xiii. 8.)

XX.

That infants are conceived and born in innocency, without sin, and that they dying, therefore, are all undoubtedly saved; which is to be understood of all infants who live in the world (Gen. v. 12; Gen. i. 17; 1 Cor. xv. 19), for the sin is not imputed; because, where there is no law, there is no transgression. Now, the law was not given to infants, but to them that could understand. (Rom. v. 13; Matt. xiii. 9; Matt. viii. 3.)

XXI.

That all actual sinners bear the image of the first Adam, in his innocency, fall, and restitution, in the offer of grace (1 Cor. xv. 49), and so pass under this threefold estate.

XXII.

That Adam being fallen, God did not hate him, but loved him still, and sought his welfare with all his heart (Gen. iii. 8; xv. 1); neither doth he hate any man that falleth with Adam; but he loves mankind, and, from his love, sent his only begotten Son to save that which was lost, and to find that which was gone astray. (John iii. 16; Matt. xviii. 11-14; Luke 15.)

XXIII.

That God never forsaketh a man till there be no remedy; neither doth he cast away his innocent creature from all eternity, but casteth away men irrecoverable in sin (literally, who will not be aided). (Job v. 4; Ezek. xviii. 23-32; xxxiii. 6.)

XXIV.

But as there is in all creatures an inclination to their young, to do them good, so in the Lord is an inclination towards men to promote their welfare (happiness); for each spark of goodliness that is in the creatures, is also infinitely in God. (Rom. i. 20; Pslm. xix. 4; Rom. x. 18.)

XXV.

That God has determined, before the foundation of the world, that the way of life and salvation should be by Christ, and that he has foreseen who would follow it (Eph. i. 4, v. 2; Tim. i. 9), and also who would follow the way of infidelity and impenitency. (Job i. 8.)

XXVI.

That no more than a father begets his child to the gallows, and a potter forms a pot to be broken, so God predestinates and creates nobody to damnation. (Ezek. xxxiii. 11; Gen. i. 17; 1 Cor. xv. 49; Gen. v. 3.)

XXVII.

That as God created all men according to his image, so hath he redeemed all that fall by actual sin to the same end; and that God, in his redemption, has not swerved from the way of his mercy which he manifested in his creation. (John i. 3-16; 2 Cor. v. 19; 1 Tim. ii. 4, 5, 6; Ezek. xxxiii. 11.)

XXVIII.

That Jesus Christ, who was in the beginning, has laid the foundation of heaven and earth, which perish or are to be changed. (Heb. i. 10; Pslm. cii. 28.) He is the Alpha and Omega, the beginning and the end, the first and the last (Rev. xxii. 13). He is the brightness of the glory and the expressed image of the substance of his Father, upholding all things by the word of his power. (Heb. i. 3.) He is the wisdom of God, begotten from all eternity, before all creatures. (Prov. viii. 20.; Mic. v. 4; Luke xi. 49.) He was in that form of God, and thought it no robbery to be equal with God; but took upon him the form of a servant, and so, in the body of the Virgin Mary, miraculously (marvellously), by the power of the Holy Ghost, and the overshadowing of the Almighty, the word is made flesh (John i. 4; Luke i. 34); being of the seed of David, as concerning the flesh (origin), God having prepared him a body. (Phil. ii. 7; Rom. i. 3; Heb. x. 5.)

XXIX.

That Jesus Christ, after being baptized, by a voice out of heaven from his Father, and by the anointing of the Holy Ghost, which appeared on his head in the form of a Dove, is ordained to be the prophet over his church, whom all men might hear (Matt. xvii.; Heb. i. 2); and that both by his doctrine and life, which he has lived here on earth, by all his doings and sufferings, he has declared and preached, as the only prophet and lawgiver of his church, the way of peace and life, the glad message of the Gospel. (Acts iii. 22, 23.)

XXX.

That Jesus Christ is come into the world to save sinners, and that the love of God towards his enemies has sent him thereunto out of heaven (John iii. 16); that Christ has died for his enemies (Rom. v. 10); that he has bought them who denied him (2 Peter ii. 1), teaching us thereby to love our enemies. (Matt. v. 44, 45.)

XXXI.

That Christ was surrendered unto the death for our sins (Rom. iv. 25), as we obtain forgiveness of sins by his death (Eph. i. 7); for himself lessening or annihilating *(sic)*, he has humbled himself, and is become obedient unto death, even the death of the cross (Phil. ii. 8), redeeming us from our vain conversation, not with silver and gold, but with his own precious blood, as of a lamb without blemish and without spot (1 Pet. i. 18-19); for he has blotted out the handwriting of ordinances that was against us (Eph. ii. 15; Col. ii. 14; Deut. xxxi. 26), and has spoiled principalities and powers, and made in that cross a show of them openly, triumphing over them in it (Col. ii. 15), and through death has destroyed him who had the power of death,—that is, the devil. (Heb. ii. 14.)

XXXII.

That the enemies of our salvation, whom Christ has conquered (vanquished), are the gates of hell, the powers of darkness; namely, Satan, sin, death, the grave, the curse and damnation, wicked men and persecutors (Ephes. vi. 12; 1 Cor. xv. 26; 1 Cor. v. 4, 5-7; Rev. xx. 10-14, 15); and these enemies we must vanquish in no other manner than Christ has vanquished. (John xxi. 12; 1 Pet. ii. 21; Rev. xiv. 4.)

XXXIII.

That the sacrifice of Christ's body and blood, offered unto God his Father, upon the cross, though a sacrifice of sweet savour, and though God be well pleased with him, doth not reconcile God unto us, who did never hate us, nor was our enemy, but reconcileth us unto God, and slayeth the enmity and hatred which is in us against God. (2 Cor. v. 19; Ephes. ii. ii. 14-17; Rom. i. 30.)

XXXIV.

That the efficacy of Christ's death is only effectual to the salvation of those who mortify their sins, and who have been planted together in the likeness of his death (Rom. vi. 3-6); who are circumcised with the circumcision made without hands; in putting off the body of the sins of the flesh, whereof Christ has become a servant of the circumcision for the truth of God to secure the promises of the Father. (Rom. xv.; Deut. xxx. 6.)

XXXV.

That there are three who bear witness in earth—the Spirit, the Water, and Blood, and these three are one in their witness, testifying that Christ in truth has died (1 John v. 8); for he gave up the ghost (John xix. 30), and out of his side, which was pierced by the spear, came water and blood, because that included (encompassed) that wherein the heart is preserved. (John xix. 36-38.)

XXXVI.

That every man being in truth dead to sin, has likewise these three witnesses in himself (1 John v. 10); for the spirit, the blood, and water of the sins, that is, the life, the food, and the enjoyment of sins, is put away. (1 Pet. iv. 1; Rom. vi. 7; 1 John iii. 9.)

XXXVII.

That Christ being dead in truth, is also buried (John xix. 39-42), and that he has lain in the grave the whole Sabbath of the Jews; but he has not seen corruption in the grave. (Pslm. xvi. 10; Acts ii. 31.)

XXXVIII.

That all men, in truth died, are also with Christ buried by baptism into death (Rom. vi. 4; Col. ii. 12), holding their Sabbath in the grave with Christ; that is, ceasing from their works as God did from his (Heb. iv. 10), expecting there, in hope of a resurrection. (Pslm. xvi. 9.)

XXXIX.

That Christ, early in the morning of the first day of the week, has risen after his death and burial (Matt. xx. 6); and he has risen for our righteousness (Rom. vi.), and is declared to be the Son of God with power, according to the spirit of holiness, by the resurrection from the dead. (Rom. i. 4.)

XL.

That those who have been planted with Christ together in the likeness of his death and burial, shall be also in the likeness of his resurrection (Rom. vi. 4, 5); for he quickens (re-creates) them, and quickens them together with himself (Col. ii. 13; Eph. ii. 5, 6); for that is their bliss, and it is done by grace. (Eph. ii. 5; 1 John v. 11-15; Tit. iii. 5-7.)

XLI.

That this re-creation and quickening of Christ, in the bath of regeneration, is the renewing of the Holy Ghost, our justification and salvation. (Tit. iii. 3-7.) This is the pure stream of the living water, clear as crystal, coming from the throne of God and the Lamb (Rev. xxii. 1); which also flows from the body of those who believe in Christ. (John vii. 38.) These are the precious promises whereby we are made partakers of the divine nature, having escaped the corruption that is in the world through lust. (2 Peter i. 4.) This is the fruit of the tree of life, which is in the midst of the paradise of God; this is the white stone, and in the stone a name written, which no man knoweth, saving he that receiveth it; this is the morning star; this is the new name—the name of God, the name of the city of God, of the new Jerusalem, which has descended from God out of heaven: it is the hidden manna, the white cloth, the eye-salve, the gold and the heavenly repast, which Christ promises them who vanquish. (Rev. ii. 7, 17, 28; Rev. iii. 5-12; xviii. 20.)

XLII.

That there are three who bear witness in heaven—the Father, the Word, and the Holy Ghost, and that these three are one in their witness, declaring the resurrection of Christ. The Father says: Thou art my son; to-day I have begotten you. (Acts xiii. 33-35.) The Son declares his resurrection, conversing forty days with his disciples. (Acts i. 3.) The Holy Ghost declares the same thing, that Christ did rise, unto his disciples on the day of Pentecost. (Acts ii.)

XLIII.

That every regenerated man who has risen with Christ, has also in himself the three above-mentioned witnesses (1 John v. 20); for Christ dwells in his heart by faith (Eph. iii. 17); and the Father dwells with his Son (John xiv. 2), and likewise, the Holy Ghost (1 Cor. x. 3); and the grace of Jesus Christ, and the love of God, and the communion of the Holy Ghost, is with them. (2 Cor. xiii. 13.)

XLIV.

That Christ having conversed forty days after his resurrection amongst his disciples (Acts i. 18), was visibly and bodily taken up into heaven, whom the heaven must receive until the times of restitution of all things, which God has spoken by the mouth of all his holy prophets since the world began. (Acts iii. 21.)

XLV.

That those who are risen spiritually, are taken up with him into the heaven, seeking the things which are above, where Christ sitteth on the right hand of God; and they set their affections on things above, not on things on earth. (Col. iii. 1, 2.)

XLVI.

That Christ being now in the heaven, sitteth on the right hand of God. (Mark xvi. 9.) He led captivity captive, and gave gifts unto men (Eph. iv. 8); that God highly has exalted him, and given him a name which is above every name; that at the name of Jesus every knee should bow, of things in heaven, and things on earth, and things under the earth; and that every tongue should confess that Jesus Christ is Lord, to the glory of God the Father (Phil. ii. 29); that he alone has received power in heaven and in earth (Matt. xxviii. 18); that God has put all things under his feet, and gave him to be head over all things to the church, which is his body, the fulness of him that filleth all in all. (Eph. i. 22, 23.)

XLVII.

That the regenerated are made to sit together in heavenly places, in Christ Jesus (Eph. ii. 6); that they sit with him in his throne (Rev. iii. 21); that they shall have power over the nations, and that they shall rule them with a rod of iron, and break them to shivers as the vessels of a potter (Rev. ii. 6–27); and that they sit upon the twelve thrones, judging the twelve tribes of Israel (Matt. xix. 28), which is to be understood spiritually, that all their enemies shall be subjected under their feet, so that wicked one will not touch them (1 John v. 18), nor the gates of hell shall prevail against them (Matt. xvi.); and that they are become pillars in the temple of God, which shall never perish. (Rev. iii. 12.)

XLVIII.

That Christ being exalted at the right hand of God his Father, far above all principalities and power, and might and dominion, and every name that is named,—not only in this world, but also in that which is to come (Eph. i. 21),—has received from his Father the promise of the Holy Ghost, which he has also poured out on his disciples on the day of Pentecost. (Acts ii. 23.)

XLIX.

That Christ, in his resurrection, ascension, and exaltation in heaven, is become the Lord Christ, Saviour, anointed, and King, dearer and more than in his humiliation, passion, and death (Acts ii. 36; Phil. ii. 7); for the end is more worthy than the means; and the sufferings and dying of Christ were the way through which he entered into his glory (Luke xxiv. 26); and, in consequence, the power of his resurrection in the new creature is more excellent and glorious than that which is in the dying to sin, the mortification of sin, and the rising from it.

L.

That to know Christ after the flesh, is of little advantage (2 Cor. v. 16, 17); and the knowledge of the lineage and the history of Christ, is nothing more than what the devil knows as well, or possibly better, than some men; but the knowledge after the spirit is serviceable for salvation, that is, to become embodied by Christ in a spiritual manner, in the likeness of Christ's birth, life, miracles, facts, sufferings, dying, burial, resurrection, ascension, and exaltation. (Rom. vi. 3–6.)

LI.

That Christ, after the flesh and history, in his operations and sufferings, is a great mystery, and holy sacrament of himself, and of his service in the Spirit, and of such heavenly things which he performs in those who shall be inheritors of the salvation (Rom. vi. 3, 6, 7; Eph. ii. 5, 6); and that he, in a spiritual manner, performs all his miracles in the regenerate which he formerly performed in the days of his flesh. He heals their leprosy, bloody flux, blindness, dumbness, lameness, paralysis, and fevers; he casts out the devils and impure spirits; he raises the dead; he checks the winds, and the sea becomes calm; he entertains, feeds thousands with barley loaves and fishes. (Matt. viii. 16, 17; Isaiah liii. 4; John vi. 27.)

LII.

That Christ (in that manner) is become a Mediator of the new Covenant, namely, priest and prophet unto his church, and that the regenerated are become also through him spiritual kings and prophets. (Rev. i. 6; 1 John ii. 20.)

LIII.

That the Holy Ghost proceeds from the Father and the Son of God (John xiv. 26; xiv. 7); that he is one only spirit, through whom Christ offered himself without spot to God (Heb. ix. 14); that he is the only comforter, whom Christ begs, obtains, and sends down unto us from the Father (John xiv. 16), which dwelleth in the regenerate (1 Cor. iii. 16), which teacheth them all things; and they need not that any man teach them, as the same anointing teaches all things. (1 John ii. 20-27.)

LIV.

That although there are diversities of gifts of the Holy Ghost, there is but one spirit, dividing to every man severally as he will (1 Cor. xii. 4-11; Eph. iv. 4); that the external gifts which the Holy Ghost poured out on the day of Pentecost on the disciples, as tongues, prophecies, and miracles, which are called the Baptism with the Holy Ghost (Acts i. 5), were only figures and introductions to better gifts,—namely, the proper gifts of the Spirit of Sanctification,—which gifts are the new creatures of our only baptism. (Eph. iv. 4; Acts ii. 23-28; Luke x. 17.)

LV.

That John the Baptist and Christ were two diverse persons: their offices, two diverse offices; and their baptism, two diverse baptisms,—the one differing from the other. (John i. 20; Acts xiii. 25; Acts i. 4, 5; Matt. iii. 2.)

LVI.

That John has taught the baptism unto repentance for the forgiveness of sins, baptising with water unto amendment of life (Matt. iii. 11), to prepare, in that manner, the way for Christ and his baptism (Luke iii. 3), bringing men to repentance and faith in the Messiah, whom he had indicated with his finger, saying: "Behold the Lamb of God, which taketh away the sin of the world." (John i. 29-31); Acts xix. 4.)

LVII.

That Christ is mightier, and has a greater office and service than John (Matt. iii. 11); that he baptises with the Holy Ghost and with fire; that he comes and walks in the way which John had prepared for him; and that the new creature comes after repentance. (Luke iii. 6.)

LVIII.

That repentance, and faith in the Messiah, are the things or conditions which we must perform on our side, that we may enjoy the promise of God (Acts ii. 38); John i. 12); that the circumcision of the heart, that is, the mortification of the sin, and the promise of the spirit, that is, the new creature, are the promises given to us for the performing of the first conditions of repentance and faith. (Deut. xxx. 6; Acts ii. 38; Gal. iii. 14; 2 Peter i. 4, 5.) Procure the promises of God, which are yea and nay and amen in Jesus Christ (2 Cor. i. 20), and in the regenerated. (Gal. iii. 16.)

LIX.

That repentance and faith are effected (brought about) in the hearts of men by the preaching of the Gospel, and by the Holy Scriptures, inwardly in the creature; while God's grace helps us by the motion and inspiration (afflatus) of the Holy Ghost, which man is able to receive or reject. (Matt. xxiii. 27; Acts vi. 10; Rom. x. 14, 15.)

LX.

That our justification before God consists, not in the performing of the works or conditions which God requires on our side, but only in the enjoying the promises, in the possession of Christ, the forgiveness of sins, and the new creature.—*Vide* Article 41.

LXI.

That God the Father begets us of his own will and with the word of truth (James i. 18), which word is not a corruptible seed (1 Peter i. 23); not the doctrine of repentance and faith that can be lost (Luke viii. 17); and that God the Father in the work of regeneration, needs not, nor employs the assistance or the means of the creature, but that the Father, the Word, and the Holy Ghost, perform that work in the soul without means, wherein the free-will of man reigns. (John i. 13.)

LXII.

That those who have not yet obtained the new creature, stand in need of the Scriptures, creatures, and ordinances of the outward or visible church, to teach, to comfort, and to excite them in order to perform better the condition of repentance and faith, to enjoy forgiveness of sins. (2 Peter i. 19; 1 Cor. ii. 26; Eph. iv. 12, 13.)

LXIII.

That the new creature which is born from God, needs not the outward Scripture, creature, or ordinances of the external churches, so that it might bear itself on it for support (1 Cor. xiii. 10–12; 1 John, ii. 17; 1 Cor. i. 15, 16; Rev. xxi. 23): because it hath three witnesses in itself, the Father, the Word, and the Holy Ghost, which are better than all Scriptures, creatures, ordinances, whatever they may be.

LXIV.

That even as (likewise) he, who was above the law, nevertheless is made under the law for our sakes, so the regenerated can and will not do other thing, from love towards their . . . than to employ the external things that therewith they might come to aid and support men, and that, therefore, the visible church and ordinances are at all time necessary for all men, whatever they may be. (Matt. iii. 15; xxviii. 19, 20; 1 Cor. viii. 9.)

LXV.

That the new creature, although being above the law and the Scripture, cannot act contrary to the law and the Scriptures, but strives that all its works may serve to confirm and establish the law (Rom. iii. 31); therefore he cannot lie, nor steal, nor fornicate, nor slay or hate any man, nor perform any carnal works: all carnal lusts and libertinism, or freedom, is against the regeneration, and a damned and execrable abomination. (Rom. vi. 15, 16, 18; 2 Pet. ii. 18, 19; John viii. 34; 1 John v. 18.)

LXVI.

That the outward visible church is an . . . figure of the real spiritual and invisible church, which consists of the spirits only of perfect and justified men, namely, of the regenerated. (Rev. i. 20; xxi. 2.)

LXVII.

That the outward and visible church consists of regenerated and believing men, as much as men can judge thereof, who bring forth fruits worthy of amendment of life (1 Tim. vii. 3–5; 2 Tim. iii. 5–10; Acts xix. 4); although hypocrites and feigners are often hidden among the repenting.

LXVIII.

That repentance is the changing of the mind from evil to good (Matt. iii. 2), and sadness for the sins before committed, with an heart humbled on account of them, with an intention of amendment for the future, and with a sincere diligence therein. (2 Cor. vii. 8, 11; Jer. xxxi. 18, 19.)

LXIX.

That when we shall have done all these things which we are able to do, we are still unprofitable servants, and all our righteousness is nothing else but a soiled cloth (Luke xvii. 10); and that we only can suppress and cut off the branches of the sin, but we are not able to pluck up the roots of sin from our hearts. (Jer. iv. 4; Deut. xxx. 6, 7.)

LXX.

That faith is a science (knowledge) of the mind of the doctrine of the law and the Gospel in the prophetic and apostolic Scriptures of the Old and the New Testaments, accompanying repentance with a confidence that God will accomplish by Christ, in us all, the promise, namely, the forgiveness of sins, the mortifying of them, with the new creature which is the eternal life, on the conditions of our sincere repentance and amendment of life. (Acts ii. 38, 39; Heb. ii. 1; Matt. i. 15.)

LXXI.

That all repenting and believing Christians are brethren in the communion of the outward visible church, wherever they may live, or by what name they may be named, be they Roman Catholics, Lutherns, Zuinglians, Calvinists, Brownists, Anabaptists, or any other pious Christians, who in truth, and by godly zeal, strive for repentance and faith, although they are implicated in great ignorance and weakness. Nevertheless, we greet them altogether with a holy kiss, deploring with our whole heart, that we, who strive for one faith, one Spirit, one Lord, one God, one body, one baptism, should be so divided and severed into so many sects and splitting, and that for so less considerable reason.

LXXII.

That the external water-baptism ought only to be administered to those who are repentant and believing, as is mentioned, and not to innocent infants or wicked men. (Matt. iii. 23; xxviii. 19, 20; John iv. 1.)

LXXIII.

That baptism put before the repentant and believing, and preached, is the spiritual baptism of Christ, that is, the baptism of the Holy Ghost and fire, the baptism for the death and resurrection of Christ, the promises of the Spirit, which he shall surely partake off, if he perseveres unto the end.

LXXIV.

That only the baptized are to taste the elements of the Lord's Supper, wherein, before the repentant and believers, are put and preached, the spiritual Lord's Supper, which is prepared from the flesh and blood of him who was crucified, and his blood poured out for the forgiveness of sins, even as the bread is broken, and the wine is poured out, and is eaten and drunken as bread and wine, in a bodily manner only by those who are flesh of his flesh, and bone of his bone, in the communion of the same spirit. (1 Cor. xii. 13; Apo. iii. 20; 1 Cor. xxi. 23, 26; John vi. 53, 58.)

LXXV.

That the outward baptism and the Lord's Supper give not, nor administer grace and regeneration to those who enjoy or partake them (see Art. 61), but even as the word which is preached; so the sacraments only serve to awaken and support repentance and faith in those who enjoy them, unto the time when Christ comes, and the day breaks, and the morning star arises in their hearts. (1 Cor. xi. 26; 2 Peter i. 9; 1 Cor. xv. 8.)

LXXVI.

That the sacraments have the same use or advantage that the preached word has; for they are a visible word, and they teach to the eyes of them that can understand, as the word teaches to the ears of them that have ears to hear (Pro. xx. 11), and that, therefore, they pertain no more to infants than the word doth.

LXXVII.

That the preaching of the word and the use of the sacraments put before the eyes the service of Christ in the Spirit, which teaches baptism, and nourisheth the regenerated through the Holy Spirit, inwardly and invisibly. (See Art. 41.)

LXXVIII.

That Christ in his outward church has appointed two sorts of servants, namely, some who are called pastors, teachers, elders, or bishops, who administer the word and sacrament: and some who are called deacons, men and women, whose office it is to serve tables and to wash the feet of the saints. (Acts vi. 2, 4; Phil. i. 1; 1 Tim. iii. 2, 8.)

LXXIX.

That the separation of the impenitent from the external communion of the church, is a figure of the eternal rejection and punishment of those who are impenitent and persevere so until the end. (Apo. xxi. 27; xxii. 14, 15; Matt. xvi. 16, 18; Matt. xviii. 18; John xx. 23; Apo. iii. 12.)

LXXX.

That none ought to be kept from the outward communion of the church but those who remain impenitent and deny the power of godliness. (2 Tim. iii. 5, 18.) And that none ought to be rejected on account of ignorance and error, or weakness, so long as they retain their repentance and faith in Christ (Rom. xiv. 1; Thess. v. 14; Rom. xvi. 17, 18); but they ought to be taught with meekness: those who are strong ought to bear the weak, and support one another in love.

LXXXI.

That one may speak a word against the Son and be forgiven; that is, one may err in the historical knowledge of God and in the matter of the outward church, and obtain forgiveness, if it springs from an unripe zeal; but whosoever speaks a word against the Holy Ghost, that is, whoever, after his enlightenment, forsakes repentance and faith in Christ, and tramples under his feet the blood of the holy covenant, turning with the dog to its own vomit again, such shall not be forgiven neither in this world nor in the world to come. (Matt. xii. 31, 32; Heb. vi. 4.)

LXXXII.

That they who are separated from the outward communion of churches, ought to be reckoned as heathen and publicans (Matt. xviii. 17); and that they ought to be shunned and avoided, so far as they might infect us. Nevertheless, we ought to be always ready to teach them, and provide them with necessaries, and by all means seek to win them, because the separation is designed only to mortify the flesh, that the spirit may be saved in the day of the Lord. (1 Cor. v. 5, 11; Matt. xiv. 19; Luke xv. 12.)

LXXXIII.

That there is no succession in that outward church where the truth is; but the succession is only from heaven; and that the new creature only has the thing signified, and the substance, whereof the visible church with its ordinances, are the figure and shadow. (Col. i. 16, 17.) The regenerated, therefore, only have power and knowledge to officiate in the visible church, for the service and benefit of others. (John vi. 45.) Nevertheless, God is not the author of confusion, but of peace and unity: and, therefore, we ought to adhere as near to the primitive institution of the visible church, or to effectuate it, as far as it is possible. Wherefore, it is not permitted that all the brethren administer the sacrament (Eph. iv. 11, 12; 1 Cor. xii. 4, 5, 6, 28, 29), except those only who are called and ordained to it.

LXXXIV.

That Christ has ordained in his visible church the vocations of masters and servants, of parents and children, of husbands and wives

(Eph. v. 22, 25; vi. 1, 4, 5, 9); and has ordered that every soul be subject to the higher powers, not only for wrath but for conscience sake; that we must pay tribute, fear to whom fear is (Rom. xiii. 1, 2, 3, 7); that we ought not to despise dominion, or speak evil of dignities (Jud. 8); that we ought to make prayer or thanksgiving for them (1 Tim. ii. 1, 2, 3), for this is good and acceptable in the sight of God our Saviour.

LXXXV.

That the office of the magistrate is a permissive ordinance of God (Rom. xiii. 1), or an ordinance of man (1 Pet. ii. 13; 1 Sam. viii. 5, 22) which God has permitted, that the one might not devour the other, as the wild beasts; so that honesty, decency, sobriety, amongst men might be maintained, and that the magistrate hereby may please God in his vocation, doing what is right and just in the sight of the Lord, in order that they may obtain a temporal blessing from God for themselves, their families, and their subjects. (2 Kings x. 30.)

LXXXVI.

That the magistrate, by virtue of his office, is not to meddle with religion or matters of conscience, nor to compel men to this or that form of religion or doctrine, but to leave the Christian religion to the free conscience of every one, and to meddle only with political matters (Rom. xiii. 3, 4), namely, injustice and wrong of one against another, so as murder, adultery, theft, and the like; because Christ alone is the King and Lawgiver of the church and the conscience. (James iv. 12.)

LXXXVII.

That the magistrate, so far as he will follow Christ and be his disciple, ought to deny himself, take up his cross and follow him. He must love his enemies and not kill them; pray for them and not hate them; feed and comfort them, but not let them die from hunger; he must visit them in prison, but not throw them there; he must not banish them out of the country, nor divest them or rob them of their goods, or appropriate them to himself. He must suffer persecution with Christ, be scolded, slandered, flogged, beaten, spit on, imprisoned, and put to death with Christ, and that by the power of the magistrate, which it is impossible to do, and to keep the sword of vengeance.

LXXXVIII.

That Christ's disciples, the members of the visible church, must judge and compose all their own differences amongst themselves, and may not go to law before magistrates (1 Cor. vi. 17), and that all their differences must be decided by yea and nay, peacefully, without using an oath. (Matt. v. 33, 37; James v. 12.)

LXXXIX.

That Christ's disciples, the members of the visible church, ought not to marry wicked and impious people of the world, but that every one must marry in the Lord (1 Cor. vii. 39, 40); that is, every man only one wife, and every woman only one man. (1 Cor. vii. 2; Acts xiii.)

XC.

That parents are bound to nourish their children, or to bring them up in the nurture and admonition of the Lord (Eph. vi. 4); and that they must provide for their house: otherwise they have denied the faith, and are worse than the infidel. (1 Tim. v. 8.)

XCI.

But in so far as any man of a particular vocation serve the Lord, so as Simeon, Andrew, James, and John, then he must forsake all, father, ships, nets,* wife, children, nay, his life, to follow Christ. (Luke x. 4-26; Mark iv. 18-22.)

XCII.

That in the necessity of the church and poor brethren, all things ought to be common (Acts iv. 32); nay, that the one church ought to assist the other church in its wants. (Gal. ii. 10; Acts xi. 30; 2 Cor. viii. 29.)

XCIII.

That the bodies of all men who have died, shall be raised out of the earth at the last day, by the almightiness of Christ, and to every one his own seed, even as the grain out of the seed corrupting in the earth.

XCIV.

That all who are remaining on the earth at the day of judgment, shall not die, but shall be changed in a moment, in the twinkling of an eye, at the last trump (1 Cor. xv. 52), for the trumpet shall sound and the dead shall be raised incorruptible, and we shall be changed: not in the essence or substance, but in the quality. For the bodies being sown spiritually in dishonour, in weakness, in corruptibility, and natural, shall rise in glory, power and incorruptibility. (1 Cor. xv. 42, 44.)

XCV.

That the bodies being risen, are to be joined to the soul, wherewith or whereto they were formerly united in life, which, until this time, are kept under the protection of the Lord. (Apo. vi. 9; Job xix. 25, 27.)

XCVI.

That it is appointed unto all men once to die, and after this the judgment. (Heb. ix. 27.) And the change of those who remain alive at the last day, shall be equivalent to death. (1 Cor. xv. 12; 1 Thess. iv. 15, 17.)

XCVII.

That there will be a general or universal day of judgment, wherein every one shall receive (according) to the things done in his body, whether they be good or bad. (2 Cor. v. 10; Acts xvii. 31.)

XCVIII.

That of that day and that hour knoweth no man, no not the angels which are in heaven, neither the Son, but the Father only. (Mark xiii. 3.) But at this time, if it be revealed unto the church or not, we dare not say anything positively.

---

* The word may be metten, " with," or mitten, nets. We have preferred the latter word.

XCIX.

That Christ shall be the Man and Judge in that day (Acts xvii. 31); that he shall come in his glory in the clouds, with all his holy angels (Matt. xxv.), with a shout and the voice of the archangel and trump of God (1 Thess. iv. 16): he shall sit on the throne of his glory, and all nations shall be gathered before him, and he shall separate them one from the other, even as the shepherd divideth his sheep from the goats, setting the sheep on his right hand, but the goats on the left. (Matt. xxv.)

C.

That the King shall say unto the sheep, the regenerated, who stand on his right hand, Come, ye blessed of my Father, inherit the kingdom of my Father, prepared for you from the foundations of the world: and so it shall be done. (Matt. xxv.)

CI.

That the King shall say unto those who stand on his left hand, the goats, which are wicked men, Depart from me, ye cursed, into everlasting fire, prepared for the devil and his angels: and so it shall be done.

CII.

That after the judgment is finished and consummated, and the last enemy, that is, death, is put under the feet of Christ, the Son also himself shall deliver the kingdom into the hands of the Father, and shall be subject to him who put all things under him, that God may be all in all. (1 Cor. xv. 24.)

[Dr. Müller says :—" I have made the translations as faithful as possible, and as literal, as far as it could be done. The incorrectness of style, and the writing, have caused much obscurity in many parts. I have occasionally altered a word, and in some instances transposed one, to make the meaning plainer. In no case is the sense altered. I have carefully avoided that. I wish I could have removed all obscurity from some of the articles, but that I found all but impossible."]

H.

There is an allusion to this letter at page 78. It should have been inserted earlier, but from some cause it was overlooked. The author is indebted to the courtesy of the authorities of Emanuel College, Cambridge, for the transcript of the MS. in their possession, and to his friend the Rev. W. Robinson, for obtaining it for him.

The men to whom this letter was addressed were from Essex. They were burnt in Smithfield on the 23rd of April, 1556. They were—

ROBERT DRAKE, minister, of Thundersly.
WM. TYMS, curate of Hockley.
RICHARD SPURGE, shewman.
THOS. SPURGE, fuller.
JOHN CARAL, weaver.
GEORGE AMBROSE, tailor.

Fox has given an account of them, and some of the letters of John Careless, given by the same historian, are addressed to Tyms. I can find no allusion to this controversy in the details of the martyrologists. It is perhaps difficult to say to whom we are indebted for the marginal notes. Mr. Robinson says :—"The spelling is modernized by me, and here and there is an (?), indicating a little doubt on my part. The figures on the first page, I am not sure about."

"A true copy of letter which Henry Hart sent to Newgate, to the prisoners there condemned to die for the confession of Christ's verity, against certain articles which they allowed, that were set forth by certain prisoners in the King's Bench, to appease the contentions that their fellow-prisoners had with them, if it might have been.

"'As ye know not what God is, otherwise than he hath shewed himself in his word, no more do you or any other man else (?) know whether he have any parts or passions or not. Wherefore, as ye ought to teach nothing which ye cannot prove, no more ought you, or any other, though they think them of the church, or the church itself, to search after secrets w^h ye Holy Ghost forbydeth you, lest you perish. Against the first article.
(?) Eccl. iii.
(?) Prov. xxv.
(?) Ps. vi. 131–4.

"'And where ye say that every one of you doth acknowledge other to be true and lively (?) members of your church, if ye maintain any errors, ye bear witness against yourselves.

"'In the second article, ye say that God and man were joined together in Christ into one person, never to be divided; and in the first, ye say that God was three persons, without beginning and ending, so that ye make quaternyty in God if ye hold the humanity which our Saviour Christ took of the blessed Virgin Mary for a person, and is not : Though ye confess all that Christ hath done, and believe it as an undoubted verity, as it is indeed, yet, if ye leave that and one which ye should do, yet shall ye perish.

"'This is of verity uncertaine faith for a man to give his life for, when ye hold and affirm in your first article that God is three persons, and then ye say in the second that he is made one person for ever. I pray you, let me know which of these ye intend to hold for the truth, when ye have well weighed the matter amongst yourselves.

"'In your fourth article you say you do believe all your

salvation, redemption, and the remission of sins, cometh unto you, wholly and solely by the mercy and favour of God in Christ, purchased unto you through his most precious death and bloodshedding only, and in no part or piece (?) by, or through, any of your own merits, works, or deservings, how many or good soever they be; and yet ye say ye do not deny nor destroy good works, but ye acknowledge and confess that all men are bound to do them, and to know and to keep God's commandments. But for all the confession of this your stronger faith, ye were best to follow St. Paul, who thought it no derogation to Christ's death nor passion, to say, Now joy I in any sufferings which suffer for you, and fulfil that which is behind or lacking of the passion of Christ in my flesh, for his body's sake, which is the congregation; for, indeed, friends, if ye do them, ye shall find them works of Christ, and, therefore, profitable; for, although ye allow good works in word, yet, if ye declare no benefit to be towards them which do them, ye were almost as good to deny them. Friends, I fear ye accept a careless man to be your teacher, and he hath taught ye as careless a faith; but yet, I say unto you, look to the matter, for it is weighty; put yourselves under the covenant of God, and do it, and see that your hearts at the least keep his commandment: which things, if ye do, you shall obtain all the benefit of Christ promised, which ye speak of, and at the end the crown of glory; but if not, ye shall be sure, by God's promise, though you gave yourselves twice, (?) to be refused and cast off out of the kingdom of God. I spare, because I want time to speak anything now of your fifth and sixth articles, lest I should lose more labour until I may hear how this is accepted at your hands.

"'By your friend, whatsoever ye say or find, (?) HENRY HART, as far as charity bindeth me, as knoweth God.

"'If your last article were true, then would ye hear one man as another, depend not of men but on the truth; for such as trust in men are cursed of God.'

("Here followeth that which the aforesaid prisoners in Newgate wrote upon the backside of the letter.) (?)

"'Before God and man, I protest this doctrine of Henry Hart to be most blasphemous to Christ's death and passion. By me, William Tyms, the   day of April, in Newgate, condemned to die for Christ's verity.'*

Colossians i. Ye shall find somewhat also for you to do in the flesh, beside all that Christ hath done, which if ye do not ye shall perish, notwithstanding all his doings.

---

* "Blessed be God for thee, my dear brother Tyms, and blessed be God again, that ever I knew thee, for in a most happy time I came first into thy company."—Letter of Careless, in Fox.

"'Also I, —— Lister, do affirm the same that our brother Tyms hath said; yea, (?) I say, moreover, that this doctrine of Henry Hart is more to the derogation of God's glory than ever was heard at any Papist mouth: from the which good Lord deliver us and all other. Signed by me, —— Lysteryd.'

"'Also I, Robert Drake, earnestly affirm the same that our brother Tyms hath said; yea, (?) I say further, that this doctrine of Henry Hart is more to the derogation of God's glory and Christ's passion than all that ever any Papist taught: from which God deliver us. Signed by me, Robert Drake.'[*]

"'And so doth George Ambrose affirm the same that is above said.'

"'Also I, Thomas Spurge, affirm the same above written, and so doth Richard Spurge, and so doth Richard Gratwick.' (?)[†]

(Another attestation apparently, but illegible, through the fold.)

"'This is to certify you and all men, that I, Simon Few, (?) do grant to the whole of Christ's Testament; but as for your false opinions and slanderous report of my faithful brethren, I utterly deny and defy with all my heart.'"

---

[*] "Ah, my loving brother Drake, whose soul now draweth nigh unto God, of whom you have received the same, full glad may ye be that ever God gave you a life to leave for his sake."—Letter of Careless, in Fox.

[†] "Ah, mine own hearts, and most dearly beloved brethren, Caral, Ambrose, and both the Spurges; blessed be the Lord on your behalf, and praised be his name, which hath given you such a glorious victory."—*Ibid.*

END OF VOL. I.

THE BAPTIST STANDARD BEARER, INC.
A non-profit, tax-exempt corporation
committed to the Publication & Preservation
of The Baptist Heritage.

SAMPLE TITLES FOR PUBLICATIONS AVAILABLE IN OUR VARIOUS SERIES:

THE BAPTIST *COMMENTARY* SERIES
Sample of authors/works in or near republication:
John Gill - *Exposition of the Old & New Testaments (9 & 18 Vol. Sets)*
(Volumes from the 18 vol. set can be purchased individually)

THE BAPTIST *FAITH* SERIES:
Sample of authors/works in or near republication:
Abraham Booth - *The Reign of Grace*
Abraham Booth - *Paedobaptism Examined (3 Vols.)*
John Gill - *A Complete Body of Doctrinal Divinity*

THE BAPTIST *HISTORY* SERIES:
Sample of authors/works in or near republication:
Thomas Armitage - *A History of the Baptists (2 Vols.)*
Isaac Backus - *History of the New England Baptists (2 Vols.)*
William Cathcart - *The Baptist Encyclopaedia (3 Vols.)*
J. M. Cramp - *Baptist History*

THE BAPTIST *DISTINCTIVES* SERIES:
Sample of authors/works in or near republication:
Alexander Carson - *Ecclesiastical Polity of the New Testament Churches*
E.C. Dargan - *Ecclesiology: A Study of the Churches*
J. M. Frost - *Paedobaptism: Is It From Heaven?*
R. B. C. Howell - *The Evils of Infant Baptism*

THE *DISSENT & NONCONFORMITY* SERIES:
Sample of authors/works in or near republication:
Champlin Burrage - *The Early English Dissenters (2 Vols.)*
Franklin H. Littell - *The Anabaptist View of the Church*
Albert H. Newman - *History of Anti-Paedobaptism*
Walter Wilson - *History & Antiquities of the Dissenting Churches (4 Vols.)*

For a complete list of current authors/titles, visit our internet site at
www.standardbearer.com or write us at:

The Baptist Standard Bearer, Inc.
No. 1 Iron Oaks Drive • Paris, Arkansas 72855

Telephone: (501) 963-3831   Fax: (501) 963-8083
E-mail: baptist@arkansas.net
Internet: http://www.standardbearer.com

Specialists in Baptist Reprints and Rare Books

Thou hast given a *standard* to them that fear thee; that it may be displayed because of the truth. -- *Psalm 60:4*

www.ingramcontent.com/pod-product-compliance
Lightning Source LLC
Chambersburg PA
CBHW020745160426
43192CB00006B/250